ALL NEW 100 MATHS LESSONS

Licence

YEAR 6

John Davis

Julie Dyer

Sonia Tibbatts

Contents

Acknowledgements

Extracts from the National Numeracy Strategy *Framework for Teaching Mathematics* © Crown copyright. Reproduced under the terms of HMSO Guidance Note 8.

Designed using Adobe Inc. InDesign™ v2.0.1

British Library Cataloguing-in-Publication Data
A catalogue record for this book is available from the British Library.
ISBN 0-439-98471-8   **ISBN 978-0439-98471-3**

Published by
Scholastic Ltd
Villiers House
Clarendon Avenue
Leamington Spa
Warks. CV32 5PR

© **Scholastic Ltd, 2005**
Text © John Davis, Julie Dyer,
Sonia Tibbatts, **2005**

Printed by Bell & Bain
123456789   5678901234

Series Consultant
Ann Montague-Smith

Authors
John Davis, Julie Dyer,
Sonia Tibbatts

Editor
Jo Kemp

Assistant Editors
Aileen Lalor and
Victoria Paley

Series Designer
Joy Monkhouse

Designers
Andrea Lewis, Catherine
Mason, Micky Pledge
Geraldine Ready and
Helen Taylor

Illustrations
Mike Phillips and
Phil Garner
(Beehive Illustration)

CD development
CD developed in association
with Footmark Media Ltd

Visit our website at
www.scholastic.co.uk

About the series

100 Maths Lessons is designed to enable you to provide clear teaching, with follow-up activities that are, in the main, practical activities for pairs of children to work on together. These activities are designed to encourage the children to use the mental strategies that they are learning and to check each other's calculations. Many of the activities are games that they will enjoy playing, and that encourage learning.

About the book

This book is divided into three termly sections. Each term begins with a **Medium-term plan** ('Termly planning grid') based on the National Numeracy Strategy's *Medium-term plans* and *Framework for teaching mathematics*. Each term's work is divided into a number of units of differentiated lessons on a specific subject.

Note: Because the units in this book follow the structure of the National Numeracy Strategy's *Framework for teaching mathematics*, the units in each term jump from Unit 6 to Unit 8. The Strategy suggests you put aside the time for Unit 7 to Assess and review.

Finding your way around the lesson units

Each term comprises 11 to 12 units. Each unit contains:
- a short-term planning grid
- three to five lesson plans
- photocopiable activity sheets.

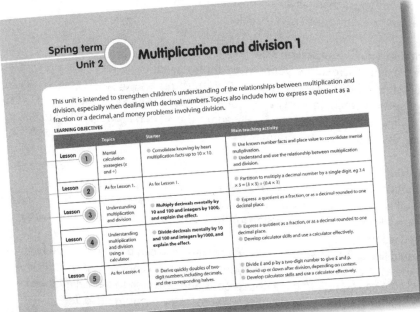

Short-term planning grids

The short-term planning grids ('Learning objectives') provide an overview of the objectives for each unit. The objectives come from the Medium-term plan and support clear progression through the year. Key objectives are shown in bold, as in the Yearly Teaching Programme in the NNS *Framework for teaching mathematics*.

Lesson plans

The lessons are structured on the basis of a daily maths lesson following the NNS's three-part lesson format: a ten-minute **Starter** of oral work and mental maths, a **Main teaching activities** session with interactive teaching time and/or group/individual work and a **Plenary** round-up including **Assessment** opportunities. In some lessons, differentiated tasks are supplied for more able and less able pupils.

However, this structure has not been rigidly applied. Where it is appropriate to concentrate on whole-class teaching, for example, the lesson plan may not include a group-work session at all. The overall organisation of the lesson plan varies from unit to unit depending on the lesson content. In some units all the plans are separate, though they provide different levels of detail. Elsewhere you may find a bank of activities that you can set up as a 'circus', or instruction and support for an extended investigation, either of which the children will work through over the course of several days.

Most units of work are supported with activity pages provided in the book, which can also be found on the accompanying CD. In addition to these core activity sheets, the CD contains additional activity sheets and differentiated versions for less able and more able ability levels. Some are available as blank templates, to allow you to make your own further differentiated versions.

How ICT is used

Ideas for using ICT are suggested wherever appropriate in *100 Maths Lessons*. We have assumed that you will have access to basic office applications, such as word-processing, and can email and research using the Internet. The QCA's *ICT Scheme of Work for Key Stages 1 and 2* has been used as an indicator of the skills the children will be developing formally from Year 1 and their progression in the primary years.

While some lessons use dataloggers or floor robots, we have avoided suggesting specific software, except for the games and interactive teaching programs (ITPs) provided by the NNS. If you do not already have them, these can be downloaded from the NNS website at: http://www.standards.dfes.gov.uk/numeracy

How to use the CD-ROM

System requirements

Minimum specification:
- PC with a CD-ROM drive and at least 32 MB RAM
- Pentium 166 MHz processor
- Microsoft Windows 98, NT, 2000 or XP
- SVGA screen display with at least 64K colours at a screen resolution of 800 x 600 pixels

100 Maths Lessons **CD-ROMs are for PC use only.**

Setting up your computer for optimal use

On opening, the CD will alert you if changes are needed in order to operate the CD at its optimal use. There are two changes you may be advised to make:

Viewing resources at their maximum screen size

To see images at their maximum screen size, your screen display needs to be set to 800 x 600 pixels. In order to adjust your screen size you will first need to **Quit** the program.

If using a PC, select **Settings**, then **Control Panel** from the **Start** menu. Next, double click on the **Display** icon and then click on the **Settings** tab. Finally, adjust the **Screen area** scroll bar to 800 x 600 pixels. Click **OK** and then restart the program.

Adobe® Acrobat® Reader®

Acrobat® Reader® is required to view Portable Document Format (PDF) files. All of the unit resources are PDF files. It is not necessary to install Acrobat Reader on your PC. If you do not have it installed, the application will use a 'run-time' version for the CD, i.e. one which only works with the *100 Maths Lessons* application.

However, if you would like to install **Acrobat® Reader®**, version 6 can be downloaded from the CD-ROM. To do this, right-click on the **Start** menu on your desktop and choose **Explore**. Click on the + sign to the left of the CD drive entitled '100 Maths Lessons' and open the folder called **Acrobat Reader Installer.** Run the program contained in this folder to install **Acrobat® Reader®.** If you experience any difficulties viewing the PDF files, try changing your **Acrobat® Reader®** preferences. Select **Edit**, then **Preferences**, within **Acrobat® Reader®**. You will then be able to change your viewing options. For further information about **Adobe® Acrobat® Reader®**, visit the **Adobe®** website at www.adobe.com.

Getting started

The *100 Maths Lessons* CD-ROM program should auto run when you insert the CD-ROM into your CD drive. If it does not, use **My Computer** to browse the contents of the CD-ROM and click on the '100 Maths Lessons' icon.

From the start-up screen there are three options: click on **Credits** to view a list of acknowledgements. You must then read the **Terms and conditions**. If you agree to these terms then click **Next** to continue. **Continue** on the start-up screen allows you to move to the Main menu.

Main menu

Each *100 Maths Lessons* CD contains:

- core activity sheets – with answers, where appropriate, that can be toggled by pressing the 'on' and 'off' buttons on the left of the screen
- differentiated activity sheets for more and less able pupils (though not necessarily both more and less able sheets in every instance)
- blank core activity sheets for selected core activity sheets – these allow you to make your own differentiated sheets by printing and annotating
- general resource sheets designed to support a number of activities.

You can access the printable pages on the CD by clicking:

- the chosen term ('Autumn', 'Spring' or 'Summer')
- the unit required (for example, 'Unit 1: Place value')
- the requisite activity page (for example, 'Multiplying and dividing'; 'Less able').

To help you manage the vast bank of printable pages on each CD, there is also a 'Practical assessment record sheet' provided on the CD that you can use to record which children have tackled which pages. This could be particularly useful if you would like less able children to work through two or three of the differentiated pages for a lesson or topic.

CD navigation

- **Back**: click to return to the previous screen. Continue to move to the **Menu** or start-up screens.
- **Quit**: click **Quit** to close the menu program. You are then provided with options to return to the start up menu or to exit the CD.
- **Help**: provides general background information and basic technical support. Click on the **Help** button to access. Click **Back** to return to the previous screen.
- **Alternative levels**: after you have accessed a CD page, you will see a small menu screen on the left-hand side of the screen. This allows you to access differentiated or template versions of the same activity.

Printing

There are two print options:

- The **Print** button on the bottom left of each activity screen allows you to print directly from the CD program.
- If you press the **View** button above the **Print** option, the sheet will open as a read-only page in **Acrobat® Reader®**. To print the selected resource from **Acrobat® Reader®**, select **File** and then **Print**. Once you have printed the resource, minimise or close the **Adobe®** screen using _ or **x** in the top right-hand corner of the screen.

Viewing on an interactive whiteboard or data projector

The sheets can be viewed directly from the CD. To make viewing easier for a whole class, use a large monitor, data projector or interactive whiteboard.

About Year 6

By the time children reach Year 6 their ability range is wide. Differentiation is therefore vitally important and care has been taken to ensure that this has been catered for in each lesson. There is also the expectation that children at this stage in their development can organise their work individually, in pairs or as a small group. During the Autumn, Spring and first part of the Summer Terms, all major mathematical topics are covered in readiness for the children's SATs in May. In the latter part of the Summer Term, once SATs have been completed, many of the practical problem-solving activities provided are set in real-life contexts so children will have realistic and challenging tasks to consider and can appreciate the importance maths plays as a key life skill. The areas covered here will also help to ensure a smooth transition into the work to be carried out at the beginning of Key Stage 3.

Termly planning grid

EVERY DAY: Practise and develop oral and mental skills (eg counting, mental strategies, rapid recall of +, - , x and ÷)

- Read and write whole numbers in figures and words and know what each digit represents.
- Order a set of positive and negative integers.
- Consolidate rounding an integer to the nearest 10, 100 or 1000.
- Use known number facts and place value to consolidate mental addition and subtraction, multiplication and division.
- Consolidate knowing by heart multiplication facts to 10 x 10.
- **Multiply and divide decimals mentally by 10 and 100 , and integers by 1000, and explain the effect**.
- Round a number with two decimal places to the nearest tenth or to the nearest whole number.
- Derive quickly division facts corresponding to tables up to 10 × 10.
- Use related facts and doubling or halving.

- Consolidate all strategies from previous year, including: add or subtract the nearest multiple of 10, 100 or 1000, then adjust; use the relationship between addition and subtraction.
- Order fractions by converting them into fractions with a common denominator.
- **Find simple percentages such as one half, one quarter, one third... of small whole-number quantities.**
- Express simple fractions as percentages.
- Use, read and write standard metric units (km, m, cm, mm, kg, g, l, ml, cl) including their abbreviations and relationships between them.
- Convert smaller to larger units (eg m to km, cm to m, g to kg, ml to l) and vice versa.

Units	Days	Topics	Objectives
1	3	Place value, ordering and rounding	• **Multiply and divide integers mentally by 10, 100 or 1000 and explain the effect.** • **Multiply and divide decimals mentally by 10 or 100 and explain the effect.**
		Using a calculator	• Develop calculator skills and use a calculator effectively.
		Problems involving 'real life', money and measures	• **Identify and use appropriate operations to solve word problems involving numbers and quantities.**
2-3	10	Understanding multiplication and division	• Understand and use the relationship between the four operations and the principles (not the names) of the arithmetic laws. • Express a quotient as a fraction or as a decimal rounded to one decimal place. Divide £p by a two-digit number to give £p. • Round up or down after division, depending on the context.
		Mental calculation strategies (× and ÷)	• Use known number facts and place value to consolidate mental division • Use related facts and doubling and halving. For example: double one number and halve the other, find the 24× table by doubling the 6× table twice.
		Pencil and paper procedures (× and ÷)	• Approximate first. • Use informal pencil and paper methods to support, record or explain divisions. • **Extend written methods to: short multiplication of numbers involving decimals;** multiplication of ThHTU x U (short multiplication); division of HTU by TU (long division).
		Problems involving 'real life', money and measures	• **Identify and use appropriate operations to solve word problems involving numbers and quantities** based on 'real life', money and measures.
		Making decisions	• Choose and use appropriate number operations to solve problems and appropriate ways of calculating: mental with jottings, written methods, calculator.
		Checking results of calculation	• Estimate by approximating (round to the nearest 10, 100 or 1000) then check results. • Check with the inverse operation when using a calculator.
4-5	10	Fractions, decimals, percentages, ratio and proportion	• Change a fraction such as 33/8 to the equivalent mixed number (4 1/8) and vice versa. • Recognise relationships between fractions: for example, that 1/10 is ten times 1/100 and 1/16 is half of 1/8. • Recognise the equivalence between the decimal and fraction forms. • Order fractions such as 2/3, 3/4 and 5/6 by converting them to fractions with a common denominator and position them on a number line. • **Reduce a fraction to its simplest form by cancelling common factors** in the numerator and denominator. • **Solve simple problems involving ratio and proportion.** • Use decimal notation for tenths and hundredths in calculations, and tenths, hundredths and thousandths when recording measurements. • Know what each digit represents in a number with up to three decimal places. • Give a decimal fraction lying between two others, eg between 3.4 and 3.5. • Round a number with two decimal places to the nearest tenth. • **Understand percentage as the number of parts in every 100.** • Express simple fractions as percentages. • **Find simple percentages of small whole-number quantities.**
6	8	Handling data	• Use the language of probability to discuss events including those with equally likely outcomes. • **Solve a problem by extracting and interpreting data in charts.** • Find the mode and range of a set of data. • Begin to find the median and the mean of a set of data.
7	2	Assess and review	

EVERY DAY: Practise and develop oral and mental skills (eg counting, mental strategies, rapid recall of +, -, x and ÷)

- **Understand percentage as the number of parts in every 100.**
- **Find simple percentages of small whole-number quantities.**
- Express simple fractions such as one half, one quarter, three quarters, one third, two thirds ... and tenths and hundredths, as percentages.
- **Order a mixed set of numbers with up to three decimal places.**
- Order a set of positive and negative integers.
- Add or subtract to the nearest multiple of 10, 100 or 1000 and then adjust.
- **Derive quickly: division facts corresponding to tables up to 10 x 10**; squares of multiples of 10 to 100 (eg 60 × 60).
- Recognise square numbers of at least 12 × 12.
- Consolidate rounding an integer to the nearest 10, 100 or 1000.
- Know imperial units.
- Round decimals to the nearest whole number.

- Recognise and extend number sequences.
- Count on in steps of 0.1, 0.2, 0.25, 0.5... and then back.
- Convert smaller to larger units and vice versa.
- Use related facts and doubling and halving.
- Use tests of divisibility.
- Use factors
- Order fractions such as 2/3, 3/4, 5/6 by converting them to fractions with a common denominator.
- Derive quickly doubles of two-digit numbers (eg 3.8 × 2, 0.76 × 2).
- **Multiply and divide decimals mentally by 10 or 100 and integers by 1000 and explain the effect.**
- Add several numbers.
- Consolidate knowing by heart multiplication facts up to 10 × 10.
- Give a decimal fraction lying between two others.

Units	Days	Topics	Objectives
8	5	Shape and space	• Classify quadrilaterals, using criteria such as parallel sides, equal angles, equal sides... • **Read and plot co-ordinates in all four quadrants.** • Recognise where a shape will be after two translations.
		Reasoning and generalising about numbers or shapes	• Make and investigate a general statement about familiar numbers and shapes by finding examples that satisfy it.
9-10	10	Measures	• **Calculate the perimeter and area of simple compound shapes that can be split into rectangles.** • Use, read and write standard metric units, including their abbreviations, and relationships between them. • Convert smaller to larger units and vice versa. • Suggest suitable units and measuring equipment to estimate and measure length, mass and capacity. • Record estimates and readings from scales to a suitable degree of accuracy. • Know imperial units. • Know rough equivalents of miles and km. • Appreciate different times around the world.
		Problems involving 'real life', money and measures	• **Identify and use appropriate operations (including combinations of operations) to solve word problems involving numbers and quantities.**
		Making decisions	• Choose and use appropriate number operations to solve problems and appropriate ways of calculating.
11	5	Mental calculation strategies (+ and –)	• Consolidate all strategies from previous year including: find a difference by counting up; add several numbers.
		Pencil and paper procedures (+ and -)	• Use informal pencil and paper methods to support, record or explain additions and subtraction. • **Extend written methods to column addition and subtraction involving decimals.**
		Checking results of calculations.	• Check with the inverse operation when using a calculator.
		Problems involving 'real life', money and measures	• **Identify and use appropriate operations to solve word problems** based on 'real life', money and measures.
		Making decisions	• Choose and use appropriate number operations to solve problems and appropriate ways of calculating: mental, mental with jottings, written methods, calculator.
12	5	Properties of numbers and number sequences	• Recognise and extend number sequences.
		Reasoning about and generalising about numbers and shapes	• Solve mathematical problems or puzzles, recognise and explain patterns and relationships, generalise and predict. • Suggest extensions asking... 'What if...?' • Make and investigate a general statement about numbers by finding examples that satisfy it. • Develop from explaining a generalised relationship in words to expressing it in a formula using letters as symbols.
		Using a calculator	• Develop calculator skills and use a calculator effectively.
13		Assess and review	

Place value

This unit looks at the multiplication and division of integers and decimals by 10, 100 and 1000 and provides opportunities for this to be carried out in the context of money and other 'real-life' word problems.

LEARNING OBJECTIVES

		Topics	Starter	Main teaching activity
Lesson	1	Place value, ordering and rounding	● Read and write whole numbers in figures and words, and know what each digit represents (Y5).	● **Multiply and divide integers mentally by 10, 100 or 1000 and explain the effect.**
Lesson	2	Place value, ordering and rounding Using a calculator	● Order a set of positive and negative integers	● **Multiply and divide decimals mentally by 10 or 100 and explain the effect.** ● Develop calculator skills and use a calculator effectively.
Lesson	3	Problems involving 'real life', money or measures	● Consolidate rounding an integer to the nearest 10, 100 or 1000.	● **Identify and use appropriate operations to solve word problems involving numbers and quantities.**

Lessons overview

Preparation
Prepare seven pieces of A4 card marked: 110 011; 101 101; 101 110; 11 001; 110 101; <; >. Copy 'Place value questions' onto acetate.

Learning objectives
Starters
● Read and write whole numbers in figures and words, and know what each digit represents (Y5).
● Order a set of positive whole numbers.
● Consolidate rounding an integer to the nearest 10, 100 or 1000.
Main teaching activities
● **Multiplying and divide integers mentally by 10, 100 or 1000 and explain the effect.**
● **Multiply and divide decimals mentally by 10 or 100 and explain the effect.**
● **Develop calculator skills and use a calculator effectively.**
● **Identify and use appropriate operations to solve word problems involving numbers and quantities.**

Vocabulary
digit, integer, place, place value, decimal point, units, ones, tens, hundreds, thousands, numeral, stands for, represents, equal to, >, greater than, larger than, bigger than, <, less than, smaller than, tenths, hundredths, thousandths, round (up or down), round to the nearest ten/hundred/thousand

You will need:
Photocopiable pages
A copy of 'Multiplying and dividing' (page 11), 'Multiplying and dividing decimals' (page 12) for each child.

CD pages
An OHT of 'Place value questions'; copies of 'Solve them!' for each child; differentiated copies of 'Multiplying and dividing', 'Multiplying and dividing decimals' and 'Solve them!' for each less able and more able child (see General resources).

Equipment
An OHP calculator; a calculator, whiteboard and number fan for each child.

Lesson

Starter

Write the following numbers on the board: 1179; 4601; 26,324; 94,002; 126; 434; 970,042; 1,326,472; 9,001,212. Ask the children to read them out loud as you point to them. Point to various digits and ask children their values. Using calculators, ask children to work in pairs to investigate how to change some of these numbers using just one addition or subtraction operation. Change 1179 to 1679, 26,324 to 26,304 and 970,042 to 978,042. Discuss answers and operations used.

Main teaching activity

Whole class: Write the following place value headings on the board: TTh, Th, H, T, U, ., t, h. Mark 45 on the chart. Ask: *Where will the digits be if you multiply the 45 by 10? What will we need to put in the units column?* Repeat multiplying by 10 twice more, making sure children understand that the number becomes ten times bigger each time and the need to use a zero as a place holder. Discuss that x 10 x 10 is the same as multiplying by 100. If necessary, put another two-digit number on the board to consolidate. Put 1700 on the chart and divide by 10. Keep dividing by 10 until you reach 1.7. Say: *If you divide by 10, then divide by 10 again, then divide by 10 a third time, this is the same as dividing by which number?* (1000) Discuss the effect with the children, ensuring that they understand that the numbers become ten times smaller each time and that there is no need, when dividing, to use a zero as a place holder for whole numbers as it has no value until decimals are reached. Repeat if necessary.

Ensure children understand that when multiplying by 10, 100 and 1000, digits move one, two and three places respectively to the left. When dividing by 10, 100 and 1000, digits move one, two and three places respectively to the right. Reinforce that the decimal point does not move, only the digits.

Divide the class in half. Ask one half to divide 230,000 by 10 six times. Ask the other to divide 230,000 by 100 three times. Make sure they record their answers at each stage. Compare answers and discuss the fact that dividing by 10 six times is the same as dividing by 100 three times.
Individual work: Hand out the 'Multiplying and dividing' activity sheet for children to complete individually.

Differentiation

Less able: Give these children the version of 'Multiplying and dividing' where they divide and multiply only by 10 and 100.
More able: Give these children the version of 'Multiplying and dividing' where they use larger numbers.

Plenary & assessment

Key a number into the OHP calculator (or individual calculators if no OHP available). Ask the children what the display will show if they multiply or divide by 10, 100 and 1000. Check understanding by asking questions, such as: *What must I do to change 27 into 2700? ...761 into 7.61? Why is 36 x 100 the same as 36 x 10 x 10?*

Lesson

Starter

Divide the children into three groups. Ask each child to write a number on their whiteboard; those in Group 1 must write a four-digit number, Group 2 a five-digit number and Group 3 a six-digit number. Choose a selection of children from each group to come to the front of the class with their numbers. Ask the rest of the children to order the numbers, smallest to largest. Ask five children to remain at the front. Give them the prepared number cards to hold. Ask the class to use the signs < > to compare chosen pairs of numbers. Finish by ordering all five numbers smallest to largest.

Main teaching activity

Whole class: Write the following place value headings on the board: Th, H, T, U, ., t, h, th. Write 4.5 on the chart. Check that everyone understands that this means four units and five tenths, or 4⁵/10. (If necessary, recap that 1/10 = 0.1 and 1/100 = 0.01 from Y5). Multiply the 4.5 by 10 and discuss the effect. Multiply the resulting 45 by 100. Discuss the effect. Repeat for division by writing 62 on the chart and dividing by 10 then by 10 again. Reinforce the teaching point from Lesson 1.

Write £250,000 on the board. Explain that a TV contestant has won 1/4 million pounds. Ask: *If it is given to him in £100 notes, how many notes will he get?* Explain that the question is the same as dividing 250,000 by 100 (2500). Ask: *How many £10 notes would he get?* (25,000) Set the following challenge, which can be solved in pairs: *How many 10p coins will he get?* (250,000 x 10, as each £1 has ten 10p coins – 2,500,000). *How many 1p coins will he get?* (25,000,000)

Individual work: Hand out the 'Multiplying and dividing by decimals' activity sheet for children to complete individually.

Differentiation

Less able: Give these children the version of 'Multiplying and dividing by decimals' where they divide and multiply only by 10 and 100.

More able: Give these children the version of 'Multiplying and dividing by decimals' where they multiply and divide by 100 and 1000.

Plenary & assessment

Pose the following questions, asking children to explain how they solved each one.
● £28 was shared between 10 people. How much did each receive?
● There are 10 people in Group A and 100 people in Group B. Group A shares £3500 between them. Group B shared £350,000. Which group would you rather be in? Why?
● Nathan cycles in a 1.5 kilometre race. Jordan's race is 100 times longer. How far is his race?

Lesson ③

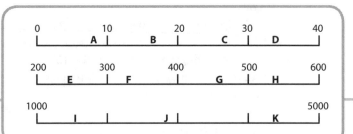

Starter

Draw the following number lines on the board:
Ask the children what the values of A–K could be. Discuss that when approximating it is best to round to the nearest 10 or 100, whichever is most appropriate. Look at the letters again and decide their values to the nearest 10 or 100. Discuss what might happen if the number ends in a 5, for example 385. Do we round up or down? Using number fans to show the answers, ask the children to round up the following numbers, to the nearest 10: 81, 276, 455, 79; to the nearest 100: 321, 851, 1672, 450; to the nearest 1000: 4567, 9320, 12,500, 231,761.

Main teaching activity

Whole class: Check that children remember what happens when multiplying or dividing by 10, 100 or 1000. Display the 'Place value questions' OHT. Discuss and solve the problems. Discuss ways of solving the last problem; elicit that they could have calculated 53p × 10 = £5.30; 5.30p × 10 = £53; £53 × 10 = £530. Or, if they remembered that 10 × 10 × 10 = 1000 they could have done £0.53 × 1000. Say: *I have £13,000. How many £10 notes would this be? …£1 coins? …10p pieces? …1p pieces?*

Individual work: Hand out the 'Solve them!' activity sheet for children to complete individually.

Differentiation

Less able: Give these children the version of 'Solve them!' where they divide and multiply only by 10 and 100.
More able: Give these children the version of 'Solve them!' which includes multi-step problems.

Plenary & assessment

Ask the children to work in pairs to invent their own word problems to share with the class.

Name	Date

Multiplying and dividing

1. Multiply or divide each number in the shapes.

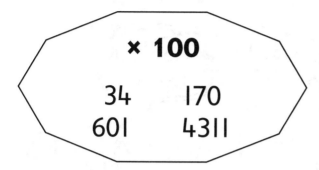

× 100

34   170

601   4311

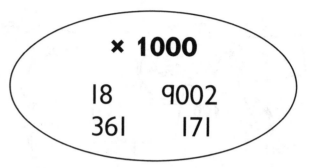

× 1000

18   9002

361   171

_____   _____

_____   _____

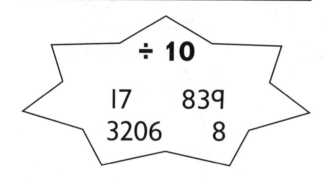

÷ 10

17   839

3206   8

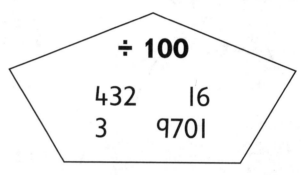

÷ 100

432   16

3   9701

_____   _____

_____   _____

2. Feed each number through the function machine. What comes out each time?

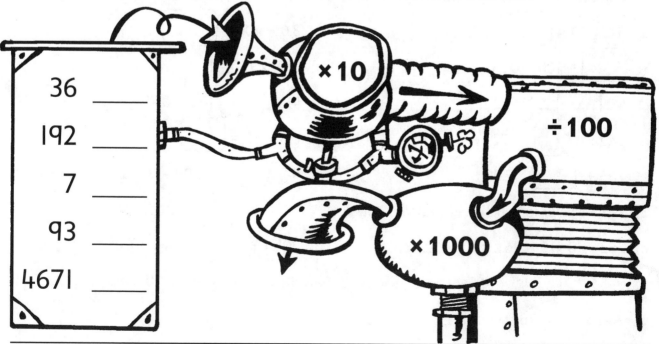

36 _____

192 _____

7 _____

93 _____

4671 _____

×10

÷100

×1000

| Name | Date |

Multiplying and dividing decimals

1. Divide and multiply each money bag by 10 and 100.

2. Complete the following sums:

a) $9.6 \div 10 = \boxed{}$

b) $\boxed{} \div 100 = 0.24$

c) $4.2 \boxed{} 100 = 420$

d) $17.2 \times \boxed{} = 172$

e) $206 \div \boxed{} = 2.06$

f) $3.6 \div 100 = \boxed{}$

g) $0.24 \times 100 = \boxed{}$

h) $41.6 \boxed{} 100 = 0.416$

i) $0.3 \div 10 = \boxed{}$

j) $9 \div \boxed{} = 0.09$

3. Write true or false beside each statement:

a) $262 \times 10 \times 10 = 26.2 \times 100$ _____

b) $345 \times 100 = 3.45 \times 10$ _____

c) $76.1 \times 100 = 7610 \div 100$ _____

d) $304.1 \div 100 = 30.41 \times 10$ _____

e) $96.3 \div 10 = 0.963 \times 10$ _____

Multiplication, division and mental methods

This unit looks primarily at multiplication and provides children with a range of methods for multiplying up to Th H T U by U only. It also provides opportunities for children to establish the link between multiplication and division.

LEARNING OBJECTIVES

		Topics	Starter	Main teaching activity
Lesson	**1**	Understanding multiplication and division	● Use known number facts and place value to consolidate mental addition and subtraction.	● Understand and use the relationship between the four operations.
Lesson	**2**	Understanding multiplication and division	● Consolidate knowing by heart multiplication facts to 10 ×10.	● Understand and use the relationship between the four operations.
Lesson	**3**	Mental calculation strategies (x and ÷)	● **Multiply and divide decimals mentally by 10 and 100 and explain the effect.**	● Use related facts and doubling and halving. For example: double one number and halve the other; find the x24 table by doubling the x6 table twice.
Lesson	**4**	Pencil and paper procedures (x and ÷) Problems involving 'real life', money and measures	● Use known number facts and place value to consolidate mental addition and subtraction.	● **Extend written methods to short multiplication of numbers involving decimals.** ● **Identify and use appropriate operations to solve word problems involving numbers and quantities** based on 'real life', money and measures.
Lesson	**5**	Pencil and paper procedures (x and ÷)	● Round a number with two decimal places to the nearest tenth or to the nearest whole number.	● **Extend written methods to:** multiplication of ThHTU x U (short multiplication).

Lessons   overview

Learning objectives

Starters
● Use known number facts and place value to consolidate mental addition and subtraction.
● Consolidate knowing by heart multiplication facts to 10 ×10.
● **Multiply and divide decimals mentally by 10 and 100 and explain the effect.**
● Round a number with two decimal places to the nearest tenth or to the nearest whole number.

Main teaching activities
● Understand and use the relationship between multiplication and division.
● Understand and use the relationship between the four operations and the principles (not the names) of the arithmetic laws.
● Use related facts and doubling and halving. For example: double one number and halve the other; find the x24 table by doubling the x6 table twice.
● **Extend written methods to short multiplication of numbers involving decimals.**
● **Identify and use appropriate operations to solve word problems involving numbers and quantities** based on 'real life', money and measures.
● Extend written methods to TH multiplication of ThHTU x U (short multiplication).

Vocabulary
product, inverse, lots of, groups of, times, multiplication, divide, division, factor, quotient

You will need:

Photocopiable pages
A copy of 'Jake's clever thoughts' (page 18) for each child.

CD pages
Differentiated copies of 'Jake's clever thoughts' for each less able and more able child (see General resources).

Equipment
Number fans; whiteboards; a dice marked x10, x100, x1000, ÷10, ÷100, ÷1000.

Lesson ①

Starter

Ask quick-fire questions, such as: 42 + 69, 98 + 37. Children display their answers on number fans. Discuss strategies for adding these pairs, for example: **Add the tens, add the units, then add both answers together.** Or, **Round the most suitable number in the pair to the nearest 10, then adjust.** For example: 92 + 49 = 92 + 50 −1 = 142 − 1 = 141

Main teaching activity

Whole class: Work out on the board, with the class, 8 x 40. Ask the children what other number facts they know using these figures. Try and elicit: 320 ÷ 40 = 8; 320 ÷ 8 = 40; 40 x 8 = 320. Tell them to write the answer to 9 x 30 on their whiteboards, plus the associated number facts. If any children find this difficult, remind them to use the known fact 9 x 3 as a starting point. Discuss the relationship between x and ÷. Establish that they are 'inverse operations'. Check the children's understanding by drawing the diagram on the left on the board:.

Establish that 7 x 60 = 420. In turn, cover each number and ask children to give a fact using the numbers left. Repeat until all four facts are established. Extend the task using decimals, for example, 3.6 ÷ 4. Explain to the children that they can use their understanding of the process above to help: 3.6 ÷ 4 can be found by 4 x ❑ = 3.6. Establish that 4 x 9 = 36, so 4 x 0.9 = 3.6. List associated number facts. Give children a few problems to practise on their whiteboards, differentiated for each ability group, for example, 3.75 x 3 for more able; whole numbers only for less able if they are not secure with decimals.
Individual work: Distribute 'Jake's clever thoughts' activity sheet and explain that the children must use the given number facts to solve the related problems on the sheet.

Differentiation

Less able: Give these children the version of 'Jake's clever thoughts' using mostly whole numbers.
More able: Give these children the version of 'Jake's clever thoughts' using a mixture of decimals and simple fractions.

Plenary & assessment

What can the class tell you about multiplication and division? Ensure that children know the term 'inverse'. Ask them to complete the following: *For every x or ÷ fact there are* ❑ *others that can be found.* Write the following on the board: 75 x 4 = 300. Ask the children to use this information to work out the following: *Four children share £3. How much does each get? What is 1/4 of 300? How many 75s in 300?*

Lesson ②

Starter

Chant together the 7 times-table. Tell the children that, in pairs, they are going to use their knowledge of this table to find the answers to other tables. Ask less able children to work on the ×70 table (1 x 70, 2 × 70, etc.), more able children to work on the ×0.7 table and the rest of the class to work on the ×700 table. Ask for a volunteer from each group to feed back their results.

Main teaching activity

Whole class: Check that all the children understand that multiplication is repeated addition. Say: *I buy four ice lollies at 96p each. How much is that?* Demonstrate the working as 96 + 96 + 96 + 96 = £3.84. Ask children if they could work it out in a different way. Let them work in pairs on their whiteboards and then share their answers with the rest of the group. Record some of their examples on the board. Hopefully the examples in the margin on page 15 will emerge, but if not, introduce them to the children.

$96 \times 4 = (90 \times 4) + (6 \times 4)$
$= 360 + 24$
$= 384$

$96 \times 4 = (96 \times 2) + (96 \times 2)$
$= 192 + 192$
$= 384$

$96 \times 4 = (100 \times 4) - (4 \times 4)$
$= 400 - 16$
$= 384$

Discuss what is happening at each stage of each method. Ask the children to work out the following, using the method of their choice: 65 x 6 and 59 x 4 (less able); 236 x 7 and 352 x 9 (average ability); 2389 x 4 and 76 x 23 (more able). Emphasise the importance of setting out each calculation clearly, as shown in the margin. When they have finished, choose one of the questions and work it out together using each method. Check they understand the processes involved.

Individual work: Give the children a range of questions to answer in their exercise books. These could be written on the board or taken from the appropriate class textbook. For most of the class, HTU x U would be appropriate.

Differentiation

Less able: This group should use numbers in the range TU x U.

More able: This group should use numbers in the range ThHTU x U and TU x TU.

Plenary & assessment

Display the following on the board:

$74 \times 8 \quad = (70 \times 8) + (70 \times 4)$
$= 560 + 280$
$= 840$

$24 \times 99 \quad = (24 \times 100) + 24$
$= 2400 + 24$
$= 2424$

Ask the children if they think the sums are correct. Encourage them to estimate the answers. Invite the children to explain why both sums are wrong, and ask volunteers to correct them.

Main teaching activity

Lesson ③

Starter

Play 'Place Value Bingo'. Ask the children to draw a 2 x 3 grid on their whiteboards. On the class whiteboard, write six different two-digit numbers. Children choose to multiply or divide each one mentally by 10, 100 or 1000 and write the answer in a space on their grid. Taking each number in turn, roll a dice marked x10, x100, x1000, ÷10, ÷100, ÷1000 to choose an operation, then ask the children to work out the answer. If the answer is on their grid, they can cross it out. Repeat until someone crosses out all of their numbers.

Whole class: Practise doubling and halving two- and three-digit numbers, such as 15, 30, 60, 120, 240, 480… 280, 140, 70, 35. Discuss how we can use this strategy to find the answer to long multiplication questions (see margin).

Try some more examples: 42 x 32, 35 x 16. Discuss which is the best number to halve and which is the best to double. For instance, if there is an odd number in the sum, it would not be possible to halve this as it would produce a fraction. Investigate other ways of using doubling and halving, for example, the x36 table can be found by doubling x9 facts then doubling again.

$25 \times 36 = \square$
$50 \times 18 = \square$
$100 \times 9 = \square$

Individual work: Ask the children how they would work out the x24 table and the x28 table. Ask them to work out each table in their books.

Differentiation

Less able: Ask this group to work out the 12 times-table by using the 3 times-table, and the 16 times-table by using 4 times-table.

More able: Ask this group to work out which tables could be used to work out the 48 times-table. They should record the 48 times-table using at least two other tables.

Plenary & assessment

As a class, work out the following by doubling the multiplier and the answer: 1 x 36 = 36, 2 x 36 = 72, 4 x 36 = ❑, 8 x 36 = ❑, 16 x 36 = ❑. Ask for ideas on how we can use this information to find the answer to 9 x 36, 12 x 36, 15 x 36, for example 9 x 36 = (1x 36) + (8 x 36).

Lessons overview

Preparation
Before Lesson 5, draw on the board the grid required for the starter.

Learning objectives
Starters
● Use known number facts and place value to consolidate mental addition and subtraction.
● Round a number with two decimal places to the nearest tenth or to the nearest whole number.

Main teaching activities
● **Extend written methods to short multiplication of numbers involving decimals.**
● **Identify and use appropriate operations to solve word problems involving numbers and quantities** based on 'real life', money and measures.
● **Extend written methods to:** TH multiplication of ThHTU x U (short multiplication).

Vocabulary
inverse, product, multiple of, repeated addition, double, halve, remainder

You will need:
Photocopiable pages
A copy of 'Multiplication problems' (page 19) for each child.

CD pages
Differentiated copies of 'Multiplication problems' for each less able and more able child (see General resources).

Equipment
Number fans (optional); individual whiteboards.

Lesson

Starter
Repeat the starter for Lesson 1, with subtraction as the focus, for example: 73 – 49 = (73 – 50) + 1. Give quick-fire questions for the children to answer on whiteboards or number fans.

Main teaching activity
Whole class: Show the class how to multiply 278 x 3, first by using the partitioning method and then by using the grid method. Estimate first by working out that 300 x 3 = 900.

Partition 278 x 3
$$200 \times 3 = 600$$
$$70 \times 3 = 210$$
$$8 \times 3 = \underline{\ \ 24}$$
$$834$$

Then draw the grid method:

	200	70	8	
3	600	210	24	= 834

Practise some examples (eg 4294 x 4) using both methods and encourage the children to estimate the answer first. Repeat the activity for U t h, linking to money. For example: *A box of chocolates costs £4.76. How much will six boxes cost?*

$$4.00 \times 6 = 24.00$$
$$0.70 \times 6 = \ \ 4.20$$
$$0.06 \times 6 = \underline{\ \ 0.36}$$
$$28.56$$

Ensure children understand that the decimal points must line up under each other. Practise examples using the partitioning and grid methods.

Individual work: Give each child a copy of the 'Multiplication problems' activity sheet, which has a range of written problems to be solved using either the grid or the partitioning methods.

Differentiation
Less able: Give this group the version of activity sheet that has problems using TU x U and money x units only.
More able: Give this group the version of activity sheet that has problems using HTU x TU.

Plenary & assessment
Ask the following questions and discuss with the class: *What different ways of multiplying have we learned this week? What important fact must we remember when we multiply numbers involving decimals? What method could we use to multiply 42 x 30?*

Lesson

Starter

0.86	4.02	1.08
3.75	8.63	6.19
1.51	2.74	1.18

Draw the following grid on the whiteboard:
Children should copy a blank version of the grid onto their whiteboards. Ask them to round each number to the nearest whole number and write the answer in the corresponding space on their blank grid. Repeat, rounding to the nearest tenth. Answers: (l to r, top to bottom) 1, 4, 1, 4, 9, 6, 2, 3, 1; 0.9, 4.0, 1.1, 3.8, 8.6, 6.2, 1.5, 2.7, 1.2.

Main teaching activity
Whole class: Extend the children's work on partitioning and grid methods of multiplying to recording in columns. Try 3782 x 5. Ask the children to estimate first: 4000 x 5 = 20,000.
Work out with the children

$$
\begin{array}{r}
3782 \\
\times \quad\quad 5 \\
\end{array}
$$

3000×5	15000
700×5	3500
80×5	400
2×5	10
	18910

Ensure children understand that when calculations are set out in columns ThHTU they must line up under each other. Try a few examples together or in pairs. Explain to the children that this method can be made more efficient by writing the result of each step of the calculation in the answer box, rather than setting out in columns, for example:

$$
\begin{array}{r}
3782 \\
\times \quad\quad 5 \\
\hline
18\,910 \\
\scriptstyle 3\,4\,1
\end{array}
$$

Ensure the children understand that the units go directly into the answer box, directly under the number that has just been multiplied. The tens are 'carried' to be added to the answer to the next stage in the multiplication. Again, try a few together on the board.
Individual work: Write ten questions for each ability group on the whiteboard in order to practise this method. Once children feel comfortable with the partitioning method and recording in columns, encourage them to use the standard format for short multiplication. The majority of the class could work on HTU x U.

Differentiation
Less able: Give this group problems that work on TU x U.
More able: Give this group problems that work on ThHTU x U.

Plenary & assessment
Display the following grids. Ask: *Can you work out the missing numbers?* Ensure that the children draw on their recent work on inverses and division. (Answers: 60 and 3076; 6, 5000, 600, 20 and 33,762)

	700	?	9	
4	2800	240	36	?

	?	?	?	7	
?	30 000	3600	120	42	?

| Name | Date |

Jake's clever thoughts

$1.2 \times 6 = 7.2$

$7.2 \div 9 = 0.8$

$360 \div 9 = 40$

$4.8 \div 0.6 = 8$

$2 \div 10 = 0.2$

$0.75 \times 4 = 3$

Jake knows these number facts.

Can you find the answers to the questions below using his thoughts?

1. Find 9×0.8. _____

2. Divide 3 by 4. _____

3. What is $7.2 \div 6$? _____

4. Find $7.2 \div 0.8$. _____

5. How many 0.2s make 2? _____

6. What is $360 \div 40$? _____

7. What is $\frac{1}{8}$ of 4.8? _____

8. How many 1.2s in 7.2? _____

Now use the following numbers to write four different number statements: 0.7, 0.6 and 0.42.

1. _____

2. _____

3. _____

4. _____

Name

Date

Multiplication problems

Solve these problems using the partitioning or grid methods of multiplication. Your teacher may tell you which method to use.

1. Exercise books cost £7.46 per packet. Chesterwood School buys eight packets.

   How much will this cost? _____

2. What is the product of 8692 and 8? _____

3. A car park holds seven rows of 53 cars on each floor.

   There are six floors. How many cars can park? _____

4. In the school library there are 286 shelves. Each shelf holds 12 books.

   How many books are in the library? _____

5. Multiply 5389 by 9. _____

6. Find the cost of 50 packets of sweets at £1.45 each. _____

7. There are 586 daffodil bulbs in a sack. How many bulbs would I get if I bought six sacks? _____

   Each sack costs £7.32. How much will I have to pay? _____

Now make up a problem for your friend to solve.

Multiplication, division and written methods

This unit deals primarily with division, showing the children a variety of methods including 'chunking' and standard long division layout. It also looks at the different ways in which the 'remainder' can be shown: as a whole number, a decimal or a fraction. Word problems are included to give children practice in working out when a remainder needs to be rounded up or down, according to the question.

LEARNING OBJECTIVES

	Topics	Starter	Main teaching activity
Lesson 1	Understanding multiplication and division Mental calculation strategies (x and ÷)	● Use known number facts and place value to consolidate mental addition, subtraction, multiplication and division.	● Understand and use the relationships between the four operations and the principles of the arithmetic laws. ● Use known number facts and place value to consolidate mental division: divide a one- or two-digit whole number by 10 or 100.
Lesson 2	Pencil and paper procedures (x and ÷) Checking results of calculations.	● Round a number with two decimal places to the nearest whole number.	● Approximate first. ● Use informal pencil and paper methods to support, record or explain divisions ● Estimate by approximating (round to the nearest 10, 100 or 1000) then check results.
Lesson 3	As for Lesson 2	● **Derive quickly division facts corresponding to tables up to 10×10.**	● **Extend written methods to** division of HTU by TU (long division). ● Check with the inverse operation when using a calculator.
Lesson 4	Understanding multiplication and division	● Consolidate rounding an integer to the nearest 10, 100 or 100.	● Express a quotient as a fraction or as a decimal rounded to one decimal place. Divide £.p. by a two-digit number to give £.p. ● Round up or down after division, depending on the context.
Lesson 5	Problems involving 'real life', money or measures Making decisions	● Order a set of positive and negative intergers.	● **Identify and use appropriate operations to solve word problems involving numbers and quantities** based on 'real life' and money. ● Choose and use appropriate number operations to solve problems, and appropriate ways of calculating: mental with jottings, written methods, calculator.

Lessons overview

Learning objectives

Starters
● Use known number facts and place value to consolidate mental addition, subtraction, multiplication and division.
● Round a number with two decimal places to the nearest whole number.
● **Derive quickly division facts corresponding to tables up to 10×10.**
● Consolidate rounding an integer to the nearest 10, 100 or 100.
● Order positive and negative intergers.

Main teaching activities
● Understand and use the relationships between the four operations and the principles of the arithmetic laws.
● Use known number facts and place value to consolidate mental division: divide a one- or two-digit whole number by 10 or 100.
● Use informal pencil and paper methods to support, record or explain divisions.
● Estimate by approximating (round to the nearest 10, 100 or 1000) then check results.
● **Extend written methods** to division of HTU by TU (long division).
● Check with the inverse operation when using a calculator.
● Express a quotient as a fraction or as a decimal rounded to one decimal place. Divide £.p. by a two-digit number to give £.p.
● Round up or down after division, depending on the context.
● **Identify and use appropriate operations to solve word problems involving numbers and quantities** based on 'real life' and money.
● Choose and use appropriate number operations to solve problems, and appropriate ways of calculating: mental with jottings, written methods, calculator.

Vocabulary
inverse, multiple of, multiplication, Venn diagram

You will need:

Photocopiable pages
A copy of 'Division bingo' (page 25) for each pair, copies of 'Up or down' (page 26) for each child.

CD pages
Copies of 'Word problems' for each child, differentiated copies of 'Division bingo' for each less able and more able pair and of 'Up or down' and 'Word problems' for each less able and more able child (see General resources).

Equipment
Individual whiteboards and pens; calculators; scissors for children to cut up 'Division bingo' if necessary;

Lesson

Starter

Write a target number on the board, such as 48. Ask children, in pairs, to think of as many ways of generating 48 as they can in a given time (eg 2 minutes). Encourage use of all four operations, fractions and decimals, for example 4/5 of 60. At the end of the allotted time, collect a selection of answers and check accuracy. Repeat for other numbers.

Main teaching activity

Whole class: Write the calculation 72 ÷ 9 = ? on the board. Ask the children how they will work this out. Elicit that they will need to use multiplication facts for the 9 times-table. Remind them that multiplication is the inverse of division. Ask for the answer (8). Next, write 480 ÷ 60 on the board. Remind children to use known multiplication facts to help them with the calculation. Elicit that 8 x 6 = 48 so 8 x 60 = 480. Give children a few examples to practise on their whiteboards.

Tell children they are going to continue their work on division by dividing by 10, 100 and 1000. Write 670 ÷ 100 on the board. If necessary, write the number under a place value chart: TH H T U · t h. Remind children that when multiplying or dividing by 10, 100 or 1000, the numbers must move along the place value chart – the decimal point does not move. Solve the calculation together, talking the process through with the children. Write 23·6 on the board and ask the children to divide it by 10 and also by 100. Collect answers and correct any misunderstandings. Practise as necessary.

Paired work: Children work in pairs on the 'Division bingo' activity sheet, which has a division game based on dividing integers by 10, 100 and 1000 and decimals by 10 and 100.

Differentiation

Less able: Provide this group with the version of the activity sheet that requires the children to divide integers by 10 and 100 only, and decimals by 10.

More able: Provide this group with the version of the activity sheet that requires children to divide both integers and decimals by 10, 100 and 1000.

Plenary & assessment

Write the following on the board: 812 ÷ 10 = 8·12; 53·78 ÷ 100 = 5·378; 0·45 ÷ 10 = 4·5; 755 ÷ 1000 = 7·55. Tell the children that each answer is incorrect and ask them to tell you why. *What mistake has been made in each one? What is the correct answer?*

Lesson

Starter

Give out calculators, either to individuals or to pairs, depending upon groupings required. Ask the children to enter 10 ÷ 6 on their calculators and respond with the answer (1·666). Ask the children what the answer is to the nearest whole number (2). Give children more calculations to round to the nearest whole number, including questions in context, such as: *Four children spend £35.60 on birthday presents. How much does each child spend to the nearest pound?*

Main teaching activity

Whole class: Ask children to approximate the answer to 768 ÷ 30. To help, check the reasonableness of their calculation. Write two or three of the approximations on the board to refer to later. Remind the children of work in Year 5, when they used multiples of the divisor for division. Work through the calculation together (see margin on page 22). Discuss how it is more efficient to subtract multiples of the divisor than single amounts of the divisor.

Refer to the approximations on the board. Were any of them close to the correct answer? If so, discuss how the approximation was made. Give children another calculation to do, for instance 652 ÷ 23. Ask them to use the 'chunking' method to complete the calculation. Collect answers and check understanding of the method. If necessary, work through another example with the class.

Individual work: Write a selection of division sentences on the board for the children to solve, for example: 37)839   42)916

Differentiation

Less able: This group should be given sentences with smaller divisors. In addition, the first two or three should contain only TU to be divided to ensure children understand the method, for example: 6)85   7)83   19)237

More able: This group can work with larger divisors, and with Th H T U, for example: 42)3285   112)5482

```
   768
 - 300  (30 x 10)
   468
 - 300  (30 x 10)
   168
 - 150  (30 x 5)
    18
Answer = 25 r 18
```

Plenary & assessment

Refer back to the first calculation in the main teaching activity: 768 ÷ 30. Remind the children that you subtracted 10 multiples of 30, then 10 more multiples of 30. Ask: *Was there a more efficient way of doing this sum?* Elicit that they could have subtracted 20 multiples of 30. Discuss that the larger the 'chunks' they subtract, the more efficient the method. Try the following together: 845 ÷ 24. Work through the children's suggestions for the size of the 'chunks' to subtract.

Lesson ③

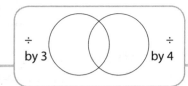

Starter

Draw a Venn diagram on the board, with one circle labelled 'Can be divided by 4' and the other labelled 'Can be divided by 3'. Write the following numbers on the board: 15, 24, 72, 36, 27, 12, 45, 56, 81, 63, 21, 32. Ask the children to use their knowledge of multiplication facts to insert the numbers into the correct part of the Venn diagram. Collect answers and check accuracy. Repeat for other times-tables if required

Main teaching activity

```
       33   r 4
 18)598
    - 54
      58
    - 54
       4
```

Whole class: Explain to children that they are going to work on the standard method of division. Refer back to Year 5, when they practised short division. Explain that they are now going to learn long division, which is an efficient way to divide by TU. Write the following calculation on the board: 598 ÷ 18. Show the standard layout (see margin). Work through the calculation with the children: *59 divided by 18 is 3. 3 x 18 is 54. Write 54 under the 59. 59 – 54 leaves 5. Bring down the 8 to make 58. 58 divided by 18 is 3. Then 3 ×18 = 54. Write 54 under the 58. 58 – 54 is 4, which is the remainder.*

Work through some more examples with the children, including the division of decimals, for example: 367·9 ÷ 19. Explain to the children that before starting any workings, the decimal point should be entered in the answer space above, in line with the point in the number to be divided.

```
      19·3 r 12
 19)367·9
    - 19
     177
   - 171
      6·9
      5 7
      1 2
```

Individual/paired work: Put a range of division sentences on the board for children to work through, for example: 27)703   19)47·29 Children should be encouraged to use the calculator to check answers by using the inverse operation.

Differentiation

Less able: Work with this group, consolidating the short division method and then introducing the long division method, using examples such as: 17)283

More able: This group should be given decimals involving larger numbers, for example: 32)213·43

Plenary & assessment

Pose the following questions: *Fifty-eight eggs are put into boxes of six. How many full boxes will I fill?*
Thirteen people share a cash prize of £875 between them. How much does each person get?
Discuss which would be the best methods to solve each question – mental, informal with jottings
or a standard method. Ask children why they would choose each method. Ask them to work
in pairs to solve each question using their chosen method. Discuss answers and correct any
misconceptions.

Lesson

Starter

Ask the children to round the number that you say to the nearest 10. Explain that you will give a few seconds
thinking time then ask for volunteers to say the rounded number. Say, for example, *Round these numbers to the
nearest 10: 24, 56, 176, 2003 …* Repeat this for rounding to the nearest 100, choosing numbers such as 54, 83,
296, 409, 837. Then ask the children to round to the nearest 1000, choosing numbers such as 1295 and 841.

Main teaching activity

a $\overline{72\,r\,1}$
$6\overline{)433}$

b   72.16
  $6\overline{)433.00}$

Whole class: Write the sum 433 ÷ 6 on the board. Ask a child to complete the calculation shown
in the margin **(a)**. Explain that there are three ways to show the remainder: as a whole number, as
a fraction or as a decimal. The method above shows the remainder as a whole number. To show it
as a fraction, explain that the divisor (6) is the denominator, and the remainder (1) is the numerator,
giving a fraction remainder of 1/6. To write as a decimal, they should continue the calculation by
adding a decimal place and two zeros. The division method then continues (see **b** in the margin).
Two decimal places is accurate enough.

Work through some more examples with the children, asking them to give the remainder in
all three ways each time. Write the following problem on the board: *A minibus holds 18 passengers.*
230 people need to travel to a football match. How many minibuses will they need? Ask the children
to work in pairs to solve the problem. Remind them to choose the most appropriate way to show
the remainder. Collect in answers. Establish that the calculation gives an answer of 12 r 14. Ask:
What does this mean? Twelve minibuses will be full and there will be 14 people left, therefore another
minibus must be hired, making a total of 13 minibuses. Discuss how remainders sometimes need to
be rounded up or down, depending on the context.

Pose the next question: *Felt pens are packed in boxes of 18. If there are 230 felt pens, how many full*
boxes can be made? Establish that we already know the answer to the calculation from the previous
question (12 r 14). However, in this context we round down – only 12 boxes can be made, so the
final answer is 12, not 13 as in the previous problem.

Next ask: *If I spend £86 on six CDs, what is the average cost per CD, to the nearest pound?* Ask
children to perform the calculation with their partner. Again, remind them about the importance
of selecting the correct form of remainder. Collect answers – establish that all calculated the
remainder as a decimal, to enable it to be written as £.p: 14·33
                                                        $6\overline{)86·00}$

Discuss the answer. (The CDs cost £14 to the nearest pound.)
Individual work: Children use the 'Up or down' activity sheet to practise examples of problems
requiring them to round up or down depending on the context.

Differentiation

Less able: This group should work on the less demanding version of the activity sheet, which
requires them to use short division only.
More able: Children in this group should be provided with the version of the activity sheet that
requires them to work on more complex problems that involve the use of long division. You may

wish to show this group how to convert a remainder that is written as a fraction (eg 1/8) to a decimal using a calculator (1/8 is the same as $1 \div 8 = 0 \cdot 125$). Give examples for the children to try.

Plenary & assessment

Choose one question from each sheet to discuss with the class. Ask children from each group to explain why they rounded their answers up or down.

Lesson ⑤

Starter

Explain that you will write four numbers on the board. Ask the children to order the numbers from smallest to largest on their whiteboards and when you say *Show me* they hold these up. Write sets of numbers such as: 621, 126, 261, 162; 543, 285, 666, 656. Include some examples of negative integers such as: 5, −2, 3, −3; and money and measures such as: £2.40, £1.50, £3.20, £2.20; and 47cm, 174cm, 74cm, 32cm.

Main teaching activity

Whole class: Pose the following problem: *The 32 children in Class 6 go on a visit to a safari park. The trip costs £450 altogether. If the coach cost £250, how much did each child pay for their safari park ticket?*

Establish the procedure for solving the problem. Read it carefully, then decide upon the appropriate operations to use. In this case, the children should realise that first they have to subtract the cost of the coach. Once this has been done, they will need to use a division method. Discuss whether this can be done mentally or whether a pencil and paper method should be used. Work through the problem together (see margin). Each ticket cost £6·25.

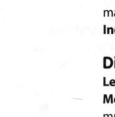

$£450 - 250 = £200.$

$$32\overline{)200 \cdot 00}\quad 6 \cdot 25$$

Write the next problem on the board and ask the children to work in pairs to solve it. Remind them that if there is a remainder, they must decide whether or not it needs to be rounded up or down. *A chocolate bar costs 32p. A pack of six of the same bar costs £1·86. Which is the cheapest way to buy the bar?* Collect answers. Discuss the method used. Ask: *Could this be done mentally or did you need to use a written method?* Establish that it is cheaper to buy a six-pack – the bars cost 31p each.

Write the final problem on the board: *A school magazine contains 21 pages. The photocopier produces 2949 pages and then breaks down. How many magazines can be made?* Ask children to work in pairs to solve the problem. Collect answers. Establish that the calculation gives the answer 140 r 9. Discuss what to do with the remainder – in this case, round down, as the question asks 'how many magazines can be made'.

Individual work: Provide children with copies of the 'Word problems' activity sheet.

Differentiation

Less able: This group should work on the less demanding version of the activity sheet.
More able: Children in this group should be provided with the version of the activity sheet with multi-step problems.

Plenary & assessment

Remind children that Units 2 and 3 involved solving real life and multi-step problems. Ask them with a partner, to produce a set of rules or guidelines to show how to solve written problems. These can be displayed in the maths area as a reminder for use in other units.

Name	Date

Division bingo

A Game for 2 Players

Preparation

Cut out the two game cards, the divisor cards and the number cards. Give a game card to each player, and put the divisor cards and number cards face down in two separate piles.

How to play

Take it in turns to pick up a divisor card and a number card. Divide the number by the divisor. If you have the answer on your game card, cross it out. Put the divisor and number cards back at the bottom of each pile. The winner is the first to cross out all the numbers on their card.

Game card 1

1·76	1·36	4·9	187	0·34
17·1	0·593	0·117	34	9·78

Game card 2

3·4	18·7	0·136	49	5·93
17·6	0·49	1·17	1·71	0·978

Divisor cards

10	100	1000

Number cards

340	176	490	593	171
1870	13·6	11·7	59·3	97·8

| Name | Date |

Up or down?

Solve each question, then decide how the answer should be written. Will you round it up, round it down, or leave it as it is?

A garden centre plants seedlings in trays of 35. How many trays can be filled with 465 seedlings?	_____
A tractor can take 24 people in a trailer on a trip around the farm. On the first day of the holidays it took 610 people around the farm. How many trips did it make?	_____
Crayons are packed in boxes of 15. How many full boxes can be made from 460 crayons?	_____
Eggs are packed in boxes of six. How many boxes are needed to pack 992 eggs?	_____
Thirty-eight people can sit in a row at a concert hall. How many rows will be needed to sit 1200 people?	_____
Fruit sweets cost 15p a tube. How many tubes can I buy for £3·22?	_____
A jug holds 750ml. How many jugs will I need to make $7\frac{1}{4}$l of squash?	_____
How many full packets of cereal bars can be made from 5000 bars if there are 12 bars in each packet?	_____
Mrs Carr pays £1350 for a new three-piece suite for her lounge. She pays for it in monthly payments of £65. How long will it take her to pay for the suite? How much will her last payment be?	_____ _____
Make up a problem for your friend to solve. Check it through carefully and make sure you know the answer before you pass it on! _____ _____ _____ _____	

Autumn term
Unit 4

Fractions, ratio and proportion

This unit looks at fractions in both practical and word-problem contexts. It shows how to order fractions by converting to a common denominator, how to find equivalents and how to reduce fractions to their simplest forms. Lesson 5 links fractions to proportion in a word-problem context.

LEARNING OBJECTIVES

		Topics	Starter	Main teaching activity
Lesson	1	Fractions, decimals, percentages, ratio and proportion	● Use related facts and doubling or halving.	● Change a fraction such as 33/8 to the equivalent mixed number (4 1/8) and vice versa.
Lesson	2	Fractions, decimals, percentages, ratio and proportion	● Consolidate all strategies from previous year, including: use the relationship between addition and subtraction.	● Recognise relationships between fractions: for example, that 1/10 is ten times 1/100, and 1/16 is half of 1/8. ● Recognise the equivalence between the decimal and fraction forms.
Lesson	3	Fractions, decimals, percentages, ratio and proportion	As for Lesson 2.	● Order fractions such as 2/3, 3/4 and 5/6 by converting them to fractions with a common denominator, and position them on a number line.
Lesson	4	Fractions, decimals, percentages, ratio and proportion	● Consolidate all strategies from previous year, including: add or subtract the nearest multiple of 10, 100 or 1000, then adjust.	**● Reduce a fraction to its simplest form by cancelling common factors** in the numerator and denominator.
Lesson	5	Fractions, decimals, percentages, ratio and proportion	As for Lesson 4.	● **Solve simple problems involving ratio and proportion.**

Lessons overview

Preparation
Prepare paper fraction strips for less able children for Lesson 3.

Learning objectives
Starters
● Use related facts and doubling or halving.
● Consolidate all strategies from previous year, including: use the relationship between addition and subtraction.
● Consolidate all strategies from previous year, including: add or subtract the nearest multiple of 10, 100 or 1000, then adjust.
Main teaching activities
● Change a fraction such as 33/8 to the equivalent mixed number (4⅛) and vice versa.
● Recognise relationships between fractions: for example, that 1/10 is ten times 1/100, and 1/16 is half of 1/8.
● Recognise the equivalence between the decimal and fraction forms.
● Order fractions such as 2/3, 3/4 and 5/6 by converting them to fractions with a common denominator, and position them on a number line.
● **Reduce a fraction to its simplest form by cancelling common factors** in the numerator and denominator.
● **Solve simple problems involving ratio and proportion.**

Vocabulary
numerator, denominator, mixed number, improper fraction, equivalent, Venn diagram, ratio, proportion, per cent, %, percentage, decimal fraction, >, greater than, bigger than, <, less than, smaller than

You will need:
Photocopiable pages
A copy of 'All mixed up' (page 31) and 'Mark up' (page 32) for each child.

CD Pages
A copy of 'Fraction wall' for each child and a class copy, a copy of the 'Fraction muncher' game for each more able child; a copy of 'All Mixed up' for each less able child, and differentiated copies of 'Cancelling fractions', 'Mark up' and 'All in proportion' for each more able and less able child (see General resources).

Equipment
Whiteboards; dice; plastic fraction sets; paper fraction strips.

Lesson ①

Starter

Ask a child to throw the dice. Use the numbers to form two-digit numbers, for example 23 from 2 and 3. Tell the children they have 1 minute to keep doubling 23. Ask: *How far can you get?* At the end of 1 minute, discuss answers and share strategies. Repeat for other numbers generated by throwing the dice.

Main teaching activity

Whole class: Check that all children understand the terms 'numerator' and 'denominator'. Draw three large pizzas on the board, each divided into six equal portions. Ask what fraction of a pizza one slice is (1/6). Remind children that six pieces make one whole one: 6/6 = 1 (Year 5).

Tell the children that you have eaten 2 1/6 of the pizzas. Ask: *How many sixths are left?* (5) *How many sixths have been eaten?* (13) Explain that 2 1/6 = 13/6 and that 2 1/6 is known as a 'mixed number'. Also, that 13/6 is known as an improper fraction because the numerator is greater than the denominator. Ask: *If I had 19/6, what would this be as a mixed number?* (3 1/6) *How many pizzas could I make from 23/6?* Try the following questions, asking the children to show the answers on their whiteboards: *Change 1 1/4 into an improper fraction. Change 11/8 into a mixed number. If each cake can be cut into 8 pieces, how many cakes do I need to hand out 30 pieces? How many pieces will I have left?*

Group work: Provide children with copies of the 'All mixed up' activity sheet. This contains practice questions requiring mixed numbers to be changed to improper fractions and vice versa.

Differentiation

Less able: This group should work on the less demanding version of the activity sheet. Plastic fraction sets may be needed if some children still require apparatus to help their understanding.
More able: Challenge the children to add simple mixed numbers involving the fractions 1/2, 1/4 and 3/4, for example, 2 1/2 + 3 3/4. Stress the need to add whole numbers first and then the fractions.

Plenary & assessment

Write the following on the board: 4 4/5 = 24/5; 3 9/12 = 4 5/12; 5 2/6 = 32/6. Tell the children that only one of these statements is correct. Ask: *Which one is it? Why are the other two incorrect? What should the correct answers be?*

Lesson ②

Starter

Explain that you will say a two-digit number. Ask the children to find quickly the number that when added to your number makes a total of 100. Now ask the children to give all the related facts. For example, for 37: 37 + 63 = 100 and 63 + 37 = 100, 100 − 37 = 63 and 100 − 63 = 37.

Main teaching activity

Whole class: Give each child a copy of the 'Fraction wall' resource sheet. Use the walls to compare fractions by asking questions such as: *One-third is equivalent to how many sixths? Six-ninths is equivalent to how many sixths? One-eighth is half of what? One-third is how many times bigger than 1/9?* and so on.

Draw the diagram on the left on the board. Ask the children: *Using the fraction walls, can you write down three equivalent fractions? How can you find a fourth equivalent without using the fraction wall?*

Write on the board 1/4 = 2/8 = 3/12 = 4/16. Identify the pattern of the numerator and the denominator and write the next two fractions in the sequence. Repeat for other fractions like 1/5 and 1/3.

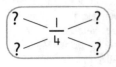

2/3 = — = — = — = —
1/6 = — = — = — = —
2/4 = — = — = — = —
2/5 = — = — = — = —
3/7 = — = — = — = —

Paired work: Ask the children to work in pairs to find equivalents of the fractions shown by creating a list and identifying the patterns formed by the numerator and denominator.

Differentiation

Less able: This group may require adult support to recognise and generate the number sequences.
More able: This group should be able to find the equivalents without having to write them in a linear format. Alternatively, the 'Fraction muncher' game could be used.

Plenary & assessment

Write the following fraction families on the board: 1/4 = 2/8 = 4/16 = 8/30 = 16/64; 1/5 = 2/10 = 3/15 = 4/25 = 5/30 = 6/35. Can the children identify the mistakes in each family? Ask: *What needs to be done to correct each mistake?*

Lesson ③

Starter

Explain that you would like the children to work out mentally one fact, then derive the three linked facts. For example, say: *What is 1000 subtract 450?* (550) The children now give the linked facts of: 1000 − 550 = 450; 450 + 550 = 1000; 550 + 450 = 1000. Repeat for other facts, such as: 1.6 + 3.8 and 420 + 730.

Main teaching activity

Whole class: Remind children of the work they did in the previous lesson on equivalence. Demonstrate a further way of finding equivalent fractions by multiplying the numerator and the denominator by the same number. Write up the following fractions as examples.

Then ask children to find equivalents of 4/9, 7/12 and 3/7 using the method shown. Explain that this method can be used to help order fractions that have different denominators. Ask the children to order 12/15, 13/15 and 9/15, smallest to largest. Ask: *Why is it so easy to do?* (They have the same denominator.) Now ask them to try 3/5, 5/6 and 2/3. Ask: *Why is this more difficult?* (The denominators are different.) Explain that the solution lies in finding a denominator that is common to the 5, 6 and 3. Establish that 30 is the common number here. Refer to the earlier method as a way to convert 3/5, 5/6 and 2/3 to thirtieths.

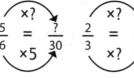

As you work through each calculation, give less information, so children identify what number they need to use as the multiplier. Repeat for 1/8, 4/12, 9/24 and 3/4, 1/2, 4/8 and 4/5.
Group work: Give out the 'Mark up' activity sheet. Tell children they have a set of fractions with each line, which need to be changed to have a common denominator. The converted fractions then need to be placed on the number line.

Differentiation

Less able: Prepare a long strip of paper marked with a number line in the same way as the activity sheet. Work with the group to change the fractions, and ask the children to write the positions of the fractions on the line.
More able: Give this group the version of the activity sheet where they have to draw their own number lines. Without the visual clues they will need to establish the most suitable common denominators.

Plenary & assessment

Ask the children: *Would you rather have 5/8 or 3/5 of a bar of chocolate?* Discuss what they would need to do to find which would be the larger piece. Ask: *Which is the bigger of the two?* (5/8 is 25/40, while 3/5 is 24/40)

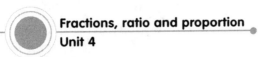

Lesson ④

Starter

Remind the children of the strategy of adding and subtracting by adding/subtracting a multiple of 10, 100 or 1000, then adjusting. Begin with examples which involve adding/subtracting multiples of 10 such as 426 + 61 and 594 – 61. Now include some examples which involve adding/subtracting a multiple of 100, then adjusting, such as 286 + 94 and 503 – 296.

Main teaching activity

Whole class: Discuss how it is sometimes easier to work with fractions if they are in their simplest form. Refer to the fraction wall and show that 3/9 can be written as 2/6 or 1/3. Ask: *What could 4/8 be written as and which is its simplest form?* Also investigate 6/9, 4/5 and 12/16.

Explain to the children that they can use division to help find a fraction's simplest form in a similar way as they used multiplication for finding equivalence. Demonstrate the method using 6/18 as an example. Ask: *What number can be divided into 6 and 18?* Children could offer a range. Accept one (eg 2) and divide the numerator and the denominator by the number: 6/18 ÷ 2 = 3/9.

Ask: *Can this fraction be divided even further?* (Yes, divide by 3: 3/9 ÷ 3 = 1/3.) Ask: *Was there a divisor that would have got to 1/3 at the first attempt?* (yes, 6) Now try other examples, like 4/16, 7/21 and so on.

Group work: Provide children with the 'Cancelling fractions' activity sheet to support the work.

Differentiation

Less able: This group should work on the less demanding version of the activity sheet.
More able: This group should use the more demanding version of the activity sheet.

Plenary & assessment

Use the 'bigger than' and 'smaller than' signs (< and >) from Unit 1 to check the children's understanding of cancelling down and simplest form. For example, ask: *Which is the largest of these pairs of fractions: 3/24 and 6/36?* (1/8 < 1/6) ... *21/28 and 105/30?* (3/4 > 1/2) ... *10/50 and 20/60?* (1/5 < 1/3).

Lesson ⑤

Starter

Repeat the Starter for Lesson 4, including some examples of adding/subtracting a multiple of 1000 then adjusting, such as 5006 – 1998 and 3002 + 496.

Main teaching activity

Whole class: Explain that proportion compares a part of something with the whole. For instance, in a packet of five sweets, two sweets are toffees and three are fudge. The toffees can be indicated as 2/5 or 2 out of 5. Then try this question: *Sally has three pens and Josh has three times as many. How many pens are there? What proportion of the pens does each child have?* (Sally has 3/12, Josh has 9/12.)

Group work: Provide the 'All in proportion' activity sheet, to solve.

Differentiation

Less able: Use the version of the activity sheet where tiles are coloured in relation to given proportions.
More able: Provide the more challenging word-based problems sheet involving proportion.

Plenary & assessment

Choose two or three problems from the main 'All in proportion' activity sheet.

Name   Date

All mixed up

Change these improper fractions to mixed numbers and vice versa.

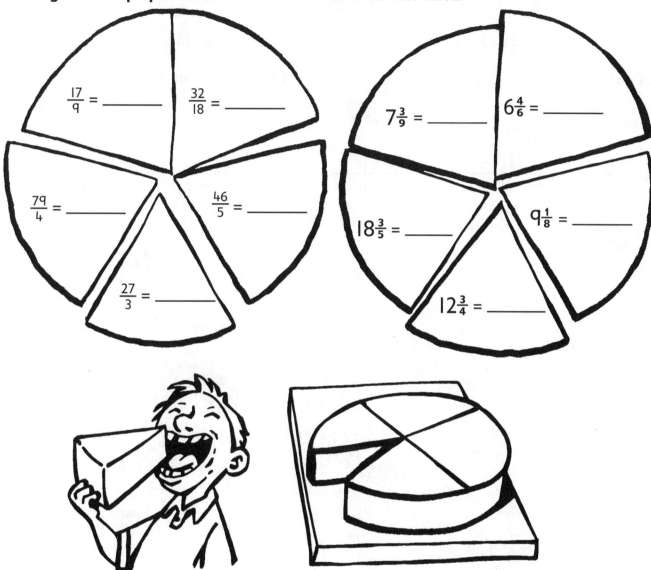

Answer the following questions.

1. Pizzas can be cut into eighths. How many slices will I have if I buy $6\frac{3}{4}$ pizzas? _____

2. Small birthday cakes are cut up into fifths. How many cakes would I have if I had $\frac{65}{5}$? _____

3. Gel pens come in packs of eight. I have 65 pens. How many packs can I make? _____

How many pens will be left over? _____

4. One sixth of a roll of fabric is used to make one curtain. I have to make 50 curtains. How many

rolls of fabric do I need? _____

Name	Date

Mark up

Mark the position of these fractions on the number line:

$\dfrac{3}{4}$ $\qquad$ $\dfrac{2}{5}$ $\qquad$ $\dfrac{7}{20}$ $\qquad$ $\dfrac{7}{10}$ $\qquad$ $\dfrac{4}{5}$ $\qquad$ $\dfrac{1}{2}$ $\qquad$ $\dfrac{9}{20}$

What must you do before you can order them? Change to have a common denominator.

Now try these:

$\dfrac{8}{12}$ $\qquad$ $\dfrac{5}{6}$ $\qquad$ $\dfrac{3}{36}$ $\qquad$ $\dfrac{1}{2}$ $\qquad$ $\dfrac{3}{4}$ $\qquad$ $\dfrac{2}{9}$ $\qquad$ $\dfrac{5}{18}$ $\qquad$ $\dfrac{1}{9}$ $\qquad$ $\dfrac{1}{4}$

Autumn term
Unit 5
Fractions, decimals and percentages, ratio and proportion

This unit looks at the links between fractions, decimals and percentages, and ratio and proportion. Children are given practice in finding simple percentages of quantities, and expressing simple fractions as percentages. In addition, decimal notation up to and including thousandths is reinforced, particularly in relation to measures.

LEARNING OBJECTIVES

	Topics	Starter	Main teaching activity
Lesson 1	Fractions, decimals, percentages, ratio and proportion	● Order fractions by converting them into fractions with a common denominator.	● **Understand percentage as the number of parts in every 100.** ● Express simple fractions as percentages. ● **Find simple percentages of small whole-number quantities.**
Lesson 2	Fractions, decimals, percentages, ratio and proportion	● **Find simple percentages of small whole-number quantities.**	● Use decimal notation for tenths and hundredths in calculations. ● **Understand percentage as the number of parts in every 100.**
Lesson 3	Fractions, decimals, percentages, ratio and proportion	● Use related facts and doubling and halving.	● Know what each digit represents in a number with up to three decimal places. ● Use decimal notation for tenths, hundredths and thousandths when recording measurements. ● Give a decimal fraction lying between two others, eg between 3.4 and 3.5. ● Round a number with two decimal places to the nearest tenth.
Lesson 4	Fractions, decimals, percentages, ratio and proportion	● Express simple fractions as percentages.	As for Lesson 3.
Lesson 5	Fractions, decimals, percentages, ratio and proportion	● Round a number with two decimal places to the nearest tenth.	● **Solve simple problems involving ratio and proportion.**

Lessons overview

Learning objectives
Starters
● Order fractions by converting them into fractions with a common denominator.
● **Find simple percentages of small whole-number quantities.**

Main teaching activities
● **Understand percentage as the number of parts in every 100.**
● Express simple fractions as percentages.
● **Find simple percentages of small whole-number quantities.**
● Use decimal notation for tenths and hundredths in calculations.

Vocabulary
equivalent, denominator, per cent, %, percentage, whole, half, quarter, tenth, hundredth, cancel, reduced to

You will need:
CD Pages
A copy of 'Percentages' and 'Dominoes' for each child, differentiated copies of 'Percentages' for each less able and more able child (see General resources).

Equipment
Whiteboards; a blank 100 square for each child; coloured pencils.

Lesson ①

Starter

Write the following sets of fractions on the class board: set 1: 6/12, 3/4, 2/3, 1/2, 1/3; set 2: 2/5, 3/20, 6/10, 1/4, 3/4, 17/20); set 3: 11/16, 1/4, 3/8, 1/2, 7/8, 1/16; set 4: 1/5, 2/3, 9/15, 4/5, 2/15. Organise children into groups of three or four, with one whiteboard per group. Ask the groups to convert the fractions in set 1 to have a common denominator and then rewrite in order of size. Allow a time limit. Can the children 'beat the clock'? Repeat for each set. Discuss findings, checking that each group chose the appropriate common denominator.

Main teaching activity

Whole class: Explain the term 'per cent' (per = for every, cent = 100). Ask: *Can you think of other words with 'cent'?* (century, centurion, centipede) Discuss how percentages equate to the number of parts in every 100.

Explain that although 100% is the whole amount, there does not have to be 100 in the group. If there are 32 children in a class, then this is 100%, the whole amount. If we want to find 25% of the class, then the percentage can be converted to a fraction to help us, for example, 25% = 1/4 , so 25% of 32 = 1/4, 1/4 of 32 = 8.

Help the class convert the following percentages to their equivalent fractions: 50%, 75%, 10%, 20%, 1%. Ask a few simple questions to check understanding, such as: *What is 10% of 70? A pair of jeans costs £20. In the sale they are 20% cheaper. How much do they cost now?*
Individual work: Give each child a copy of the 'Percentages' activity sheet, which has a range of written problems to be solved.

Differentiation

Less able: Give this group the version of 'Percentages' that sets problems using simple percentages.
More able: Give this group the version of 'Percentages' that sets problems extending beyond the percentages used in the main lesson.

Plenary & assessment

Write the following numbers on the board: 10, 25, 7, 40, 13, 63. Ask children, in pairs, to choose three of the numbers and make up statements which result in the chosen number as the answer, for example: *A coat costs £70. It is reduced by 10%. I save £7.* Or, *A coat costs £70. It is reduced by 10%. It now costs £63.*

Lesson ②

Starter

Write the following numbers on the board: 10, 15, 45, 3, 5, 17, 150, 1, 225, 96, 30, 12, 4, 75, 83. Ask the children to draw a 4 x 2 grid on their whiteboards, choosing a different number from the list above to go in each box. Play 'Percentage Bingo' by asking questions that have answers from the list above, for example: *What is 10% of 150? What is 20% of 20?* The first child to cross out all eight answers on their board is the winner.

Main teaching activity

Whole class: Remind children that 1/10 can be written as 0·1 and 1/100 as 0·01. If necessary, show this pictorially (see margin).

Give out the blank 100 squares and ask the children to colour in one square. Ensure that they understand that this is equivalent to 1/100 or 0·01 or 1%. Ask them to colour in the following numbers of squares, in a different colour each time, writing each set as a decimal, a fraction and a percentage: 10 squares; 20 squares; 25 squares and 40 squares. Discuss the relationships between decimals, fractions and percentages.

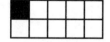

Group work: Give out the 'Dominoes' activity sheet. Ask children to cut out the dominoes. Working in mixed-ability groups of four, ask children to arrange the dominoes to form a continuous loop by matching equivalent percentages, decimals and fractions. Establish a group to work with the teacher, made up of those children who are finding it particularly difficult to understand the links between fractions, decimals and percentages

Plenary & assessment

Choose three dominoes from the set that do not go together. Draw them on the board and ask children to explain why they do not match. Ask for volunteers to bring out the correct dominoes.

Lessons   overview

Preparation
Prepare the multilink pattern described in the main lesson, or draw it on the board.

Learning objectives

Starters
- Use related facts and doubling and halving.
- Express simple fractions as percentages.
- Round a number with two decimal places to the nearest tenth.

Main teaching activities
- Know what each digit represents in a number with up to three decimal places.
- Use decimal notation for tenths, hundredths and thousandths when recording measurements.
- Give a decimal fraction lying between two others, eg between 3.4 and 3.5.
- Round a number with two decimal places to the nearest tenth.
- Solve simple problems involving ratio and proportion.

Vocabulary
place value, tenth, hundredth, thousandth, in every, for every

You will need:

CD Pages
A copy of 'Number lines' and 'Ratio and proportion' for each child; differentiated copies of 'Number lines' for each less able and more able child (see General resources).

Equipment
Whiteboards; number fans; 30cm rulers, with mm markings; metre sticks, calculators; multilink cubes.

Lesson

Starter

Write the following facts on the board: 1 x 28 = 28; 2 x 28 = 56; 4 x 28 = 112; 8 x 28 = 224; 16 x 28 = ? Discuss how each answer has been arrived at. What is the missing answer? Ask children questions such as: *What is 5 x 28? What is 12 x 28?* Make sure they understand how to use the information to help them with their calculations. Discuss answers, recapping strategies used.

Main teaching activity

Whole class: Draw a decimal place value chart on the board: T U · t h th. Place digits on the chart and discuss values, for example, 0·02 = 2/100; 0·007 = 7/1000; 0·46 = 46/100. Begin to relate this to measurements. Tell children a class is running in a charity race. They have to run for 1km. Ask: *How many metres in a kilometre?* Say: *After 0·735km, two of the class stop for a rest.* Discuss the value of each digit: 7/10km, 3/100km and 5/1000km. Establish that this equals 700m, 30m and 5m. Ask: *How many metres in 1km? So how far is left to run?*

Repeat for other distances, ensuring children understand the value of each digit and its value in relation to distance. In particular, ensure children know that 1/1000km= 1m.

Individual/paired work: Ask children to measure various items around the classroom, such as an exercise book, the height of a table, and so on. Results should be written both in centimetres and as a decimal fraction of a metre, for example, 38cm = 0·38m.

Differentiation

Less able: These children may need to be supported in the writing of measurements as decimal fractions.

Plenary & assessment

Write 67·5cm on the board. Ask for ideas on how this could be written in metres. Elicit that there are 0 metres, 6 tenths, 7 hundredths and 5 thousandths = 0·675m.

Lesson 4

Starter

Use whiteboards or number fans to show the answers to quick-fire questions expressing simple fractions as percentages, such as: 1/5, 3/5, 1/4, 3/4, 1/100, 1/10, 6/10, 1/20, 7/20, 63/100.

Main teaching activity

Whole class: Draw the following number line on the board:

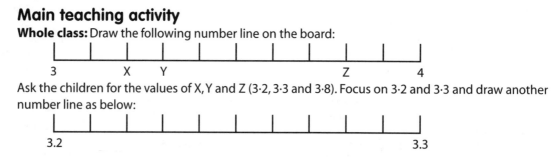

Ask the children for the values of X, Y and Z (3·2, 3·3 and 3·8). Focus on 3·2 and 3·3 and draw another number line as below:

Ask: *How can we find the values of the numbers in between?* Elicit that we can mark the divisions in hundredths. Mark on each of the divisions, 3·21, 3·22, 3·23 etc.

Tell the children they are going to focus on 3·22 to 3·23. Ask them to draw a number line for 3·22 to 3·23, drawing the divisions in between and labelling each division. Discuss findings, establishing that the new divisions are thousandths (3·221, 3·222, 3·223 etc.).

Use the number lines on the board, plus the one on the children's whiteboards, to round decimals to two decimal places to the nearest tenth, and decimals to three places to the nearest hundredth. For example, on the number line 3·2 to 3·3, point to 3·23 and ask: *Is 3·23 nearer to 3·2 or 3·3?* Choose various numbers on each of the number lines and ask children to round to the nearest tenth or hundredth.

Individual work: Provide the children with the 'Number lines' activity sheet. This has blank number lines for children to fill in and use to round decimals to the nearest tenth.

Differentiation

Less able: Provide this group with the version of the activity sheet with rounding to the nearest whole number only.

More able: Provide this group with the version of the activity sheet that extends children to work on rounding to the nearest hundredth.

Plenary & assessment

Remove any number lines from the whiteboard and ask children to cover up their activity sheets. Without these visual aids, ask children to round the following numbers to one decimal place, in other words to the nearest tenth: 5·39, 4·41, 8·356, 2·75. Focus on 8·356 and 2·75. Ask for an explanation of the procedure that was needed to round 8·356 to the nearest tenth. Ask: *What about 2·75 – what happens when the last digit is a 5?*

Tell the children they are now going to round to two decimal places. Ask: *What decimal position will this be?* (hundredths) Ask them to round the following numbers to two decimal places: 23·592, 4·335, 19·044.

Lesson ⑤

Starter

Play 'Decimal swap' in pairs. Give children calculations to do on calculators, which give answers to two decimal places (eg 26·2 ÷ 3). The first child does the calculation and the other child in the pair rounds the answer to the nearest tenth, then the nearest whole number. Swap and repeat for different numbers.

Main teaching activity

Whole class: Explain the term 'ratio' – a comparison of part to part: *I have one toffee **for** every five humbugs.* Explain that this is written as 1:5, and is a total of six items, one toffee and five humbugs. Explain the term 'proportion' – how many in each group: *I have one toffee **in** every five sweets.* Explain that this is written as 1/5 and is a total of five items, one toffee and four other sweets.

ROSES	WEEDS
2	1
4	2
6	3
8	4

On the board, write: *Fred the gardener has two roses for every weed in his garden.* Then say: *He has eight roses, so how many weeds are there? …six roses, how many weeds?* For some children, it may be necessary to build up a chart so that they can see the relationship (see margin). Then ask: *If he has six weeds, how many roses will there be?*

Elicit how they would write down the ratio of roses to weeds (2:1) Ask: *What proportion of his plants are weeds?* Explain that there are three items in each group – two roses and one weed. Therefore, 1/3 are weeds. Ask: *What proportion are roses?* (2/3) Draw on the board, or use multilink to make the following pattern:

Blue	Blue	Green	B	B	G	B	B	G	B	B	G

Elicit that one in every three is green, so the proportion is 1/3 green, 2/3 blue. The ratio is one green for every blue, so is written 1:2. Ask the following questions: *If there were 30 squares, how many would be green? …blue? If there were 300 squares, how many would be green? …blue?* Encourage children to use their knowledge of finding fractions of quantities to help find the answers..

Individual work: Ask children to draw strips in their exercise books, colouring them in to match given ratios and proportions, for example, ask them to draw a strip divided into 18 equal parts and say: *Colour this strip red and yellow in the ratio of 2:4.* Ask them to draw a strip divided into 20 equal parts and say: *Colour this strip with three blue sections in every five.*

Differentiation

Less able: This group may need to be supported in this activity in order to access the correct vocabulary.

More able: The 'Ratio and proportion' activity sheet containing written problems can be used for this group. If using this sheet, you will need to work through the following question with this group to prepare them for the level of understanding needed. *There are 32 children in a class, in the ratio of three boys to five girls. How many are girls?* Explain that they need first to add up the parts (3 boys + 5 girls = 8 parts). Next, divide the number of children in the class by the number of parts (32 ÷ 8 = 4). Therefore: 3 boys x 4 = 12; 5 girls x 4 = 20, so there are 20 girls. If necessary, work through another question: *Richard, Joss and Sanjay have been given £80 to divide in the ratio 2:3:5. How much does each child get?*

Plenary & assessment

Ask four boys and three girls to come to the front of the class. Ask for the ratio and proportion of boys and girls. Invite two more girls to come to the front. Ask: *How do the ratio and proportion change?*

Handling data

This unit gives children practice in constructing and interpreting a range of graphs – pie charts, bar charts, line graphs and conversion graphs. In addition, it explains the terms mean, range, mode and median and gives practice in using these in context.

LEARNING OBJECTIVES

	Topics	Starter	Main teaching activity
Lesson 1 Lesson 2	Handling data	Use, read and write standard metric units (km, m, cm ,mm, kg, g, l ml,cl), including their abbreviations and relationships between them. Convert smaller to larger units (eg m to km, cm or mm, g to kg, ml to l) and vice versa.	**Solve a problem by extracting and interpreting data in charts.**
Lesson 3	Handling data	As for Lesson 1.	As for Lesson 1.
Lesson 4	Handling data	Use related facts and doubling or halving, for example, double or halve the most significant digits first.	Find the mode and range of a set of data. Begin to find the median and mean of a set of data.
Lesson 5	Handling data	As for Lesson 3.	**Solve a problem by extracting and interpreting data in charts and graphs.**
Lesson 6	Handling data	**Multiply and divide decimals mentally by 10 or 100, and integers by 1000, and explain the effect.**	Use the language of probability to discuss events, including those with equally likely outcomes.
Lesson 7	Handling data	As for Lesson 6.	As for Lesson 6.
Lesson 8	Handling data	As for Lesson 6.	As for Lesson 6.

Lessons overview

Preparation
Copy 'Space days' and 'Charity graph' onto acetate as OHTs. Check current rates of exchange for Lesson 5.

Learning objectives
Starters
 Use, read and write standard metric units (km, m, cm, mm, kg, g, l, ml, cl), including their abbreviations and relationships between them. Convert smaller to larger units (eg m to km, cm or mm, g to kg, ml to l) and vice versa.
 Use related facts and doubling or halving, for example, double or halve the most significant digits.
 Multiply and divide decimals mentally by 10 or 100, and integers by 1000, and explain the effect.
Main teaching activities
 Solve a problem by extracting and interpreting data in charts and graphs.
 Find the mode and range of a set of data.
 Begin to find the median and mean of a set of data.
 Use the language of probablility to discuss events, including those with equally likely outcomes.

Vocabulary
proportion, data, range, mode, median, mean, improper fraction, mixed number, graph, axis, axes, classify, outcome, label, title, diagram

You will need:

CD Pages
OHTs of 'Space days' and 'Charity graph'; a copy of 'Zarg the alien', 'Varik and friends' and 'Cool down' for each child, differentiated versions of 'Zarg the alien' for each less able and more able child (see General resources).

Equipment
An OHP; whiteboards.

Lesson ①

Starter

Explain that you will write on the board some abbreviations for metric units. Ask the children to give each unit's full name, and give an example of how it could be used. Use km, m, cm, mm, kg, g, l, ml, cl. Now say: *Convert 2.125km to metres. How many metres is it? Change 500 ml to litres.*

Main teaching activity

Whole class: Show the OHT of 'Space days'. Explain that the data is represented by sectors – like the pieces of a pie. Each sector represents the proportion of items in that sector. Ask: *What proportion of a Monday does Zarg spend in each lesson?* Establish that ¼ or 25% of the time is spent learning Martian (2 hours). This leaves 6 hours spent equally on astrophysics and intergalactic travel (3 hours each). Now use the OHT to show how his friend on Pluto spends his day. Ask: *What fraction of a Monday does Yardok spend on each subject? Which of the two spends the most time learning astrophysics?* Establish that we cannot tell because we do not know how long a school day is on Pluto. Tell the children a school day is 18 hours. Ask: *Now is it possible to find out who spends most time on each subject?* Stress that although the sector on Zarg's chart is bigger that on Yardok's, this does not mean it is a greater amount. It needs to be related to the overall amount in the whole chart.

Individual work: Give out the 'Zarg the alien' activity sheet, which provides practice interpreting and drawing pie charts.

Differentiation

Less able: This group should work on the less demanding version of the activity sheet.
More able: This group should be provided with copies of the version of 'Zarg the alien' where they are required to draw their own pie chart from the information given. This group may need support in the drawing activity.

Plenary & assessment

Check children's understanding of pie charts by revisiting the OHT of 'Space days'. This time change the number of hours in each school day and ask the children to give the value of each sector.

Lesson ②

9.2	8.6	3.7	6.1
4.2	5.9	3.3	2.9
4.8	5.7	6.5	2.4

Starter

Draw this grid on the board. Ask the children to draw a similar grid, without the numbers, on their whiteboards. In the spaces in their grids the children should write the complement to make each box total 10. Repeat so each box totals a different number eg 13.

Main teaching activity

Whole class: Show the 'Charity graph' OHT. Explain that the graph shows the amount of money collected by a group of children who are raising funds for charity. Point out that the data is grouped and that each block shows a range of amounts. Ask the children to tell you the range for each block on the graph. Follow this up with other questions. *How many children collected between £15 and £19.99? Look at the block £0 to £4.99. What is the largest amount that could have been collected by this group?* (£4.99 x 5) *What is the smallest amount?* (0 x 5). Point out that the graph cannot tell us exactly how much was raised, as each block does not give an exact amount. Establish how many children were collecting for charity altogether (50).

Paired or individual work: Ask the children to imagine that the group has been collecting for a further two months. What could the graph look like now? Ask the children to produce a graph of their predictions.

Differentiation

Less able: You may need to provide support for this group to help them with their predictions.
More able: Ask this group to think of other situations in which a graph of this kind showing grouped data might be used. Suggest they collect data and produce their own graph.

Plenary & assessment

Show the children 'Charity graph' OHT again. Revise the data shown. Then review the children's predictions as to how it might have changed. Establish that more children will appear in the last three blocks and fewer in the first three blocks, as the amount of money raised will have increased. Draw the predictions on the OHT. Explain that there is not a set answer as it is not possible to predict the outcome accurately. Establish that the number of children still adds up to 50. More able children may have added one or more blocks, £30–£34.99 and £35–£39.99.

Lesson ③

Starter

Play the game 'Show me' on whiteboards. Ask children to show the double of each number you call out. Start with these examples: 72, 126, 3.8, 0.7, 0.15. Explain that one way to solve these questions is to double the most significant figure first.

Main teaching activity

Whole class: Write the following numbers on the whiteboard: 3, 7, 2, 5, 3, 2, 1, 2, 4. Ask: *Which number appears the most?* (2) Explain that this is the 'mode' or the most frequent number. Write the following sets of numbers on the whiteboard: 11, 12, 13, 11, 10, 9, 11, 7 (11); 4, 3, 3, 3, 2, 4, 3, 4, 4, 6, 5, 6, 5 (3 and 4). Ask: *Which is the mode of each set?*

Amount of pocket money	£2	£4	£5	£6	£10
Number of children	5	8	4	3	3

Explain that sometimes data is in groups, known as 'modal groups'. Draw this pocket-money chart on the whiteboard. Then ask: *Which amount of pocket money do most children receive?* (£4) Say: *This is the modal group.*

Look at the first set of numbers again. Explain that you are now going to find the 'range'. Ask for the smallest size (1). Ask for the largest size (7). Ask: *What is the difference between them?* (6) This is the 'range'. Go on to find the range of the other three sets of data that have already been used.

Explain that yet another way of interpreting data is to find the 'median'. To do this the data has to be arranged in order of size, for example, for the numbers 1, 7, 12, 8, 13, 3, 1, the order would be 1, 1, 3, 7, 8, 12, 13. The median would be 7 because it is the middle number. Then find the medians of the other sets of data used previously. Explain what happens when there are two middle numbers because there is an even set of numbers in the group. In this case add the middle numbers and divide by 2.

Lastly, tell children they are going to find the 'mean' or 'average' of a set of data. Ask them to imagine that a parent wants to know how well their child is doing in spelling tests. It would take too long to go through every result, so the teacher would give an average score. For example, Shannon's test scores over a week were 13/20, 16/20, 12/20, 19/20 and 15/20. Ask children to estimate her average score. Then show them how to work it out. Add the scores (75). Divide by the number of tests (5): 75 ÷ 5 = 15. So, on average Shannon gets 15/20. Sometimes she is below her average (13 and 12) and sometimes she is above her average (16 and 19).

Individual work: Children work on the 'Varik and friends' activity sheet, which contains questions relating to mode, range and median.

Differentiation

Less able: This group should focus on questions 1 to 4. Work with them to ensure they receive support, particularly with questions 3 and 4.

More able: Encourage this group to work through the activity sheet as quickly as possible so they can move on to question 5, which deals with finding the mean.

Plenary & assessment

Ask for volunteers to explain the meaning of the words 'mode', 'median', 'range' and 'mean'. Encourage them to give real-life contexts in which they would be used. For example, the mode of a group of children's trainers sizes, the median in a survey of children's heights.

Lesson 4

Starter

Repeat the Starter for Lesson 3, but this time ask the children to halve the numbers that you say. Say, for example: *Find half of 68, 84, 92, 156.*

Main teaching activity

Whole class: Give out copies of the 'Cool down' activity sheet. Tell the children that the graph shows the results of a science experiment comparing how quickly hot water cools in different containers. A is a metal mug and B is a plastic disposable cup. Ensure children understand how to read the graph. Then ask them to fill in the missing information on the chart. Ask the following questions. *How many minutes does it take for A to reach 50°C?* (19 minutes approximately) *How many minutes does it take for B to reach the same temperature?* (12 minutes approximately) *For how many minutes is the temperature in container A above 45°C?* (25 minutes)

Discuss what might happen if the temperature of each container was measured for a further 20 minutes. Ask: *Would there be a point at which A and B were the same temperature? Would the temperatures eventually drop to 0°C?* Establish that temperatures would become equal to room temperature and would fall no lower.

Group work: Ask children to plot another set of data on the graph for container C, an insulated foam cup with a lid, using the data on the left.

Time (minutes)	0	10	15	20	30	40	50	60
Container C (Temperature in °C)	90	85	82	77	68	59	50	45

Differentiation

Less able: Provide support to ensure children plot the points in the correct positions on the graph.

More able: Do not provide this group with figures. Challenge them to plot what they think the rate of cooling would be and complete their own chart.

Plenary & assessment

Show on an OHP the results produced by the groups. Ask the children to pose questions about the results for others in the class to answer.

Lesson 5

Starter

Provide the children with the answer to a division calculation (eg 9). They have to write on their whiteboards as many facts as possible that will have this answer, for example, 63 ÷ 7 = 9. Give them a time limit, say 45 seconds, then share the responses. Move on to other numbers (eg 6 or 8). Encourage use of fractions, decimals and percentages, eg 3/9 of 27.

Main teaching activity

Whole class: Draw a grid on the whiteboard showing the vertical and horizontal axes. With the children, plot the following information. Josh and Sarah take part in a charity bicycle ride at a steady rate of 2km per 1/2 hour. Plot the journey over 180 minutes. (See diagram left.) Explain that points in between each marked division have a value. Ask questions like the following. *How long did it take for the children to travel 6km? How long did it take the children to travel 11km?* Explain that this is a conversion graph to show the relationship between two units of measurement and that intermediary points have values.

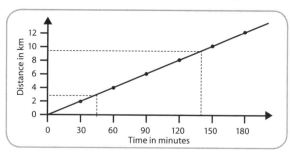

Individual work: Give out current rates of exchange from the local bank or the internet, or cut out the details from a newspaper. Ask children to plot their own conversion graph to change £s to another currency. Avoid using the Euro as this is featured in Term 2. Calculators could be used with conversions.

Differentiation

Less able: Choose a currency for this group that will be straightforward to convert.

More able: When this group has completed the graph, challenge them to make up questions based on it for the rest of the class to answer.

Plenary & assessment

Use the graph from the main teaching activity. Tell children that another child has joined the charity ride. Although she travels at 2km per 1/2 hour, she takes a 15-minute break after each hour of cycling. How would this be plotted on the graph? (It would be plotted as a straight line, keeping the same distance value, for 15 minutes of time.)

Lessons

Preparation

It may save time in all three lessons if duplicated sheets are provided for the children to record the results of their investigations.

Learning objectives

Starters

● **Multiply and divide decimals mentally by 10 or 100, and integers by 1000, and explain the effect.**

Main teaching activities

● Use the language of probability to discuss events, including those with equally likely outcomes.

Vocabulary

fair, unfair, likely, unlikely, likelihood, equally likely, certain, uncertain, probable, possible, impossible, chance, good chance, poor chance, no chance, equal chance

You will need:

Equipment
Collections of round coins, some bronze, some silver; 1–6 dice; coloured counters, especially red, blue and green; small bags.

Lesson

Starter

Revise what will happen when a decimal number is multiplied by 10, ie the digits will move one place to the left, eg 17.4 x 10 = 174 and 1.635 x 10 = 16.35. Try other examples with the children, varying the vocabulary as much as possible, eg *Make 24.9 ten times bigger. What is 9.04 times 10? What is the product of 10 and 152.75?*

Also revise that, when a number is divided by 10, the digits will move to the right eg 19.75 ÷ 10 = 1.975 and 456.7 ÷ 10 = 45.67. Again, work through other examples such as How many tens are there in 473.2. Divide 19.04 by 10. What is the quotient of 10 and 607?

Main teaching activity

Whole class: Tell the children they are going to investigate probability (the likelihood that something will or will not happen). First discuss the concepts of 'impossible' and 'certain'. If a ball is thrown into the air, for example, it is impossible for it to continue moving upwards. On the other hand, it is certain that the sun will rise tomorrow. Show the children an example of a simple probability scale in which impossible is 0, certain is 1 and all other probabilities lie somewhere between these two. These can be described using other phrases such as 'likely', 'unlikely', 'equally likely', 'no chance', 'good chance', 'poor chance', 'even chance'. Explain that probability and its connection with the study of statistics is an important area of mathematics and affects many ordinary situations like the outcome of sports events, weather conditions, insurance claims and traffic movements.

Paired work: Children, working in pairs, should start with an activity that has only two possible outcomes. When a coin is tossed, it is equally likely to come down heads or tails. This is what is known as an even chance. Children should predict how many heads and how many tails they would expect to get if the coin was tossed ten times. What result might be expected if the number of tosses was increased to 20, 50 or 100? They should test out their theories and record the results.

Differentiation

Less able: Keep the number of attempts down to small manageable amounts. Assist with methods of recording or provide this group with recording sheets that have already been prepared.

More able: This group could experiment with two coins, perhaps one bronze and one silver. *How many different ways are there for the coins to settle now? What is the probability of throwing a pair of heads or a pair of tails?*

Plenary & assessment

Review the outcomes of the coin tossing activities. How close were the children's results to their predictions? Did the number of tosses significantly affect the findings?

Lesson 7

For the **Starter** repeat the activities carried out in the starter for Lesson 6, but this time revise multiplying and dividing decimal numbers by 100, for example, 1.752 x 100 = 175.2 and 379.6 ÷ 100 = 3.796. During the **Main teaching activity** pairs of children should work with six-sided dice. They should investigate the likelihood of throwing odd/even numbers and the likelihood of throwing individual numbers 6, 4, 1. Review and discuss the results of the investigation in the **Plenary & assessment.** Ask children to try and plot the results on the 0 to 1 probability scale that was discussed in Lesson 6

Lesson 8

As the **Starter** activity children should revise multiplying and dividing an integer by 1000, or example, 527 x 1000 = 527,000 and 435,000 ÷ 1000 = 435. For the **Main teaching activity** provide groups of children with eight counters and a small bag. Five of the counters should be coloured red, two blue and one green. Encourage them first to think about possible outcomes in terms of fractions. They should predict the chances of pulling out each different colour and then test out their ideas. Remind them to replace the counter each time it has been taken out and to record their results fully. Check the findings during the **Plenary & assessment** session. Pool the results of all the groups together. Help children to appreciate that the larger the number of results collected, the more likelihood there is of getting closer to the ratio 5:2:1.

Shape and space

This unit explores the properties of quadrilaterals and gives practice in visualising shapes from given information. In addition, it covers plotting co-ordinates in all four quadrants.

LEARNING OBJECTIVES

		Topics	Starter	Main teaching activity
Lesson	1	Shape and space	● **Understand percentage as the number of parts in every 100.** ● **Find simple percentages of all whole–number quantities.**	● Classify quadrilaterals, using criteria such as parallel sides, equal angles, equal sides...
Lesson	2	Shape and space	● Express simple fractions such as one half, one quarter, three quarters, one third, two thirds…, and tenths and hundredths, as percentages.	As for Lesson 1.
Lesson	3	Reasoning and generalising about numbers or shapes	● **Order a mixed set of numbers with up to three decimal places.**	● Make and investigate a general statement about familiar numbers and shapes by finding examples that satisfy it.
Lesson	4	Shape and space	● Order a set of positive and negative integers.	● **Read and plot co-ordinates in all four quadrants.**
Lesson	5	Shape and space	● Derive quickly: division facts corresponding to tables up to 10 x 10; squares of multiples of 10 to 100 (eg 60 x 60).	● Recognise where a shape will be after two translations.

Lessons overview

Preparation

Information may need to be put on the main class demonstration board before the start of some lessons.

Learning objectives

Starters
● **Understand percentage as the number of parts in every 100.**
● **Find simple percentages of small whole-number quantities.**
● Express simple fractions such as one half, one quarter, three quarters, one third, two thirds..., and tenths and hundredths, as percentages.
● **Order a mixed set of numbers with up to three decimal places.**
● Order a set of positive and negative integers.
● Derive quickly: division facts corresponding to tables up to 10 × 10; squares of multiples of 10 to 100 (eg 60 × 60)

Main teaching activities
● Classify quadrilaterals, using criteria such as parallel sides, equal angles, equal sides...
● Make and investigate a general statement about familiar numbers and shapes by finding examples that satisfy it.
● **Read and plot co-ordinates in all four quadrants.**
● Recognise where a shape will be after two translations.

Vocabulary

quadrilateral, parallelogram, kite, trapezium, square, rectangle, rhombus perpendicular, parallel, polygon, diagonal, place value, tenth, hundredth, thousandth, axis, axes, quadrant, acute angle, obtuse angle, symmetrical, origin, opposite, intersect

You will need:

Photocopiable pages
A copy of 'Visualising shapes' (page 48) for each child. 'Shape maker' (page 49).

CD pages
An OHT of 'Odd one out' and 'Grids', and a copy of 'Grids' for each child; differentiated copies of 'Visualising shapes' and 'Shape maker' for each more able and less able child, and 'Shape translation' for each less able child (see General resources).

Equipment
Whiteboards; pens; plastic shapes: square, rectangle, trapezium, rhombus, kite and parallelogram; dotty paper; protractors; nail boards; elastic bands; tracing paper; card template of parallelogram.

Lesson ①

	100%	50%	25%	12 ½%	75%	10%
£4000						
£12,000						
£28,000						
£46,000						

Starter
Ask children to draw quickly on their whiteboards the grid right. Then ask them to fill it in with the appropriate amounts. Discuss strategies used, for example halving numbers, quartering numbers, adding two columns together.

Main teaching activity
Whole class: Draw on the board: parallelogram, kite, trapezium, square, rectangle, rhombus. Ask the children to name each shape. Remind them that the shapes are all quadrilaterals. Recap vocabulary such as perpendicular, parallel, acute angle, obtuse angle, symmetrical. Tell the children they are going to list the properties of each shape using the criteria of sides, angles and lines of symmetry.
Individual work: Ask children to list the properties of the shapes in their books using the method described above.

Differentiation
Less able: Work with this group using large plastic shapes where necessary as a visual aid.
More able: When the task is completed, ask this group to draw some quadrilaterals of their own, especially a parallelogram, kite and trapezium, using rulers and protractors.

Plenary & assessment
Choose a set of properties, for example angles, and read them out to the class. Ask children which shapes these could describe. Now read out another set of properties, for example sides, and ask: *Which shapes are now eliminated? Why? Which shapes remain?* If more than one shape is left, read out the symmetry properties to establish which shapes you were describing.

Lesson ②

Starter
Explain that you will say a fraction and the children should write the corresponding percentage on their whiteboards. Ask them to hold these up when you say *Show me.* Say, for example, 1/2, 1/4, 3/4, 1/3, 2/3, 1/10, 7/10.

Main teaching activity

Whole class: Recap the properties of the sides for each of the shapes studied in the previous lesson. Ask: *Do all trapezia have one pair of parallel sides and one pair of sides of equal length?* Elicit the answer 'no'. Establish that children understand that a trapezium must have one set of parallel sides that must be unequal in length, but that the other sides can be equal or unequal in length. Draw some examples to illustrate the point (see margin). Explain the symbol used to show parallel lines. Tell the children they are going to investigate the diagonals of quadrilaterals. Draw two squares of different sizes and draw in the diagonals. Ask for the properties, for example: the diagonals are the same length and they intersect at right angles (see margin). They also bisect at the centre of the square.

Group work: For each shape (rhombus, kite, rectangle, trapezium and parallelogram) children should draw three different examples on dotty paper and put in the diagonals. For each shape ask: *What is the common property?* Encourage children to come up with a general statement for each shape, for example: the diagonals of a kite intersect at right angles.

Differentiation
Less able: Some children may find the quadrilaterals easier to construct using nail boards and elastic bands. Provide support when children are making the statements.

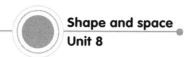

More able: Ask this group to measure the angles of the quadrilaterals they have drawn to see if a pattern emerges. Work towards the statement: The internal angles of a quadrilateral always total 360°.

Plenary & assessment
Show children the OHT of 'Odd one out'. This shows sets of kites, trapezia and parallelograms. In each set there is an odd one out. Ask children to identify the incorrect shape explaining why it is incorrect.

Lesson ③

Starter
Write the following numbers on the board in this order: 3.270, 3.720, 3.027, 3.727, 3.702. Tell children that the numbers have been ordered from lowest to highest but that two of them have been put in the wrong place. Ask: *Which two are incorrect? Why are they in the wrong order?* Ensure the children can explain why that is using the correct place value terminology, for example, tenths, hundredths, thousandths. Repeat with similar lists, such as: 26.137, 26.317, 26.731, 27.317 and 26.713.

Main teaching activity
Whole class: Tell the children they are going to draw a quadrilateral on their whiteboard based on given information: *My quadrilateral has two sets of parallel sides. What could it be?* They should produce a range of squares, rectangles and parallelograms. Ask: *What further information would be needed to make the description of a shape more precise, for example for a square?* Elicit that you would need the following information: all four sides are equal; all four angles are right angles.

Try another one. *My quadrilateral has only one set of parallel lines.* Children should produce a range of trapezia. Ask: *What other information could be given to identify the type of trapezium?* This could include, for example, non-parallel sides of equal length, two acute angles, two obtuse angles.
Individual work: Give out dotty paper and the 'Visualising shapes' activity sheet. Explain that the instructions given could produce more than one type of quadrilateral.

Differentiation
Less able: This group should work from the version of 'Visualising shapes' where the instructions are more precise and less open to interpretation.
More able: This group should work from the version of 'Visualising shapes' where the instructions include visualising shapes through the properties of the diagonals.

Plenary & assessment
Ask children to give instructions for visualising a shape, invite the rest of the class to draw it.

Lesson ④

Starter
Ask each child to write a number between –100 and 500 on their whiteboard. Choose six or seven children to come to the front of the class with their boards, and ask the rest of the class to order them. Repeat with others. Put negative numbers into context by asking: *The temperature is –2°C. It rises by 5°C. What is the new temperature?* (3°C) *The temperature is –4°C. It falls by 6°C. What is the new temperature?* (–10°C) *Put these temperatures in order, lowest first: 13°C, 26°C, –3°C, –13°C, 0°C.*

Main teaching activity
Whole class: Show the 'Grids' OHT, which contains two co-ordinate grids. Work with Grid A, which shows the first quadrant. Recap important vocabulary from Year 5, ensuring children are conversant with 'x axis', 'y axis', 'quadrant' and 'origin'.

Point to point A on the grid and ask the children for the co-ordinates (2, 1). Remind children how to write down a co-ordinate. Also point out that the numbers are enclosed in brackets. Plot points B, C and D, joining them to make a parallelogram. Ask for the co-ordinates of each point.

Now look at Grid B, which illustrates all four quadrants. Explain the numbering of each quadrant (first is top right, second is top left, third is bottom left and fourth is bottom right). Label the x and y axes, explaining that the x axis in the second and third quadrants and the y axis in the third and fourth quadrants are negative numbers. Draw a parallelogram in the second quadrant. Ask for the co-ordinates. Check children understand that the x co-ordinates will be negative. Repeat for the third and fourth quadrants, drawing attention to the negative co-ordinates.

Individual work: Give out copies of 'Shape maker'. Ask the children to complete each shape, writing the co-ordinates of each vertex.

Differentiation

Less able: This group should work from the version of 'Shape maker' that contains completed shapes. Children have to write the co-ordinates.

More able: Give this group the version of 'Shape maker' where just two vertices have been plotted and they have not been joined.

Plenary & assessment

Return to the 'Grids' OHT. Label a point A at (3, 2) and a point B at (−1, 2) on Grid B. Ask: *Where could points C and D be marked to draw a trapezium?* There will be a number of possible answers. Encourage answers that use all four quadrants.

Lesson ⑤

Starter

Explain that you will ask division facts which the children can derive from the multiplication tables. Ask *What is 40 divided by 8? 56 divided by 7? 32 divided by 4?* Now ask the children to say the square of the number you say, for example: *Say the square of 5, 8, 10, 12, 3, 11…* When the children are confident with this ask: *What is the square of 10? What is the square of 20? How did you work that out?* Encourage children to use the square facts that they have just rehearsed in order to work this out. Continue with the square of 30, 40, 50… up to 100.

Main teaching activity

Whole class: Show the 'Grids' OHT and provide children with their own copies, as well as the 'Shape translation' activity sheet. This shows a parallelogram drawn in the first quadrant. Ask the children to write down the co-ordinates of the parallelogram in the space provided on the sheet. Put the parallelogram template onto the OHT and explain that you are going to slide it into a new position within the first quadrant. Its orientation will remain the same. Explain that this is called translation. Describe the translation, for example, three units up, two units right and so on. Ask for the co-ordinates of the new position. Continue to translate the parallelogram, ensuring that it moves into all four quadrants.

Individual work: Children complete the translation of the parallelogram into all four quadrants themselves on the 'Shape translation' activity sheet. It may be necessary for the children to trace the template and use it to translate the shape until they feel confident.

Differentiation

Less able: This group should use the version of 'Shape translation' which asks them to translate fully into each quadrant without the shape lying astride any axis.

More able: Encourage this group to use the standard method of recording a translation, for example A, B, C, D to A¹, B¹, C¹, D¹ is $\begin{pmatrix} -3 \\ 4 \end{pmatrix}$

Plenary & assessment

Show the 'Grids' OHT again. Place the card parallelogram in quadrant four. Ask children to describe the translation from the parallelogram in quadrant one to quadrant four. Repeat to different quadrants.

Name	Date

Visualising shapes

Read carefully each of the descriptions below. Visualise each shape, then draw it accurately on your dotty paper.

Remember: There are alternatives, so you may have different answers from others in your group. Always use a ruler.

1. three quadrilaterals that have just one set of parallel sides

2. a quadrilateral that has two sets of parallel sides of equal length

3. a quadrilateral that has two obtuse angles and two acute angles

4. two quadrilaterals that have four right angles

5. a quadrilateral that has only two right angles

6. two quadrilaterals that have two sets of parallel sides

7. a quadrilateral with no parallel sides (a challenge!)

■ SCHOLASTIC

photocopiable

Name

Date

Shape maker

Complete each shape to make a parallelogram, then write the co-ordinates of each vertex.

1st quadrant A = (   )

B = (   )

C = (   )

D = (   )

2nd quadrant A = (   )

B = (   )

C = (   )

D = (   )

3rd quadrant A = (   )

B = (   )

C = (   )

D = (   )

4th quadrant A = (   )

B = (   )

C = (   )

D = (   )

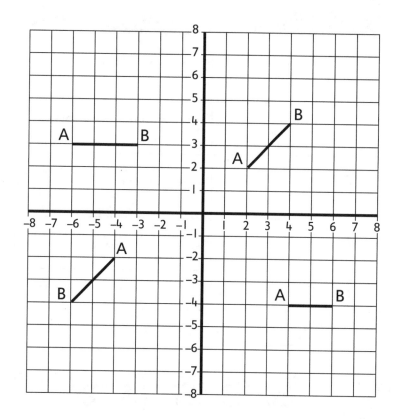

1st quadrant

2nd quadrant

3rd quadrant

4th quadrant

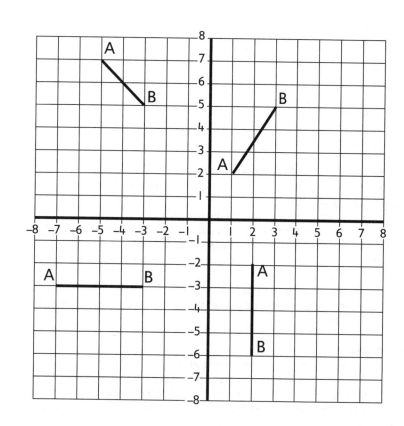

Measures

This unit concentrates on measures in the form of 'time' and 'perimeter'. It introduces time zones around the world and extends work on time to include 24-hour clock and time elapsed. Perimeter of rectangles and compound shapes are explored in practical situations.

LEARNING OBJECTIVES

		Topics	Starter	Main teaching activity
Lesson	1	Measures Problems involving 'real life', money or measures	● Derive quickly: division facts corresponding to tables up to 10 × 15; squares of multiples of 10 to 100.	● Appreciate different times around the world. ● **Identify and use appropriate operations (including combinations of operations) to solve word problems involving numbers and quantities**.
Lesson	2	Measures Problems involving 'real life', money or measures	● Recognise squares of numbers to at least 12 x 12.	As for Lesson 1.
Lesson	3	Measures	● Consolidate rounding an integer to the nearest 10, 100, 1000. ● Know imperial units. ● Round decimals to the nearest whole number.	● Use, read and write standard metric units, including their abbreviations, and relationships between them. ● Convert smaller to larger units and vice versa.
Lesson	4	Measures	● Recognise and extend number sequences. ● Count on in steps of 0.1, 0.2, 0.25, 0.5… and then back.	● **Calculate the perimeter and area of simple compound shapes that can be split into rectangles.**
Lesson	5	Measures	● Convert smaller to larger units and vice versa.	As for Lesson 4.

Lessons   overview

Preparation
Note that if a different time-zone map is used, or if the website worldtimezone.com is accessed, the time zones may be marked differently from the Scholastic map (+ times to the east and – times to the west).

Learning objectives
Starters
● Derive quickly squares of multiples of 10 to 100.
● Recognise squares of numbers to at least 12 × 12.
● Consolidate rounding an interger to the nearest 10, 100, 1000.
● Know imperial units.
● Round decimals to the nearest whole number.
● Recognise and extend number sequences.
● Count on in steps of 0.1, 0.2, 0.25, 0.5… and then back.

Main teaching activities
● Appreciate different times around the world.
● **Identify and use appropriate operations (including combinations of operations) to solve word problems involving numbers and quantities.**
● Use, read and write standard metric units, including their abbreviations, and relationships between them.
● Convert smaller to larger units and vice versa.
● **Calculate the perimeter and area of simple compound shapes that can be split into rectangles.**

Vocabulary
time, Greenwich Mean Time, International Date Line, 12-hour clock, 24-hour clock, estimate, approximate, integer, kilogram (kg), gram (g), litre (l), millilitre (ml), kilometre (km), metre (m), centimetre (cm), millimetre (mm), multiple of, sequence, perimeter, distance, edge, metric, area, length, width, breadth, square centimetre, measure, measurement

You will need:
Photocopiable pages
A copy of 'Finding the time' (page 55) and 'Measure by measure' (page 56) for each child.

CD Pages
A copy of the 'World time zones' resource sheet for each child; a copy of 'All the way around' and 'Calculating area' for each child, differentiated copies of 'Finding the time' and 'All the way around' for each less able child, differentiated copies of 'Measure by measure' and 'Calculating area' for each more able and less able child (see General resources).

Equipment
A globe; whiteboards and pens; rulers; tape measures; plastic cups; measuring jug; weighing scales; centimetre-squared paper; counting stick.

Lesson ①

Starter

Explain that you will ask division facts which the children can derive from the multiplication tables. Ask: *What is 35 divided by 7? 81 divided by 9? 64 divided by 8?* Ask the children to say the square of the number that you say, for example: *What is the square of 4, 2, 9, 7, 11, 8, 12…* including all the squares up to 12 × 12.

Main teaching activity

Whole class: Give out copies of 'World time zones'. Explain to the children that there are different time zones around the world. Show the globe to reinforce understanding of the fact that when it is daylight in the British Isles it will be dark in places like New Zealand and Australia. Refer to the resource sheet, explaining that times are recorded as before or after GMT. Also that the time zones on the sheet show how many hours before or after GMT the time is, according to the country's position east or west of the International Date Line. To the west it is earlier than GMT (–) and to the east it is later (+). Ask questions relating to the sheet, such as: *It is 3.00pm in France. What time is it in New York?* Draw the chart on the left on the board. Ask children to copy it onto their whiteboards and fill in the missing information. Alternatively, complete it with the whole class. Note that more than one answer could be placed in the bottom space.

GMT	2.00pm	6.30pm	3.30am
Brazil			
Los Angeles			
China			
	4.00pm	8.30pm	5.30am

Activity	Time in the UK	Time in ……………

Individual work: Ask each child to complete a simple timetable of a typical day, for example: *I get up at 7.00am. I eat breakfast at 8.00am. I start school at 9.00am.* Children should then choose a country and list what time it would be there as they are doing each activity. Use the type of recording box shown in the margin.

Differentiation

Less able: This group may benefit from having a chart already prepared for them.
More able: When this group has completed the task, move them on to look at large countries where the time zone varies from one part of the country to another, such as the east and west coasts of the USA.

Plenary & assessment

Using the resource sheet, choose a city where the time difference from London is considerable, for example, Los Angeles (8 hours earlier) or Sydney (10 hours later). Discuss what problems this may cause in an international context, for example, businesses around the world find it hard to communicate, families have to arrange phone calls at mutually appropriate hours. Ask the more able group to report back on time zones in the USA. Ensure the discussions help children to understand and appreciate time zones and that they can use the time zone chart accurately.

Lesson ②

Starter

Ask the children to write down the square numbers to 100 (4, 9, 16, 25, 36, 49, 64, 81, 100). Remind them that they can use these multiplication facts to find the squares of larger numbers, for example, if 6 x 6 = 36 then 60 x 60 = 3600. Ask children to calculate the squares of 20, 30, 40… to 100. Discuss the answers and correct any misconceptions, such as 40 x 40 = 160.

Main teaching activity

Whole class: Ask the following question: *If I leave my house at 9.05am and reach my destination at 1.25pm, how long did it take me?* Draw a timeline on the board and explain how we can use it to find time elapsed.

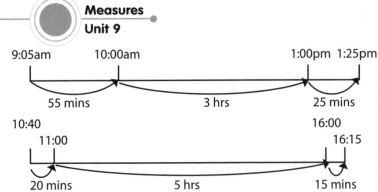

Now add each stage of the calculation (55 minutes + 25 minutes = 80 minutes = 1 hour 20 minutes, then 1 hour 20 minutes + 3 hours = 4 hours 20 minutes). Try some more examples on the board, inviting children to come to the front of the class to complete each stage. Include 24-hour clock times as well as 12-hour clock times (see the second example on the left).

Then ask this question: *A rounders match takes 40 minutes. At a school's tournament, seven matches are played. How many minutes of rounders were played?* Discuss 7 x 40 = 280 minutes. *There are 60 minutes in an hour, so 280 ÷ 60 = 4 hours 40 minutes.*

Individual work: Provide children with copies of 'Finding the time' activity sheet, which provides a range of real-life word problems on the topic of time.

Differentiation
Less able: A differentiated version of the activity sheet is provided for this group.
More able: When this group has finished the activity sheet, challenge them to make up their own time scenario and make up questions about it for a friend to answer.

Plenary & assessment
Ask the following question: *A bus driver works for seven hours. His route takes 50 minutes for a round trip. How many trips did he make? How long was his rest break?* Establish what operation is needed this time (division). Then discuss how the problem can be solved: 7 x 60 minutes = 420 minutes, 420 ÷ 50 = 8 with 20 over. Therefore, he drives the route eight times, with a 20-minute rest period.

Lesson

Starter
Tell the children that if they wanted to work out the calculation 602 – 287, they could first estimate the answer by rounding the integers to 600 and 300. The answer will therefore be about 300. Ask the children to find the approximate answers to the following questions, rounding off numbers to the nearest 10, 100, 1000 or whole number as appropriate: 36.9 – 8.6, 779 – 213, 7.6 x 3.9, 1872 + 3899, 41.7 ÷ 5.8, 492 + 89 + 503, 27.4 x 3.8, 50.2 – 9.6, 2046 – 205, 63.9 ÷ 7.7. Discuss answers and ask children to explain their choices when rounding up or down.

Main teaching activity
Whole class: Remind everyone that there are 1000m in a kilometre, 1000ml in a litre, 1000g in a kilogram, 1000mm in a metre and 100cm in a metre. Show the children that 3kg 125g can be written in two other ways, by converting to grams (3125g) or as a decimal fraction of a kilogram (3.125kg). If written as a decimal fraction, only the kg unit is used, not the g. Ask the children to write 4732g in two other ways on their whiteboards. Discuss the answers. Then try the following as a whole class.

465m	=	km	or	km	m
1.25l	=	ml	or	l	ml
76m	=	cm	or	km	
2km 5m	=	km	or	m	

For each of these, stress the importance of place value, especially the use of zero as a place-holder. You may need to draw a place value chart on the board as each measurement is converted. For example, 2km 5m:

T	U	.	t	h	th
	2	.	0	0	5

Repeat this activity, if necessary, for kilograms and litres. By the end of the lesson, children should know the equivalent of one thousandth of a kilometre, a kilogram and a litre in metres, grams and millilitres.
Individual work: Provide children with the 'Measure by measure' activity sheet, which gives them practice in converting measurements. You will also need to provide rulers, tape measures and weighing scales, plus a measuring jug and some plastic cups for children to use for question 4. Explain to the children how they should use these.

Differentiation
Less able: Provide this group with the version of 'Measure by measure' that contains examples relating to the conversion of larger units to smaller units.
More able: This group should work on the more demanding version of 'Measure by measure', which will extend their thinking about converting smaller to larger units.

Plenary & assessment
Refer to the place value chart on the board. Ask the children where they would place 1m, 10m, 100m and 1000m. Repeat the process for 1g, 10g, 100g and 1000g and for 1ml, 10ml, 100ml and 1000ml. Check that they understand the importance of the zero when writing these measurements, for example, 1m = 0.001km.

Lesson (4)

Starter
Tell the children that the beginning of the counting stick is 0, then count along it in 0.1 increments. Ask the children to count again, with you, forward and back along the stick. Point to positions on the stick and ask the children to say which number belongs there. Repeat the activity counting in increments of 0.25 or 0.5 or 0.6.

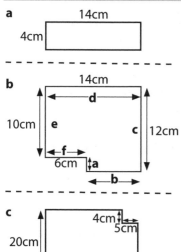

Main teaching activity
Whole class: Remind the children of the meaning of the word 'perimeter'. Ask them how they can find quickly the perimeter of the rectangle **[a]** in the margin. Elicit one of these two methods: either (14 + 4) x 2 or (14 x 2) + (4 x 2). Draw some simple rectangles on the board and ask children to calculate the perimeter. Then draw shape **[b]** on the board, explaining that it is not to scale. Ask children to find the perimeter. Ask: *What information is missing?* (the length of two of the sides) *What can be done to find these two lengths?* Establish that length *a* can be found by subtracting side *e* from side *c* (12cm – 10cm = 2cm). Also, side *b* can be found by subtracting side *f* from side *d* (14cm – 6cm = 8cm). Now the perimeter can be found.

Ask the children to draw the shapes shown in **[c]** in the margin on their whiteboards and work in pairs to establish the perimeters. Discuss answers and correct any misunderstandings. If necessary, work during individual activity time with any children who are finding it difficult to calculate the missing measurements.

Individual work: Hand out the 'All the way round' activity sheet for children to work on individually.

Differentiation
Less able: This group work on the differentiated version of 'All the way round', which consolidates finding the perimeter of rectangles before moving on to compound shapes.
More able: Once this group has completed the activity sheet challenge them, in pairs, to make up word problems involving perimeter. For example: *A farmer owns a rectangular field measuring 270m by 450m. He sells a 60m by 60m square of land in one of the corners for house building. What is the perimeter of his field now?*

9cm

5cm

Plenary & assessment

Ask: *If Sasha has three tiles measuring 9cm by 5cm, how can she arrange them to give the following perimeters: 48cm and 64cm?* (two different answers) Discuss the solutions, ensuring children understand that only the outside of the shape is counted, not the individual perimeters of each shape.

Lesson ⑤

Starter

Tell the children they are going to convert centimetres to metres, metres to kilometres, millilitres to litres and grams to kilograms, as in Lesson 3. Remind them to be careful with place value and the position of the zero as a place-holder. Answers can be displayed on whiteboards or written as a list to be checked at the end. Change to km: 360m, 2401m, 18m, 4kg 25m. Change to litres: 8643ml, 290ml, 15ml, 2l 109ml. Change to kg: 1kg 302g, 19g, 400g, 9736g. Discuss the answers and check that the decimal points and/or zeros are correctly positioned.

a

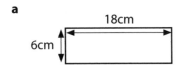

18cm

6cm

Main teaching activity

Whole class: Draw the shape **[a]** left on the board. Ask children to find the perimeter (48cm). Tell them that you now want to find out how much surface area the rectangle covers. Explain that area is not the space inside a shape but the amount of surface the shape covers. Ask children for suggestions as to how they could find the surface area, reminding them of work covered in Year 5. Elicit the method of multiplying length by width or breadth. Remind children that this is written as area = length x width or $a = l \times w$. Stress that the answer will always be in square centimetres or whatever unit is being used (square metres, square kilometres and so on).

b

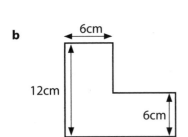

6cm

12cm

6cm

14cm

Now draw a compound shape (see **[b]**). Ask for suggestions as to how the area might be calculated now. Establish that the shape will need to be divided into two smaller rectangles that can be labelled *a* and *b* (see **[c]** left). Explain that there is more than one way to divide the shape, as shown, and that both ways are acceptable. Establish that the area of *a* is found by multiplying 12 by 6 = 72 in the top diagram of **[c]**. The area of *b* will be 6 x 8 = 48. So the total area will be 72 + 48 = 120 square centimetres, or 120cm².

Try another shape together as a class (see **[d]** left). This time, divide the shape into three sections and then find the area.

Individual work: Distribute copies of the 'Calculating area' activity sheet. Children have to find the area of compound shapes, and there are also real-life problems to solve.

c

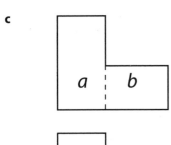

a   *b*

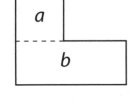

a

b

Differentiation

Less able: Provide this group with the version of 'Calculating area' where the shapes provided are more straightforward.

More able: Provide this group with the more demanding version of the activity sheet. You may need to work with this group, as one set of questions involves finding the surface area of a box.

Plenary & assessment

Ask the following question: *A gardener creates a vegetable plot with a perimeter of 36m. The plot is rectangular. Of all the possible rectangles, which would give the greatest surface area for his vegetables?* Ask children for strategies they could use to solve this problem. Then ask them to work in pairs to solve it. What do they discover about the best possible length x width to use? (9 x 9) Do they recognise what type of number the size of the area is? (It is a square number.).

d

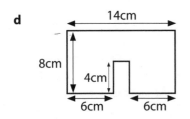

14cm

8cm

4cm

6cm   6cm

Name	Date

Finding the time

1. Sita got into the pool at 1.30pm. She swam for 50 minutes.

At what time did she get out? _____

2. A pie was put into the oven at 5.10pm. It came out at 5.50pm.

How long was it in the oven? _____

3. Children at St Saviour's School finish their lunch break at 1.10pm.

They have 50 minutes for lunch. At what time does the lunch break start? _____

4. Mark went jogging at 18:26. He jogged until 19:05. For how long was he jogging?

_____

5. Jade got up at 7.40am. It took her 25 minutes to get ready, 6 minutes to pack
her bag and 20 minutes to walk to school. At what time did she arrive at school?

_____

6. A cake takes 95 minutes to cook. It comes out of the oven at 6.05pm.

At what time was it put in the oven? _____

7. Class 6 went on a moorland hike. They started out at 09:40 hours and finished at 15:25 hours.

How long did the hike last? _____

8. A train leaves the station at 22:50 and arrives at its destination at 01:05.

How long did the journey last? _____

9. The programme for a school play gives the start time as 18:45 and the finish time as 21:25.

How long does the play last? _____

10. Calculate how long you spend in school each day.
Of that time, how long is spent **a)** in lessons **b)** having break times?

_____

_____

Name	Date

Measure by measure

1. Write each of the measurements in two other ways.

2kg 361g   = _____ and _____

4726g   = _____ and _____

36cm   = _____ and _____

146m   = _____ and _____

6km 860m   = _____ and _____

27ml   = _____ and _____

3060ml   = _____ and _____

2. Measure the length of your exercise book. Write the answer in these three different ways.

_____ cm _____ mm _____ m

3. Measure the height of your table. Write the answer in these three different ways.

_____ cm _____ mm _____ m

4. Estimate how much water the plastic cup holds. Use the measuring jug to check your answer. Write the answer in three different ways.

_____ estimate _____ ml _____ l _____ ?

5. Choose two items to weigh, such as your exercise book or pencil case. Write the answers below.

Item 1 _____ g _____ kg

Item 2 _____ g _____ kg

Measures (2)

This unit gives practice in measuring to a fine degree of accuracy and encourages children to practise the skills of estimating. It also provides practice in reading measurements from scales in the context of mass and capacity. Children are taught the relationship between imperial and metric measurements, and are given practice in converting between miles and kilometres.

LEARNING OBJECTIVES

	Topics	Starter	Main teaching activity
Lesson 1	Measures	● Use related facts and doubling or halving.	● Use, read and write standard metric units (km, m, cm and mm) including their abbreviations, and the relationships between them. ● Convert smaller to larger units and vice versa.
Lesson 2	Measures	● Use tests of divisibility. ● Use factors.	● Suggest suitable units and measuring equipment to estimate and measure length, mass or capacity. ● Record estimates and readings from scales to a suitable degree of accuracy.
Lesson 3	Measures	● Order fractions such as 2/3, 3/4 and 5/6 by converting them to fractions with a common denominator.	● Use, read and write standard metric units (km, m, cm and mm) including their abbreviations, and the relationships between them. ● Convert smaller to larger units and vice versa.
Lesson 4	Measures	● Use tests of divisibility. ● Use factors.	● Know imperial units (mile). ● Know rough equivalents of miles and km.
Lesson 5	Making decisions Problems involving 'real life' money and measures	● Derive quickly doubles of two-digit numbers (eg 3.8 × 2, 0.76 × 2).	● Choose and use appropriate number operations to solve problems and appropriate ways of calculating. **● Identify and use appropriate operations to solve word problems involving numbers and quantities.**

Lessons   overview

Preparation
Copy 'Reading from scales' onto acetate to show on the OHP. Before Lesson 2, prepare the various equipment needed for the two versions of the 'How good are your estimates?' activity sheets.

Learning objectives
Starters
● Use related facts and doubling or halving.
● Use tests of divisibility.
● Use factors.
● Order fractions such as 2/3, 3/4 and 5/6 by converting them to fractions with a common denominator.
● Derive quickly doubles of two-digit numbers (eg 3.8 × 2, 0.76 × 2).

Main teaching activities
● Use, read and write standard metric units (km, m, cm and mm) including their abbreviations, and the relationships between them.
● Convert smaller to larger units and vice versa.
● Suggest suitable units and measuring equipment to estimate and measure length, mass or capacity.
● Record estimates and readings from scales to a suitable degree of accuracy.
● Know imperial units (mile). Know rough equivalents of miles and km.
● Choose and use appropriate number operations to solve problems and appropriate ways of calculating.
● Identify and use appropriate operations to solve word problems involving numbers and quantities.

Vocabulary
metric unit, kilometre, metre, centimetre, millimetre, estimate, approximate, division, imperial unit, mile, pound, ounce, pint, convert, factor, inch, foot, yard, standard unit

You will need:
Photocopiable pages
A copy of 'How good are your estimates?' (page 62), and 'Solve these 1' (page 63) for each child.

CD Pages
An OHT of 'Reading from scales'; a copy of 'Inch by inch' for each child, differentiated copies of 'How good are your estimates?' for each less able child and of 'Solve these 1' for each less able and more able child (see General resources).

Equipment
An OHP; metre sticks; tape measures marked in cm/mm; 30cm rulers; calculators; whiteboards; measuring sticks/tape measures marked in cm/inches; trundle wheel; a set of weighing scales; an apple; a clear jar containing uniform-sized counting apparatus such as marbles, coloured beads or multilink; a sheet of triangular isometric paper and six 1p coins.

Lesson ①

Starter

Tell the children they are going to work on the 27x table. Ask for strategies that they could use based on knowledge of other tables. Elicit the fact that they could use the 9x table then multiply by 3, or take the 20x table and the 7x table and add the results. Ask children to choose one method and then work out the 27x table. How quickly can they do this? Check the answers. Repeat the process for the 24x table. What different strategies could be used now? (Double the 12x table; 8x table multiplied by 3; double the 6x table and double again.)

Main teaching activity

Whole class: Ask children to list common units of length. Look for kilometre, metre, centimetre, decimetre and millimetre. Tell the children that these are all metric measurements. Rehearse the relationship between them. Remind the children that 1000m = 1km, 100cm = 1m, 10cm = 1dcm and 10mm = 1cm. Also explain the vocabulary. Say: *'Kilo' means 1000, 'centi' means 1/100. This helps us to know how big units are. A centimetre is 1/100 of a metre. If 'milli' means 1/1000, how many millimetres are there in 1 metre?* Then ask some quick-fire questions relating to converting smaller into larger units. Use the following examples. *How many centimetres are there in ¾ of a metre? How many millimetres are there in 6 metres? How many centimetres are there in 3.6 metres? How many millimetres are there in 12.5 centimetres? How many metres are there in 4.2 kilometres?* Remind children of previous work, when they wrote measurements in different ways, for example: 9076m = 9km 76m = 9.076km. Try a few as revision, for example, write these measurements in two different ways: 126cm, 1.3m, 2km 5m.

Paired work: Provide a range of measuring equipment, such as rulers, metre sticks, tape measures and so on. Tell the children they are to measure a range of objects in the classroom, such as the height of the table, length of books, circumference of a friend's head, etc. Stress that they need to choose the correct equipment for the task. Tell them also that the measurements need to be recorded in two different ways using the type of chart shown below. Encourage accuracy, ie

Object	Estimate	Measurement 1	Measurement 2
Maths book	25cm	25cm	0.25m

measuring to the nearest millimetre. Ensure children estimate lengths before measuring each object.

Differentiation

Less able: Ensure this group is confident about using the equipment available. Check that measurements start from zero and not from the edge of the ruler, for example.
More able: Encourage this group to find the perimeters of large objects, for example the playground, with tape measures and trundle wheels and then show their results in scale drawings.

Plenary & assessment

Recap on the relationships between the metric units of length. Ask questions: *A table is 1200mm in length. How would this be written in a) centimetres, b) metres?* Check that children can convert between the units. Ask children to investigate other units of length in preparation for Lesson 3.

Lesson ②

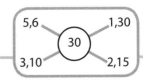

Starter

Ask: *How can we tell is a number is divisible by 2, 5 or 10?* Recap on the meaning of the term 'factor', then write the following numbers on the board: 30, 48, 96, 16, 40, 25, 50, 81. Ask the children, working in pairs, to list the factors for each number as above. Check the answers. Ask: *What do you notice about the number of factors for 16, 25 and 81?* (Square numbers have an odd number of factors.) Try another square number to check this statement.

Main teaching activity

Whole class: Discuss the importance of estimating when calculating or solving problems. Explain that it helps to check whether final answers are reasonable. Ask children to study carefully a 30cm ruler and to fix in their mind set distances like 1cm, 10cm, 30cm. Now ask them to put the rulers out of sight and to estimate the length of a thumb, an exercise book, the height of the table, the length of their arm and so on. Ask them to write the estimated measurement down each time. Then, with a partner, they should check their answers, seeing how close to the estimates they were. Discuss strategies that can be used, such as visualising the ruler or using a 'span' to help them. Tell children that once estimations have been made they need to measure objects accurately to find the true amount. Show them the OHT of 'Reading from scales', which illustrates some measuring apparatus. Using an OHT pen, mark on the different scales to show different amounts, asking the children to read the scales accurately. When displaying the OHT, explain how scales are marked in divisions that are labelled. Explain that the label x 25g would mean divisions of 25g.

Individual/paired work: Provide children with the 'How good are your estimates?' activity sheet. This is in two sections: the first gives practice in estimating; the second involves reading from scales.

Differentiation

Less able: This group will require support for section two of their version of the worksheet. Alternatively, you may wish to set up practical reinforcement tasks involving estimating and reading from scales using various containers filled with water and/or jars filled with beads.

More able: Once the activity sheet has been completed, challenge this group, working in pairs, to set up practical tasks and to make up their own scale, reading questions for a partner to solve.

Plenary & assessment

Return to the 'Reading from scales' OHT. Ask children to come to the board and mark on given measurements. Mark positions on the equipment and pose questions such as: *If I add 75g more flour to the scales, what amount will the dial show now?*

Lesson ③

Starter

Write the following fractions on the board: 2/3, 2/18, 2/9, 3/4, 5/6, 5/9, 1/6 and 1/2. Ask children, working in pairs, to order the fractions, smallest first. Discuss the answers insisting the children explain their method. Ask: *Did you remember to convert to a common denominator? Which denominator did you choose? How can we easily find a common denominator?*

Main teaching activity

Whole class: As a result of their research started in Lesson 1, find out the names of any units of imperial measurement that the children have collected. Discuss words like inch, foot, yard and mile. Explain that although Britain uses metric units, there are still imperial measurements in use, such as mile, pint and pound. Explain that the children are going to learn how to convert kilometres to miles and vice versa. Write the following information on the board: 1km = 0.62 miles; 1 mile = 1.6km; 1 km = 5/8 of a mile; 5 miles = 8km. Then, using calculators, ask children the following question: *Anytown is 24km away from Bettertown. How many miles is this?* Explain that they will need to multiply 24km by 0.62. This equals 14.88 miles or 15 miles rounded to the nearest mile. Ask the children to convert kilometres to miles using this method. Try 13km, 83km and 10km.

Pose the next question: *The distance from Bigtown to Smalltown is 17 miles. How many kilometres is this?* Ask children how this could be calculated. Elicit 17 x 1.6 = 27.2km or 27km to the nearest kilometre. Try converting these distances to kilometres: 32 miles, 50 miles and 3 miles. Practise other examples if necessary.

Paired work: Draw the distance chart on the left on the board. Explain how it can be used to find the

Distance in miles							
Squareville							
173	Circelton						
84	203	Deciham					
16	121	53	Trichester				
400	45	200	860	Addstown			
333	560	370	296	18	Subtractown		
192	641	110	703	1000	1076	Multipool	

distances between towns and cities. Ask the children to draw the chart in their books, converting the miles to kilometres.

Differentiation

Less able: This group will need support initially to remind them of the conversion method being used. Also check on their understanding of rounding distances to the nearest kilometre.

More able: Once the task has been completed, encourage this group to make up a similar chart of imaginary place names in which kilometres have to be converted into miles.

Plenary & assessment

Refer back to the information given at the beginning of the lesson: 1km = 5/8 mile and 5 miles = 8km. Explain that these approximations can be used for quick conversions, although they are, of course, less accurate. Point out that 5 miles = 8km, so 10 miles = 16km and 12½ miles = 20km. Also, if 1km = 5/8 mile then 12km = 12 x 5 ÷ 8 = 7½ miles. Give the children some examples to try.

Lesson

Starter

Repeat the Starter for Lesson 2. Invite the children to suggest how to find out if a number can be divided by 9. (Add the digits, and if the total is more than 9, add the total digits. If the result is 9, then the original number can be divided by 9.) Put some numbers on the board for children to investigate if this method is accurate, eg 549, 289, 369, 108.

Main teaching activity

Whole class: Recap on the imperial measurements listed in Lesson 3 (inch, foot, yard, etc). Explain that many years ago people measured length by pacing with their feet. Unfortunately, feet are different sizes, so the length had to be standardised (12 inches = 1 foot). Tailors measured cloth by holding it between the tip of the nose and the tips of the fingers. This also created different lengths, so again this length was standardised (3 feet = 1 yard). Ask: *If 1 yard (yd) = 3 feet (ft) and 1 foot (ft) = 12 inches ("), how many inches are there in a yard?* (36")

Write down metric equivalents for imperial units: 1 inch = approximately 2.5cm and 1 metre = 39 inches (3ft 3"). Rehearse these equivalents. Ask children how they can convert between these units. Elicit that if 1 inch = 2.5cm, multiply the number of inches by 2.5. Say: *Try converting the following: 6 inches, 9 inches, 15 inches. Use calculators if necessary. When converting centimetres to inches, divide by 2.5. Try converting the following: 24cm, 14cm, 30cm.* Ask children to work in pairs to measure two or three objects in either centimetres or inches and convert to the metric/imperial equivalent. Share outcomes with the rest of the class.

Group work: Provide children with copies of the 'Inch by inch' activity sheet. This provides practice in using centimetres and inches and converting between the two.

Differentiation

Less able: Provide this group with support when they are multiplying numbers and rounding off measurements. Calculators may help with some of the calculations.

More able: Extend this group to making conversions between feet and metres and vice versa. For example, to convert 6 metres into feet, multiply 6m by 39 inches (234") and then divide by 12 to find the number of feet (19.5).

Plenary & assessment

Review the work that children have carried out in their groups. Recap on some of the conversions they have made, for example: *How many inches in 10cm?* (4) *How many centimetres in 16 inches?* (40)

Lesson

Starter

Ask the children to write quickly on their whiteboards the doubles of the numbers that you say. Say, for example: *Write the double of 34, 27, 3.2, 0.8, 0.76.* Keep the pace sharp.

Main teaching activity

Whole class: Write this question on the board: *A garden centre is situated on a busy main road. It is open every day until 7.00pm. It sells a variety of rose bushes that are kept in five plots of land measuring 7 metres by 12 metres each. The owner wants to enclose the plots with new fencing wire. How much fencing must he buy?* Ask the children to look carefully at the question and then ask what information is needed to solve the problem. Establish that they need first to find the perimeter of each plot of land and then multiply this answer by 5. Discuss the information given. Is there any that does not help to solve the problem? (Yes, the location of the garden centre and its opening times.) Establish that when solving problems children need to:

1 read the question carefully to identify key words and numbers – these can be underlined
2 decide what operation(s) will need to be done
3 estimate the answer
4 decide which method of calculation is required
5 check to see that the answer is correct and makes sense.

Ask children to complete the calculation of the question. Discuss the answer and the strategies used. Then write up the next problem: *The roses at the garden centre cost £5.95 each. Jayne buys five of them, three pink and two yellow. How much change does she get from £30?* Ask children to complete the calculation and discuss the methods used. Some children will need to use a pencil and paper method, whereas more able children might calculate mentally. Check answers. Some children will have worked out the cost of the plants and given that as the answer, forgetting that the question asked for the change. Discuss the importance of re-reading the question to check what answer is required.

Write up another question: *I buy 2000 pencil cases and pack them into boxes of eight. How many full boxes can I make? Each box costs £7.50. How much money do I make?* Discuss the best way to solve this. Can it be done mentally? Should pencil and paper be used, or a calculator? Elicit that the figures involved would necessitate a calculator, although children would still need to understand the operations required to work out the question. Ask children to work out the answers on their calculators. Recap on the sequence of tasks needed to solve written problems.

Group work: Provide children with the 'Solve these 1' activity sheet, which gives practice in solving real-life problems. Children should be encouraged to recognise and explain any patterns and relationships and should be prepared to generalise on their findings and predict outcomes.

Differentiation

Less able: This group should work from the less demanding version of the activity sheet.
More able: This group should work from the more demanding version of the activity sheet, where the problems are more complex and include some items from the Year 7 framework.

Plenary & assessment

Choose a question from each of the activity sheets to solve together. For each question, work through the strategies that the children used. Recap on the list of instructions for solving problems.

Name	Date

How good are your estimates?

Section 1

1. Look carefully at the jar of counters. How many do you think are in there? How did you work it out?

2. Look at the piece of isometric paper. How many triangles do you think there are? How did you work it out?

3. This jar holds 500 sweets when full. About how many are in the jar at the moment?

4. This jug holds $1\frac{1}{2}$ litres when full. About how many millilitres does it contain at present?

5. Look carefully at the 1p coins. Estimate how many you would need to make a straight line 1 km long. How did you work it out?

6. How many words do you think are in your reading book? How could you work this out?

7. Estimate the height of the classroom door. How could you measure it? Measure it accurately. How close were you?

Name   Date

Solve these 1

Solve the following word problems.

1. A sales person drives an average of 4560 kilometres each month.
How far will she drive in a year?

_____

2. The Sales Manager drives 3000 kilometres a month.
What is this in miles? **(Remember: 1km = 0.62 miles)**

_____

3. A class of 32 children take part in a Maths Challenge. I want to give each of them a prize.
Would it be cheaper for me to buy pencils at 65p each or novelty rubbers at £3.00 for a box of 5?

_____

4. Use the above menu to answer the following questions.

a) What two snacks could I buy for exactly £4.65? _____

b) A family buys two pizzas, a veggie burger and chicken bites.
How much change do they get from £10?   _____

c) I have £5. Can I buy two cheeseburgers and a hot dog?   _____

d) Is it possible to buy three different snacks without spending more than £5? If so, what can I buy?

_____

5. A theatre presented five performances of the play The Magic Wand. A total of 1860 people attended during the week. What was the average size of the audience each night?

_____

This unit looks at the use of positive and negative numbers in practical situations, and also provides information on the essential rules for ordering and rounding off decimal numbers.

LEARNING OBJECTIVES

	Topics	Starter	Main teaching activity
Lesson 1	Mental calculation strategies (+ and −) Pencil and paper procedures (+ and −)	● **Multiply and divide decimals mentally by 10 or 100 and integers by 1000 and explain the effect.**	● Consolidate all strategies from previous year including: find a difference by counting up. ● Use informal pencil and paper methods to support, record or explain additions and subtractions.
Lesson 2	Pencil and paper procedures (+ and −)	● Consolidate + and − strategies from previous year including: add several numbers..	● **Extend written methods to column addition and subtraction involving decimals.**
Lesson 3	Checking results of calculations	● Derive quickly doubles of two-digit numbers.	● Check with the inverse operation when using a calculator..
Lesson 4	Measures	● Consolidate + and − strategies from previous year including: add several numbers.	● **Extend written methods to column addition and subtraction.**
Lesson 5	Problems involving 'real life', money or measures Making decisions	● Use factors.	● **Identify and use appropriate operations to solve word problems involving numbers** based on 'real life', money or measures. ● Choose and use appropriate number operations to solve problems, and appropriate ways of calculating: mental, mental with jottings, written methods, calculator.

Lessons overview

Preparation
At the beginning of most lessons information will need to be written up on the class board for the children to use.

Learning objectives
Starters
● **Multiply and divide decimals mentally by 10 or 100 and integers by 1000 and explain the effect.**
● Consolidate + and − strategies from previous year including: add several numbers.
● Derive quickly doubles of two-digit numbers.
● Use factors.
Main teaching activities
● Consolidate + and − strategies from previous year including: find a difference by counting up.
● Use informal pencil and paper methods to support, record or explain additions and subtractions.
● **Extend written methods to column addition and subtraction.**
● Check with the inverse operation when using a calculator.
● **Extend written methods to column addition and subtraction.**
● **Identify and use appropriate operations to solve word problems involving numbers** based on 'real life', money or measures.
● Choose and use appropriate operations to solve problems, and appropriate ways of calculating: mental with jottings, written methods, calculator.

Vocabulary
inverse, factor, add, addition, subtraction, more, digit, place value

You will need:
Photocopiable pages
A copy of 'Addition and subtraction' (page 69) and 'Down the column' (page 70) for each child.

CD Pages
A copy of 'Opposites attract', 'Decimal numbers' and 'Solve these 2' for each child, differentiated copies of 'Opposites attract' for each less able child, and of 'Addition and subtraction', 'Down the column', 'Decimal numbers' and 'Solve these 2' for each less able and more able child (see General resources).

Equipment
Number fans; whiteboards.

Lesson ①

Starter

Ask the children to show you the answer to the following questions, either on number fans, show-me cards or whiteboards. Questions can be read out or written on the board. *What is: 0.7 x 100 (70), 23 ÷ 10 (2.3), £4.70 ÷ 10 (£0.47), 6 ÷ ? = 0.6 (10) How many times smaller is 150 than 1500? (10) How many £10 notes can you get for £600? (60) 1.03 x ? = 1030. (1000) What must I do to change 9 to 0.009 or 900? (÷1000; x100) How many millimetres are in 1cm and 1m? (10; 1000).*

a
```
   9742
+  6381
  15000
   1000
    120
      3
  16123
```

Main teaching activity

Whole class: Explain to children that they are going to revise addition and subtraction strategies from Year 5 in preparation for extending these to standard written methods. Discuss informal pencil and paper methods the children might use. Write 9742 + 6381 on the board. Ask children to estimate the answer first to help check its reasonableness at the end of the calculation. Record on the board as you work out the answer with the children. **[a]**

Check with the original estimate. Is the answer reasonable? Remind children that it is important that the units line up under the units, that tens line up under tens and so on. Set another calculation for the children to work out on their whiteboards. Share the answer and discuss the calculation.

b
```
   7472
-  3661
     39   (3700)
+   300   (4000)
   3000   (7000)
    472   (7472)
   3811
```

Write 8419 – 4247 on the board. Ask the children to estimate the answer first. Complete the calculation on the board with the class, using the 'adding on' number line method (see below). Ask the children to work out 6840 – 2906 using the above method. Share the calculations and discuss the result. Next, write 7472 – 3661. **[b]** Remind the children that they could also use a column method to subtract, as shown in the margin. Show the children how they can add on until they reach the next significant number in each stage. Give children a calculation to try this method out. **[c]** Collect answers and discuss. Ask: *Which method did you find easiest?*

Group work: Give children copies of the 'Addition and subtraction' activity sheet, which provides practice using the methods outlined above.

c
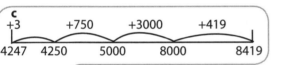
```
+3      +750      +3000      +419

4247  4250    5000     8000      8419
```

```
   3000
+   750
+   419
+     3
   4172
```

Differentiation

Less able: This group should work on the less demanding version of the activity sheet.
More able: This group should work from the version of the activity sheet with two sections. Then challenge them to prepare word-based problems that will test out the different methods, eg: *If a crowd of 8642 is watching a football match and 2037 leave early, how many are left?*

Plenary & assessment

Pose the following question. *Last year 10,482 people visited Anytown Zoo during the months of July and August. During September and October only 6973 people visited. What was the difference in visitors during the two periods? (3509)* Ask children to use the method they feel most comfortable with to calculate the answer. Discuss strategies and why some may consider one method easier than another.

Lesson ②

Starter

Write the following on the board: 27 + 39 + 43. Ask the children what strategy they would use to work it out. (adding tens, adding units and then adding both numbers; looking for pairs that make multiples of 10; starting with the largest number). Then try 63 + 69 + 62 + 66. Ask: *What method could be used here?* ((60 x 4) + (3 + 9 + 2 + 6))Write the following on the board, telling children to add them mentally using the most efficient strategy each time: 42 + 43 + 44 + 45; 36 + 42 + 18 + 24; 17 + ? + 53 = 92; 40 + 90 + 60 + 50; 33 + 28 + ? = 89. Collect answers once they have completed and discuss methods:.

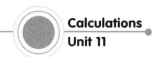

```
  493      599
+ 106    - 495
  599      104
```

```
  2 1 5 1
  3 2 6 5
-  1 7 4 6
   1 5 1 9
```

Main teaching activity

Whole class: Explain to the children that they are going to learn the standard column methods of addition and subtraction. Write the questions in the top box in the margin on the board. Show the children how to add each column, carrying the tens into the next column and so on. Remind them that digits should be placed correctly, with units, tens, hundreds and so on lining up underneath each other. Provide a few examples for the children to try.

Now write the following on the board: 3265–1746. Explain the decomposition method to the children, working it through on the board with them. Ensure they understand that the bottom row is taken from the top row and not vice versa. Tell them that 6 cannot be taken away from 5, so take 10 from the 6 tens, and so on. Work through another example with the children, asking them to explain each step in the process.

Individual/paired work: Children should work on the 'Down the column' activity sheet.

Differentiation

Less able: Provide this group with the less demanding version of the activity sheet.
More able: This group should work through the core page as quickly as possible and then concentrate on the more able version.

Plenary & assessment

Write the following numbers on the board: 1274, 39, 864, 19 and 2021. Ask children to find the total using the column addition method. Check that they all understand the importance of writing digits in the correct place. Discuss the various methods used during the last two lessons. Ask: *Which do you find the quickest and most efficient? When would you use these methods? When would it be quicker to use mental methods? Which of these calculations would you do mentally and for which would you use a written method: 126 – 34, 472 + 320, 1276 – 904, 18932 + 7641, 9062 – 4387?*

Lesson ③

Starter

Tell children that you are going to call out a number. They must double it, showing the answers on their whiteboards. Encourage a quick response – all the answers should be worked out mentally. Numbers to be doubled could include: 2.6, 0.47, 3½, 0.37, 9.4.

a
```
    4 2 6
+   □ □ □
  1 4 1 3
```

b
```
  1 3 1 0 1
  1 4 1 3    check    426
-   4 2 6         +  987
    9 8 7           1413
                      1 1
```

c
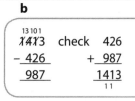
```
    □ □ □
-   4 9 3
    1 0 6
```

d
```
  493    check    599
+ 106         -  493
  599            106
```

e
```
  9 8 2          9 8 2
- □ □ □        -  3 2 7
  3 2 7         _____
```

Main teaching activity

Whole class: Write the calculation in the margin [a] on the board. Ask the children for suggestions as to how they could find the missing numbers in the calculation. Elicit that they could subtract 426 from 1413. Explain that addition and subtraction are inverse operations. Carry out the calculation and then check (see [b] in the margin).

Ask the children to try another one on their whiteboards. Check calculations and discuss strategies. Now try calculation [c]. Ask the children how the numbers already given can be used to find the numbers that are missing. Remind children that addition and subtraction are inverse operations. Elicit that 493 + 106 should equal the missing number. Tell the children to work through the calculation on their whiteboards (see [d] in the margin).

Ask the children to try the calculations in [e] on their whiteboards. Check the results and discuss strategies. What did they have to do to solve the second calculation? Establish that in this example the calculation was 982 – 327 to find the missing number-the inverse operation was not used this time. Remind children again that addition and subtraction are inverse operations and can be used to check the results of calculations.

Group work: Children should work from the 'Opposites attract' activity sheet.

Differentiation

Less able: Provide this group with the less demanding version of the activity sheet.
More able: Once the activity has been completed, challenge this group to devise some addition and subtraction calculations in which random missing numbers have to be found.

Plenary & assessment

Write the following on the board: 3689 − 1642 = 2047; 847 − 350 = 497; 8724 + 917 = 9641. Ask: *What method would you use to check each answer is correct?* Make sure they offer correct use of the inverse operation. Choose one of the examples and work it out as a class.

Lesson

Starter

Repeat the Starter for Lesson 2. Use addition sentences such as 32 + ☐ + 39 = 98, 41 + 19 + 34 = ☐. Invite the children to explain the strategies that they used, such as starting with the largest number, and looking for pairs that make multiples of 10 and doing these first.

a
```
  £43.50
+   8.25
+   3.79
   55.54
```

b
```
    7 11 1
  £8.2̸5̸
−   3.79
    4.46
```

Main teaching activity

Whole class: Write the following problem on the board: *In a sports shop I spend £43.50 on trainers, £8.25 on a pair of shorts and £3.79 on a whistle. How much do I spend altogether?* Establish that column addition would be an efficient method to use. Ask the children to work out the answer, reminding them that units should be under units, tens under tens and that the decimal points should line up (see [a] left). Check what the children have written.

Now ask: *What is the difference in price between the shorts and the whistle?* Ask children to use an efficient column subtraction method to work this out, as shown left [b]. Again, check the position of the decimal points when setting out the column and also when calculating the answer.

Move on to the following question: *A builder has a 12.5kg sack of sand. He uses 3250g to make cement. How much sand is left?* Establish that the calculation requires subtraction and ask children how they would set it out. Elicit that the units of measurement need to be the same and that either 12.5kg needs to be converted to grams or 3250g needs to be converted to kilograms. Both methods are acceptable. Ask the children to make the conversion and write as column subtraction. Demonstrate on the board (see [c] and [d] left).

c
```
     4 1
  12.5̸00
−  3.250
   9.250  9kg 250g
```

d
```
    4 1
  125̸00
−  3250
   9250  9250g
```

Check place value and the position of the decimal point. Remind children to place the decimal point in the answer box before undertaking any calculation. Work out the problem and discuss the answers. Elicit from the children that [c] will give an answer in kg and g and that [d] will provide an answer in g only. If necessary, give the children another example to try.

Group work: Provide children with copies of the 'Decimal numbers' activity sheet. This provides practice in adding and subtracting decimal numbers.

Differentiation

Less able: Provide this group with the version of the activity sheet with just one section.
More able: Provide this group with the more able version to work through all sections.

Plenary & assessment

Write on the board 4.6kg − 780g. Ask the children the following questions to ensure understanding: *What do you need to remember when setting this out as a column subtraction?* Elicit converting to the same unit, lining up units, tens, and so on, lining up decimal points. *How can we check the answer?* Elicit using the inverse operation.

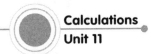
Lesson ⑤

Starter

Recap on the term 'factor'. Tell the children that factors can help when multiplying and dividing large numbers. Show the following: 42 x 24. Ask the children for factors of 24 (1 and 24, 2 and 12, 3 and 8, 4 and 6). Using 3 and 8, the calculation could be done as follows: 42 x 24 = 42 x 8 = 336 and 336 x 3 = 1008. By breaking 24 into its factors, the calculation can be carried out mentally. Ask children to try 27 x 18 and 36 x 16. Collect and discuss answers.

Write on the board 756 ÷ 27. Show that the same method can be used when dividing, for example: 756 ÷ 3 = 252 ÷ 9 = 28. Ask children to try 800 ÷ 32 and/or 768 ÷ 24. Again, collect and discuss answers.

Party menu for 24	
Pizzas	£54.40
Burgers	£40.88
Sandwiches	£43.92
Chicken pieces	£58.56
Spaghetti	£47.76

Main teaching activity

Whole class: Write the following question on the board. *Grant is planning his eleventh birthday party. He has to make his food choices from the following menu.* (See margin.) *What is the difference in price between the cheapest and dearest item? Grant decides to buy chicken pieces and spaghetti. How much does it cost? What change does he get from £110?* Ask the children, working in pairs, to calculate the answers on their whiteboards. Discuss their answers.

Were there any questions that could be done mentally? For instance, the last question required the children to subtract £106.32 from £110. This can be done mentally by counting up. Choose one part of the question and ask a child to work it out on the class board. Ask the rest of the class to check the answer by using the inverse operation.

Then ask the next question. *Grant's Mum decides to add one more item to his choice. The food now costs £147.20. What extra item did she buy?* Ask children, again in pairs, to complete the calculation and feed back on the method used. Tell them they are now going to work on similar problems themselves. They will need to decide the most efficient method to use – mental or pencil and paper – for each calculation

Group work: Provide children with the 'Solve these 2' activity sheet to work through.

Differentiation

- **Less able:** This group should work from the less demanding version of the activity sheet. Adult assistance should be given to help children convert the word problems into numerical calculations.
More able: This group should work from the version of the activity sheet where the problems are more complex.

Plenary & assessment

Choose one of the problems from the 'Solve these 2' activity sheet. Discuss the strategies used to solve it. Recap on what the children have learned from this unit of work. They should appreciate the following: when to choose suitable methods of calculation (mental or pencil and paper); how to use the inverse operation, especially for checking; the importance of setting out calculations accurately, especially with regard to the positioning of the decimal point.

Name	Date

Addition and subtraction

Work out the answers to each of the calculations below.

Calculate some of them using a number line and some using the column method. Use the space below for any workings.

1. 6537 + 2914 = _____

2. 8728 + 3947 = _____

3. 8030 + 1286 = _____

4. 1723 + 406 + 4975 = _____

5. 9071 + 89 + 620 = _____

6. 7841 – 3221 = _____

7. 9042 – 3719 = _____

8. 6271 – 4028 = _____

9. 9004 – 4811 = _____

10. 10 000 – 8729 = _____

Name	Date

Down the column

Work out the answers to each of the calculations below.

Use the standard column methods of addition with carrying, and subtraction using decomposition.

Section 1	
264 + 322 =	576 + 215 =
1462 + 389 =	98 – 49 =
1256 – 392 =	4012 – 2111 =
462 + 197 =	762 + 983 =
217 – 84 =	672 – 489 =

Properties of number and number sequences

This unit looks at number sequences and patterns, with particular reference to triangular and square numbers. Children are required to explain patterns, make generalised statements and predict terms in sequences.

LEARNING OBJECTIVES

	Topics	Starter	Main teaching activity
Lesson 1	Properties of numbers and number sequences Using a calculator	● Consolidate knowing by heart multiplication facts up to 10 x 10.	● Recognise and extend number sequences. ● Develop calculator skills and use a calculator effectively.
Lesson 2	Properties of numbers and number sequences Reasoning and generalising about numbers or shapes Using a calculator	● Count on in steps of 0.1, 0.2, 0.25, 0.5… and then back.	● Recognise and extend number sequences. ● Solve mathematical problems or puzzles, recognise and explain patterns and relationships, generalise and predict. ● Suggest extensions asking 'What if…?'. ● Develop calculator skills and use a calculator effectively.
Lesson 3	Properties of numbers and number sequences Reasoning and generalising about numbers or shapes	● Give a decimal fraction lying between two others.	As for Lesson 2.
Lesson 4	Reasoning and generalising about numbers or shapes	● **Find simple percentages of small whole-number quantities.**	● Make and investigate a general statement about numbers by finding examples that satisfy it. ● Develop from explaining a generalised relationship in words to expressing it in a formula using letters as symbols.
Lesson 5	Reasoning and generalising about numbers or shapes	● **Multiply and divide decimals mentally by 10, 100 or 1000 and explain the effect.**	As Lesson 4.

Lessons overview

Preparation
Set up the counting stick for use in the starter of Lesson 2. Have pegs and peg boards ready for those who need them in Lesson 5.

Learning objectives
Starters
● Consolidate knowing by heart multiplication facts up to 10 x 10.
● Count on in steps of 0.1, 0.2, 0.25, 0.5, and then back.
● Give a decimal fraction lying between two others.
● **Find simple percentages of small whole-number quantities.**
● **Multiply and divide decimals mentally by 10, 100 or 1000 and explain the effect.**
Main teaching activities
● Recognise and extend number sequences.
● Develop calculator skills and use a calculator effectively.
● Solve mathematical problems or puzzles, recognise and explain patterns and relationships, generalise and predict. Suggest extensions asking 'What if …?'.
● Make and investigate a general statement about numbers by finding examples that satisfy it.
● Develop from explaining a generalised relationship in words to expressing it in a formula using letters as symbols.

Vocabulary
sequence, square number, predict, pair, rule, row, column

You will need:
Photocopiable pages
A copy of 'All square' (page 76) and 'What's it worth?' (page 77) for each child.

CD Pages
A copy of 'What's it worth?' for each child and a differentiated copy of 'All square' for each more able child (see General resources).

Equipment
Calculators; counting stick; counters; squared paper or isometric paper; interlocking cubes; number fans; whiteboards; dice; pegs and peg boards.

Lesson ①

Starter

Ask the children to chant the 8 times-table. Tell them they are going to continue to count in multiples of 8 from 8 x 10. Continue until children stumble over the multiples. Discuss the strategy they could use quickly (for example, add 10 and subtract 2). Try again. Does this strategy help children to continue the sequence more quickly? Repeat for multiples of 80 or 0.8. Try counting in multiples of 8 from a given starting point that is not a multiple of 8, such as 18 or 25.

Main teaching activity

Whole class: Write the following number sequence on the board: 15, 30, 45. Explain that each number is a term in a sequence. Ask the children to identify the pattern. Ask: *If the sequence continued, what would be the seventh term? What would be the tenth term?* Model another sequence, say 2.5, 4, 5.5, ?, 8.5, ?, ?. Ask children to fill in the missing terms. What are the steps in the sequence? Show how, if steps are equal, a calculator can be used to continue a sequence. On the calculator pad, press 1.5 + =. Explain that each time the = key is pressed 1.5 is added to the sequence. Show that the steps in a sequence are not always equal, for example: 2, 5, 9, 14, 20. Ask: *What is happening in this sequence?* The pattern increases by 1 each time: + 3, + 4, + 5 and so on.
Paired work: Ask children to work in pairs to make up number sequences for their partner to solve.

Differentiation

Less able: Suggest that this group works through some of the sequences in the times-tables (eg 4x, 6x, 8x) before branching out.
More able: Move this group quickly on to sequences where the gap between the numbers consists of two different steps, for example, 2, 5, 11, 14, 20 and so on (+3, +6).

Plenary & assessment

Choose some of the children's number sequences for the class to solve. Then challenge them with the following sequence: 2, 5, 11, 23, 47. Ask: *Who can work out the next term? How does the sequence increase?* (Each term is double the previous number.)

Lesson ②

Starter

Use a counting stick to support counting in amounts of 0.2. Start at different parts of the stick and count forwards and backwards. Repeat for other amounts such as 0.25, 0.75 and so on.

Main teaching activity

Whole class: Recap on square numbers from Year 5. Ask: *What are square numbers?* List all the square numbers to 100. Ask: *How can larger square numbers be calculated? What, for example, is 20^2?* Responses should include partitioning (10 x 20 = 200, 2 x 200 = 400) and using 2^2 as a starting point ($2^2 = 4$ so $20^2 = 400$). Remind children that it pays to estimate before doing calculations, to help check the reasonableness of the answer. Ask the children to estimate 16^2 then check with a calculator. How close were they? Extend more able children by asking them to estimate 2.5^2.
Group work: Provide children with the 'All square' activity sheet.

Differentiation

Less able: Work with this group during the lesson to provide extra support.
More able: This group should be provided with the version of 'All square' which involves finding the squares of decimal numbers.

Plenary & assessment

Recap on square numbers to 100. Given this information, ask children to list square numbers to 10,000. What do they notice? Can anyone provide the answer to 200²?

Lesson ③

```
3   3.1  3.2  3.3  3.4  3.5  3.6  3.7  3.8  3.9   4
|___|____|____|____|____|____|____|____|____|___|

3.1                                            3.2
|___|____|____|____|____|____|____|____|____|___|

3.11                                          3.12
|___|____|____|____|____|____|____|____|____|___|
```

Starter

Draw three number lines on the board, marked in divisions of 10, and label them as above.
Indicate various points on the number line and ask children to give the values. Then, without giving any visual clues, ask children to write down decimal numbers lying between the numbers given, for example: *Give me a decimal number between 6.12 and 6.13.*

Main teaching activity

Whole class: Provide children with counters, squared paper or other suitable apparatus, such as interlocking cubes. Ask them to make the pattern shown in the margin, either using the equipment or drawing on the paper.

Ask the children to add the next row. *How many counters/squares are needed? What about the next row?* Continue until ten rows have been created. Ask the children to list how many counters/squares they have used row by row to create the following sequence: 1, 3, 6, 10, 15, 21, 28, 36, 45, 55. Explain that these are triangular numbers. Ask: *Can you spot how the pattern increases?* (add 2, add 3, add 4, add 5...) *Can you predict the next two numbers in the sequence?*

Paired work: Ask the children, working in pairs, to write the first 20 triangular numbers. Ask them to choose any two adjacent numbers and add them together. They should try this at least four times. Ask: *What do you notice about your answers? Have you seen these numbers before?*

Differentiation

Less able: Suggest to this group that they focus on some of the lower pairs of adjacent numbers when adding.
More able: Challenge this group to continue with the pattern of triangular numbers so that they are dealing with three-digit numbers.

Plenary & assessment

Ask the children to explain what they have discovered when adding pairs of adjacent numbers. Elicit that two adjacent triangular numbers add up to a square number. Check some of the pairs to prove the statement. Tell children they need to know square numbers to 100 and at least the first ten triangular numbers.

Lesson ④

Starter

Ask children, on their number fans or using whiteboards, to show you the answers to the following questions relating to percentages: Show me 10% of 300, 150, 280, 170. *Show me 50% of 60, 250, 110, 86. Show me 25% of 200, 500, 600, 1000. Show me 30% of 60, 90, 140, 400.*

Main teaching activity

Whole class: Explain that in mathematics, letters sometimes represent numbers. This is called algebra. Write up the following example. If $x = 4$, what is 2 times x? (8) Show children that this can be written as $2x$ and that the multiplication sign is not needed. Try these examples: If $x = 4$ what is 8*x*? …12*x*? …9*x*? Can they combine this technique of using letters to write formulae? Remind them of formulae they know already, for example: area = length x width (*a* = *l* x *w*) and perimeter = (length + width) x 2 (*p* = (*l* + *w*) x 2). Show the children how to devise simple formulae. Give an example: *If sweets cost 7p, how much will it cost for any number of sweets?* Work through the process with the children, asking the following questions: *What do we want to find out? The cost, so call this c. What do we know? Sweets are 7p each, so c = 7. How many do we want? We don't know, so call the missing number n. So, the cost = 7p x the number of sweets or c = 7n.* Try it out together. Ask: *I want 6 sweets, how much will this cost?* (c = 7n so c = 7p x 6 = 42p)

Ask children to write the formula or equation for the cost of sweets at 4p each. Elicit that c = 4n. Then, as a class, work on the following. (1) *What is the number of months in y years?* (m = 12y) (2) *What is the formula for finding the nth term of this sequence: 4, 8, 12, 16, 20?* (n = 4n) (3) *There are x carrots in a field. How many carrots will each rabbit get if there are 6 rabbits?* (x/6) Before children work on their own, show and explain these additional algebra statements: n ÷ 5 = n/5; n x n = n²; a x b = ab; 3 x n = 3n.

Individual work: Give out copies of the 'What's it worth?' activity sheet. This will provide the children with practice in basic algebra.

Differentiation

Less able: This group should focus only on Section 1 of the activity sheet and some will need adult support.

More able: Encourage this group to move on to Section 2 of the activity sheet as soon as possible. Once this is complete, challenge them to write their own word problems and then make up simple formulae for solving them.

Plenary & assessment

Write the following on the board and ask children to explain what they mean: d/n; xy; 12n; p². Invite children to make up a question to go with each statement. Then ask the rest of the class to work it through to see if they are correct.

Lesson ⑤

Starter

Ask children to draw a 2 x 5 grid on their whiteboards. Draw a corresponding grid on the class board and write a decimal number in each box, such as 1.7, 26.34. Ask children to take it in turns to throw a dice. They should multiply the first decimal in the box by the dice score and write it in the correct box on their grid. Throw the dice again and repeat for the next decimal number. Check answers as you go.

Main teaching activity

Whole class: Draw the following pattern on the board and fill in the chart shown.
Ask: *What would the next two sequences be?* (6–8 and 7–10)

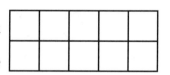

no of ✓	no of ✗
3	2
4	4
5	6

Draw another pattern, again asking the children to work out the next two terms in the sequence.

Term	✓	✗
1	1	1
2	2	3
3	3	5
4	?	?
5	?	?

✓ ✓✓ ✓✓✓
✗ ✗✗✗ ✗✗✗✗✗

Ask: *Can you see the pattern?* Elicit the fact that it is necessary to double the number of ticks and then subtract one to find the number for x. Ask: *Can you use this information to find the twentieth term …the fortieth term …the one-hundredth term without having to draw pictures to fill in the chart?* The twentieth term would be 20 ticks and 39 crosses (double 20 and then subtract 1). Repeat for the fortieth and one-hundredth terms.

Individual/paried work: Give out squared or isometric paper, or apparatus like coloured pegs and peg boards. Tell children they are going to create a pattern up to the fifth term and then give it to a partner to work out the eighth, tenth and twelfth terms. Emphasise that there must be a relationship between the two aspects of their pattern, it cannot just occur randomly.

Differentiation

Less able: This group may benefit from using apparatus rather than paper. Suggest that they start with very simple patterns.

More able: Encourage the children in this group to extend the sequence even further. Can they find out what the twentieth, fiftieth and one-hundredth term might be?

Plenary & assessment

Invite children to show their patterns. Discuss the relationship between the two aspects of the sequence. Ask: *Is it possible to work out any term in the sequence by using a formula?* Try also to include sequences that do not work, as a teaching point. (Note: You may wish to make these up yourself to avoid highlighting any children who have not been able to grasp the concept behind the pattern relationship.)

Name	Date

All square

Calculate the squares of these numbers.

Remember to estimate first and then show you working out. If you need more space for your working out, use the back of this sheet.

22^2	Estimate		Working out	Answer
	Calculator check		I was correct ☐ wrong ☐	

30^2	Estimate		Working out	Answer
	Calculator check		I was correct ☐ wrong ☐	

42^2	Estimate		Working out	Answer
	Calculator check		I was correct ☐ wrong ☐	

55^2	Estimate		Working out	Answer
	Calculator check		I was correct ☐ wrong ☐	

68^2	Estimate		Working out	Answer
	Calculator check		I was correct ☐ wrong ☐	

75^2	Estimate		Working out	Answer
	Calculator check		I was correct ☐ wrong ☐	

Name		Date

What's it worth?

Fact box: Use this important information to help you.

$3 \times n = 3n$	$n \div 5 = \dfrac{n}{5}$	$n \times n = n^2$	$a \times b = ab$	$6 \times n \times n = 6n^2$

Section 1

Find the value of each equation if $a = 4$, $b = 6$, $c = 5$, $d = 9$ and $e = 3$.

ab _____

$2c$ _____

$\dfrac{d}{e}$ _____

$7b^2$ _____

$cd + de$ _____

c^2 _____

$bc/10$ _____

$40 - a^2$ _____

Section 2

Find the value of n in each of these equations

$4n - 3 = 21$ _____

$n/5 = 40$ _____

$6n + 12 = 48$ _____

$42 = n - 9$ _____

$9n = 108$ _____

$n^2 = 121$ _____

$n = 16/4 + 18$ _____

$3n^2 = 75$ _____

EVERY DAY: Practise and develop oral and mental skills (eg counting, mental strategies, rapid recall of + and - facts)

- Consolidate rounding an integer to the nearest 10, 100 and 1000.
- Consolidate knowing by heart multiplication facts up to 10 x 10.
- **Multiply decimals mentally by 10 and 100 and explain the effect.**
- **Divide decimals mentally by 10 and 100 and explain the effect.**
- **Derive quickly: division facts corresponding to tables up to 10 x 10;** squares of multiples of 10 to 100 (eg 60 x 60); doubles of two-digit numbers including decimals and the corresponding halves.
- Use factors (eg 35 x 18 = 35 x 6 x 3).
- Use related facts and doubling or halving. For example: to multiply by 25, multiply by 100 then divide by 4.
- Use closely related facts: for example, multiply by 49 or 51 by multiplying by 50 and adjusting.
- Order fractions such as 2/3, ¾ and 5/6 by converting them to fractions with a common denominator, and position them on a number line.

- Know what each digit represents in a number with up to three decimal places
- **Order a mixed set of numbers or measurements with up to three decimal places.**
- Round a number with two decimal places to the nearest tenth or the nearest whole number.
- **Understand percentage as the number of parts in every 100.**
- Express simple fractions as percentages.
- Order a set of positive and negative integers.
- **Find simple percentages of small whole-number quantities.**
- Use, read and write standard metric units (km, m, cm, mm…) including their abbreviations, and relationships between them.
- Count on in steps of 0.1, 0.2, 0.5, and then back.

Units	Days	Topics	Objectives
1	3	Place value, ordering and rounding	• Find the difference between positive and negative integers or two negative integers and order a set of positive and negative integers.
		Using a calculator	• Develop calculator skills and use a calculator effectively.
		Fractions, decimals, percentages, ratio and proportion	• **Order a mixed set of numbers** or measurements **with up to three decimal places.** Round a number with two decimal places to the nearest tenth or nearest whole number.
2-3	5	Mental calculation strategies (x and ÷)	• Understand and use the relationship between multiplication and division. • Partition to multiply a decimal number by a single digit, eg 3.4 x 3 = (3 x 3) + (0.4 x 3). • Use closely related facts. • Use factors (eg 35 x 18 = 35 x 6 x 3).
		Understanding multiplication and division	• Express a quotient as a fraction, or as a decimal rounded to one decimal place. Divide £ or p by a two-digit number to give £ and p. • Round up or down after division, depending on context. • Use brackets. • Understand and use the relationships between operations and the principles of the arithmetic laws.
		Using a calculator	• Develop calculator skills and use a calculator effectively.
		Pencil and paper procedures (x and ÷)	• **Extend written methods to: long multiplication of a three-digit by a two-digit integer;** short division of HTU by U (mixed number answer); division of HTU by TU (long division, whole number answer); **short division of numbers involving decimals.**
4	5	Making decisions	• Choose and use appropriate number operations to solve problems, and appropriate ways of calculating.
		Problems involving 'real life', money and measures	• **Explain methods and reasoning.** • **Identify and use appropriate operations to solve word problems involving numbers and quantities** based on 'real life', money… including converting pounds to foreign currency and vice versa.
		Checking results of calculations	• Check the sum of several numbers by adding in reverse order. Check with an equivalent calculation
5.1	5	Fractions, decimals and percentages	• Order fractions such as 2/3, 3/4 and 5/8 by converting them to fractions with a common denominator, and position them on a number line. • **Use a fraction as an 'operator' to find fractions of numbers or quantities.** • Begin to convert a fraction to a decimal using division. • **Find simple percentages of small whole-number quantities.**
		Using a calculator	• Develop calculator skills and use a calculator effectively.
5.2	3	Shape and space	• Recognise where a shape will be after a rotation through 90º about one of its vertices. • Recognise where a shape will be after reflection: in a mirror line touching the shape at a point (sides of the shape not necessarily parallel or perpendicular to the mirror line; in two mirror lines at right angles (sides of the shape all parallel or perpendicular to the mirror line).
		Assess and review	

EVERY DAY: Practise and develop oral and mental skills (e.g. counting, mental strategies, rapid recall of +, –, x and ÷ facts)

- Consolidate all strategies from previous year, including: find a difference by counting up; use the relationship between addition and subtraction; add several numbers.
- Use known number facts and place value to consolidate mental addition and subtraction.
- Find the difference by counting up.
- Use the relationship between addition and subtraction.
- Consolidate knowing by heart multiplication facts up to 10 x 10.
- **Derive quickly: division facts corresponding to tables up to 10 x 10; doubles of two-digit numbers; multiples of 10 to 1000 and the corresponding halves.**
- Develop the x17 table by adding facts from the x10 and x7 tables.
- **Multiply and divide decimals mentally by 10 or 100 and explain the effect.**
- Use, read and write standard metric units including their abbreviations, and the relationship between them.
- Convert smaller units to larger units and vice versa.

- Know imperial units.
- Know rough equivalents of lb and kg, oz and g, miles and km, litres and pints or gallons.
- **Understand percentage as the number of parts in every 100.**
- **Find simple percentages of small whole numbers.**
- Recognise squares of numbers to least 12 x 12.
- Use tests of divisibility.
- Count on in steps of 0.1, 0.2, 0.25, 0.5, and then back.
- Consolidate rounding an integer to the nearest 10, 100 or 1000.
- Round a number with two decimal places to the nearest tenth or the nearest whole number.
- **Order a mixed set if numbers or measurements with up to three decimal places.**
- Order a set of positive and negative integers.
- Order fractions such as 2/3, 3/4 and 5/6 by converting them to fractions with a common denominator, and position them on a number line.

Units	Days	Topics	Objectives
7	5	Pencil and paper procedures (+ and –)	• **Extend written methods to column addition and subtraction of numbers involving decimals.**
		Problems involving 'real life' money and measures	• **Identify and use appropriate operations (including combinations of operations) to solve word problems involving numbers and quantities**, including converting pounds to foreign currency and calculating percentages such as VAT.
		Using a calculator	• **Explain methods and reasoning.**
8	5	Shape and space	• Recognise and estimate angles. • **Use a protractor to measure** and draw **acute and obtuse angles to the nearest degree.** • Check that the sum of the angles of a triangle is 180°, for example, by measuring or paper folding. • Describe and visualise properties of solid shapes such as parallel or perpendicular faces or edges. • Visualise 3-D shapes from 2-D drawings and identify different nets for a closed cube.
		Measures	• **Calculate the perimeter and area of simple compound shapes that can be split into rectangles.**
9	5	Measures	• Record estimates and readings from scales to a suitable degree of accuracy. • Convert smaller units to larger units and vice versa. • Know imperial units. • Know rough equivalents of lb and kg, oz and g, miles and km.
		Problem solving involving 'real life', money and measures	• **Identify and use appropriate operations (including combinations of operations) to solve word problems involving numbers and quantities** based on 'real life', money or measures.
10	5	Fractions, decimals, percentages, ratio and proportion	• **Solve simple problems involving ratio and proportion.**
		Handling data	• Find the mode and range of a set of data. • Begin to find the median and mean of a set of data. • **Solve problems by representing, extracting and interpreting data in tables, graphs, charts and diagrams.**
11	5	Properties of numbers and number sequences	• Make general statements about odd and even numbers including the outcome of products. • Know and apply simple tests of divisibility. • Recognise prime numbers to at least 20. • Find simple common multiples. • Factorise numbers to 100 into prime factors.
		Reasoning or generalising about numbers or shapes	• Develop from explaining a generalised relationship in words to expressing it in formula using letters as symbols. • Solve mathematical problems and puzzles, recognise and extend patterns and relationships, generalise and predict.
		Assess and review	

This unit looks at the use of positive and negative numbers in practical situations like measuring temperature. It also provides information on the essential rules for ordering and rounding off decimal numbers using measurements collected during sporting events.

LEARNING OBJECTIVES

	Topics	Starter	Main teaching activity
Lesson 1	Place value, ordering and rounding Using a calculator	● Consolidate rounding an integer to the nearest 10.	● Find the difference between a positive and a negative integer, or two negative integers, and order a set of positive and negative integers. ● Develop calculator skills and use a calculator effectively.
Lesson 2	Fractions, decimals, percentages, ratio and proportion	● Consolidate rounding an integer to the nearest 100.	● **Order a mixed set or** measurements **with up to three decimal places.**
Lesson 3	As for Lesson 2.	● Consolidate rounding an integer to the nearest 1000.	● Round a number with two decimal places to the nearest tenth or nearest whole number.

Lessons overview

Preparation

Prepare the number line and put it out of sight at the front of the class. Prepare the 'Digit (+ and –) and decimal point cards' and the OHT of 'Golfing score card'.

Learning objectives

Starters
● Consolidate rounding an integer to the nearest 10 , 100 and 1000.

Main teaching activities
● Find the difference between a positive and a negative integer, or two negative integers, and order a set of positive and negative integers.
● **Order a mixed set of numbers or** measurements **with up to three decimal places.**
● Round off a number with two decimal places to the nearest tenth of nearest whole number.
● Develop calculator skills and use a calculator effectively.

Vocabulary

digit, one-, two-, three-, four- and five-digit numbers, integer, positive, negative, minus, above/below zero, decimal, decimal fraction, decimal point, decimal place, order, calculator, display, key, enter, sign change, round to nearest ten, hundred, round (up or down), nearest, clear, constant, operation key

You will need:

Photocopiable pages
A copy of 'Goals galore' (page 83) and 'Mini Olympics' (page 84) for each child.

CD pages
A set of 'Digit (+ and –) and decimal point cards' for each child and a class set, an OHT of 'Golfing score card'; differentiated copies of 'Goals galore' and 'Mini Olympics' for each less able and more able child (see General resources).

Equipment
A large –10 to 10 number line; an OHP calculator; a calculator with 'sign change' keys for each child; washing line and pegs.

Lesson

Starter

Revise the fact that when rounding a number to the nearest 10, if it is less than 5 it moves back to the previous 10, and if it is exactly 5 or more it moves on to the next 10. Distribute the digit cards among the class and choose volunteers to stand up with their cards. They put up a series of random cards to make two-digit, three-digit and four-digit numbers that the rest of the class have to round to the nearest 10, for example, 52 becomes 50, 76 becomes 80, 154 becomes 150, 645 becomes 650, 1374 becomes 1370 and 5976 becomes 5980.

Main teaching activity

Whole class: Tell the children they are going to work with positive and negative numbers, but keep the positive/negative number line covered to start with. Children should put the –10 to 10 digit cards in front of them and shuffle them. Say: *Put the numbers in order, with zero in the middle, the negative numbers on the left and the positive numbers on the right.* Display the number line. Choose children to come out and find the differences between numbers by pointing to the moves they are making on the number line, reminding them that negative numbers go left and positive numbers go right, for example: 4 to – 6 (10), –3 – 5 (2), –2 to + 8 (10) and 3 to – 7 (10). Illustrate a practical use of this sort of calculation by giving an example involving temperatures: *The temperature rises from –2 degrees Celsius to 7 degrees Celsius. How many degrees has it risen? What is the temperature difference if it fell from 3ºC to –4ºC?*. Introduce other examples.

Individual/paired work: Explain to the class the meaning of the term 'goal difference' as applied to football league tables (the difference between the number of goals scored and the number conceded). Then, working individually or in pairs, children should complete the 'Goals galore' activity sheet.

Differentiation

Less able: Give these children a copy of 'Goals galore' with only four teams. Provide a –10 to 10 number line so they can physically count the steps as they move from one number to another.
More able: Working in pairs, these children should progress to work though the 'Goals galore' sheet with ten teams.

Plenary & assessment

Display the 'Golfing score card' on the OHP and ask children a series of questions about it. Discuss the meaning of 'par for the course' (the standard number of shots it should take to go round the whole course). For example, if a course is par 60 and the scores are Smith 63, Brown 58, Jones 65, Davis 55, Evans 59, you could ask the following questions: *How far over par is Smith?* (3) *How far under par is Davis?* (–5) *What is the difference between the scores of Evans and Jones?* (from 59 (–1) to 65 (5) is 6 shots). Note that hole distances in golf are still measured in yards.

Lesson ②

Starter

Repeat the starter from Lesson 1, this time asking children to round off numbers to the nearest 100. Individual volunteers use digit cards to generate three-, four- and five-digit numbers which the others round off. Remind them that 50 is the halfway point this time, for example, 354 becomes 400, 9427 becomes 9400 and 17523 becomes 17500.

Main teaching activity

Whole class: In this lesson, children will learn about ordering a set of decimal numbers. Have a set of digit cards and a decimal point card, plus a washing line and pegs, ready at the front of the room. Ask a child to select three digits, say 7, 3 and 2. Ask the children, using the cards and the point card, to make a series of four decimal numbers, such as 73.2, 0.372, 3.27 and 237. Put each of the numbers on the washing line in turn and ask children to say them out loud and in full, avoiding the word 'point', for example: *seventy-three and two tenths, three hundred and seventy two thousandths, three and twenty-seven hundredths, two hundred and thirty-seven.* Write all the selected numbers on the whiteboard and ask children to arrange them in order of size smallest to largest (0.372, 3.27, 73.2 and 237). Reinforce place value by asking the value of individual digits in these numbers. For example, say: *What is the value of the 3?* Repeat the process with another set of cards.

Paired work: Working in pairs, children use digit cards and the decimal point card to make their own sets of four decimal numbers. Make sure they can say the numbers in full to each other and then order them smallest to largest. Answers should be recorded in maths books.

Differentiation

Less able: It may be necessary to provide this group with numbers to order that only have one digit on the left of the decimal point, for example: *Order the following 5.84, 4.58, 4.85 and 8.45.*
More able: Ask children to suggest a decimal fraction that lies between two others, for example, 5.26 and 5.27. Invite children to make a decimal number with their cards, such as 8.6, and attach it to the washing line. Ask: *If a 1 card is fastened onto the line, where must it be placed to make the largest possible number?* (81.6) *And the smallest possible number?* (8.16)

Plenary & assessment

Revise solutions children have produced during group work. Discuss the methods they used to order the numbers. Write a series of decimal numbers on the whiteboard to three decimal places. Ring certain digits within these numbers and ask children to give you the value, for example: *In 53.742, what is the value of the 2?* (two thousandths) *In 7.645, what is the value of the 6?* (six tenths)

Lesson

Starter

Repeat the game from Lesson 1, but this time ask children to produce four-, five- and six-digit numbers. The other children round them off to the nearest thousand. Remind children that 500 is the halfway point this time, for example, 2374 becomes 2000, 19,768 becomes 20,000 and 142,503 becomes 143,000. Revise work done in the previous lessons. For example, ask: What is 24,526 rounded to the nearest 10? … the nearest 100? … the nearest 1000? (24,530, 24,500 and 25,000 respectively)

Main teaching activity

Whole class: Remind children of previous work on rounding numbers to the nearest tenth. Draw a number line with 1.6 at one end and 1.7 at the other. Mark ten divisions and write in 1.64 on the line. Explain that you need to round 1.64 to the nearest tenth. The class must decide whether round down or round up (they should round down). Repeat with 1.65 (round up). Continue with further examples and extend by asking them to round to the nearest whole number (again model this using number lines on the board).

Tell the children there are a number of practical situations when it is necessary to round off decimal numbers to the nearest tenth and the nearest whole number. Point out that a lot of these are to do with measurements of distance. Use the example of some children in school throwing a beanbag as part of a mini Olympics athletics event. Put some distances they might have thrown on the whiteboard and ask children to round them off to the nearest tenth and the nearest whole number so they are easier to record on a graph. Some examples might be 7.52 metres (7.5 metres and 8 metres), 10.65 metres (10.7 metres and 11 metres) and 12.71 metres (12.7 metres and 13 metres).
Group work: Provide children with a copy of the 'Mini Olympics' activity sheet, where measurements have to be rounded off to the nearest whole number and the nearest tenth. It may be possible to take measurements from the class's own efforts during a PE or games lesson and to use these as well.

Differentiation

Less able: Work with this group during the lesson on the differentiated 'Mini Olympics' activity sheet to reinforce their knowledge of rounding a decimal measurement to its nearest whole number. Stress that they round down if the number of tenths is less than 5 and round up if it is 5 or more.
More able: These children should move on to the 'Mini Olympics' activity sheet where they have to round more measurements with a greater degree of accuracy.

Plenary & assessment

Mark a number line on the whiteboard from 1 to 2, divided into tenths and hundredths. Point to different positions on the line and ask children to round each to the nearest tenth and the nearest whole number. For example, 1.45 would be 1.5 and 1, while 1.87 would be 1.9 and 2.

Name	Date

Goals galore

Work out the goal difference for these six football teams, who have completed their league programme.

In each case, take the 'goals against' away from the 'goals for'.

	Goals for	Goals against	Goal difference
Ayr Albion	84	69	
Rigby Rangers	53	64	
Topham Town	54	62	
Clark City	65	41	
Ulwell United	82	89	
Sutton Swifts	72	63	

Now answer these questions.

1. Which teams have scored more goals than they let in?

_____

2. Which teams have let in more goals than they have scored?

_____

3. Which team has the best goal difference?

_____

4. Which team has the worst goal difference?

_____

5. Put the teams in order, going from best goal difference to worst goal difference.

_____

6. What is the difference between the results of:

Rigby Rangers and Topham Town? _____

Ayr Albion and Sutton Swifts? _____

Clark City and Ulwell United? _____

Name	Date

Mini Olympics

- **Some children have been taking part in a 'throwing the beanbag' event on sports day.**
- Round each child's throw to the nearest metre and then to the nearest tenth of a metre. The first one has been done for you.

Child number	Distance thrown	Nearest metre	Nearest tenth of a metre
1	6.57m	7m	6.6m
2	7.52m		
3	10.65m		
4	12.71m		
5	9.08m		
6	8.79m		
7	11.26m		
8	9.72m		
9	13.69m		
10	8.45m		

Follow up:

Put the children in the order in which they finished, longest throw first.

_____

Which child threw the furthest and by how much? _____

Multiplication and division 1

This unit is intended to strengthen children's understanding of the relationships between multiplication and division, especially when dealing with decimal numbers. Topics also include how to express a quotient as a fraction or a decimal, and money problems involving division.

LEARNING OBJECTIVES

	Topics	Starter	Main teaching activity
Lesson 1	Mental calculation strategies (× and ÷)	● Consolidate knowing by heart multiplication facts up to 10 × 10.	● Use known number facts and place value to consolidate mental muliplivation. ● Understand and use the relationship between multiplication and division.
Lesson 2	As for Lesson 1.	As for Lesson 1.	● Partition to multiply a decimal number by a single digit, eg 3.4 × 3 = (3 × 3) + (0.4 × 3)
Lesson 3	Understanding multiplication and division	● **Multiply decimals mentally by 10 and 100 and integers by 1000, and explain the effect.**	● Express a quotient as a fraction, or as a decimal rounded to one decimal place.
Lesson 4	Understanding multiplication and division Using a calculator	● **Divide decimals mentally by 10 and 100 and integers by 1000, and explain the effect.**	● Express a quotient as a fraction, or as a decimal rounded to one decimal place. ● Develop calculator skills and use a calculator effectively.
Lesson 5	As for Lesson 4	● Derive quickly doubles of two-digit numbers, including decimals, and the corresponding halves.	● Divide £ and p by a two-digit number to give £ and p. ● Round up or down after division, depending on context. ● Develop calculator skills and use a calculator effectively.

Lessons overview

Preparation
Prepare an OHT of 'Random times and share machines'. Copy and cut out a set of 'Digit (+ and –) and decimal point cards' for each pair.

Learning objectives
Starters
● Consolidate knowing by heart multiplication facts up to 10 × 10.
● **Multiply decimals mentally by 10 and 100 and explain the effect.**
● **Divide decimals mentally by 10 and 100 and integers by1000, and explain the effect.**
● Derive quickly doubles of two-digit numbers, including decimals, and the corresponding halves.

Main teaching activities
● Understand and use the relationship between multiplication and division.
● Use known number facts and place value to consolidate mental multiplication.
● Partition to multiply a decimal number by a single digit, eg 3.4 × 3 = (3 × 3) + (0.4 × 3).
● Express a quotient as a fraction, or as a decimal rounded to one decimal place.
● Divide £ and p by a two-digit number to give £ and p.
● Round up or down after division depending on context.
● Develop calculator skills and use a calculator effectively.

Vocabulary
times, multiply, multiplied by, multiplication, product, integer, multiple of, inverse, share, division, divide, divided by, divided into, divisible by, quotient, decimal place, remainder, double, estimate, round up, round down, fraction, recurring, product, halve, half

You will need:
Photocopiable pages
Two copies of 'Speed check' (page 90) for each child (they are invited to complete them with and without a calculator).

CD pages
An OHT of 'Random times and share machines', a set of 'Digit (+ and –) and decimal point cards' for each pair; a copy of 'Eating out' for each child; differentiated copies of 'Speed check' and 'Eating out' for each less able and more able child (see General resources).

Equipment
An OHP; number fans; a number line; calculators; stopwatch or classroom clock; pairs of ten-sided dice (0–9).

Lesson ①

Starter
Show the grids for the games 'Random times' and 'Share machines'. These could be written or projected onto the whiteboard. Revise children's knowledge of multiplication and division facts up to 10 x 10, especially with the 6 and 8 times-tables. Children either give the answers verbally as the spaces are indicated, show the answers using number fans or come out to fill in the answers on the whiteboard. Alternate between multiplication and division games to sharpen up thinking and response.

Main teaching activity
Whole class: Tell the children they are going to play a game called 'Keep it in the family' using decimal numbers. Explain that this activity will revise the close relationship between multiplication and division. Revise the meaning of the word 'inverse'. Use some simple examples, such as: If $12 \times 9 = 108$ and $9 \times 12 = 108$, the inverse is also true that $108 \div 9 = 12$ and $108 \div 12 = 9$. Then write the calculation $3.56 \times 4 = 14.24$ on the whiteboard. Remind the children that the same rules apply to decimal numbers and that if one member of the 'family' is known, we know the other three as well: $4 \times 3.56 = 14.24$, $14.24 \div 4 = 3.56$ and $14.24 \div 3.56 = 4$. Repeat the process with other examples, like 4.12×6 and 8.74×3.

Paired work: Children should work in pairs. Shuffled digit cards drawn at random and a decimal point card can be used to generate numbers. Children should devise questions with missing numbers for a partner to complete. Boxes should be used to indicate missing numbers. For example, $6.45 \times 3 = a$, $a \times 6.45 = 19.35$, $19.35 \div a = 6.45$ and $a \div 6.45 = 3$. Calculators can be used to check calculations. Remind children to put the answer back into the question to check that it works.

Differentiation
Less able: Focus first on statements given to one decimal place, eg 7.3×4 and 4.8×5. Reinforce with these children that decimal numbers can be multiplied in any order.

More able: These children should progress quickly onto using a decimal point in both numbers, eg 3.2×7.4. They should estimate the answer first and then work out the first family member using a calculator. The other numbers are then written without the aid of a calculator.

Plenary & assessment
Check through examples produced during the group work activities. Once the first family member was known, how quickly could the children complete the others? Can the children start with a division fact and provide the other family members from there? Can children use a calculator to find missing numbers in statements such as $453.25 \div \square = 9.8$ and use the inverse operation to check their answers?

Lesson ②

Starter
Repeat the activities used in Lesson 1. Use the 'Random times' and 'Share machines' grids with different times-tables. Now try 7 and 9 times-tables.

Main teaching activity
Whole class: Review multiplication methods taught in the autumn term. Remind children about the effect of multiplying decimal numbers by 10 or 100, and the use of doubling and halving strategies when multiplying, eg $24.2 \times 2 = 48.4$ (double) $24.2 \times 4 = 96.8$ (double again). Repeat for $\times 6$ (trebling strategy).

$2 \times 3 = 6.0$
$0.3 \times 3 = 0.9$
$0.04 \times 3 = 0.12$

Also, remind children about the work done in the autumn term on short multiplication of decimal numbers (see Autumn Term, Unit 2, Lesson 4). Go through an example on the whiteboard, eg 2.34 × 3. Encourage estimation first and then suggest that children partition the numbers, for example see left:

Then add the parts together to get 7.02. Stress that the decimal points should be lined up underneath each other before addition takes place. Work through other examples, such as 5.17 x 5 and 4.83 × 6. Move on to show an example of a larger decimal number using the same method, for example: 13.72 × 4 (see margin).

$13.00 \times 4 = 52.0$
$0.70 \times 4 = 2.8$
$0.02 \times 4 = 50.08$
$= \underline{54.88}$

Individual work: Working individually, children should complete the 'Speed check' activity sheet. They should attempt this activity against the clock, using a stopwatch if one is available or timing themselves to the nearest minute using the classroom clock.

Differentiation

Less able: Ensure that children understand how the grid system works on their differentiated version of the 'Speed check' activity sheet, and that they appreciate the value of the numbers in the tenths column, to the right of the decimal point.

More able: This group should work through the 'Speed check' activity sheet with more difficult calculations. Then ask them to check the inverse operation of the multiplication facts they have calculated on the activity sheet.

Plenary & assessment

Check through the work children have produced on the activity sheets. Play a 'hit the target' type activity as follows. Provide the answer to a decimal number multiplication calculation and ask children to provide you with the question. For example, if you say 0.6 they could answer 0.6 × 1 or 0.3 × 2; if you say 1.8 they could answer 0.6 × 3 or 0.9 × 2. Encourage the children to provide their own 'answers' for other members of the class to work out.

Lesson

Starter

Revise multiplying decimal numbers by 10 and 100. Work through some examples to show the movement of the digits to the right relative to the decimal point, for example, 0.5 × 10 = 5 and 0.5 × 100 = 50. Try other examples: 0.8, 2.3, 6.8. Then introduce numbers written to two decimal places, for example, 0.42 × 10 = 4.2 and 0.42 × 100 = 42. Use other examples: 0.73, 1.27 and 13.59. Extend to multiplying integers by 1000.

Main teaching activity

Whole class: On the whiteboard write an example of division that produces a remainder, for example, 31 divided by 5. Establish that this is 6 remainder 1. Write up 31 ÷ 5 = 6 r 1 and demonstrate this on a number line if necessary. Tell the children that 1 ÷ 5 is 1/5 and that 31 ÷ 5 = 6 and 1/5. Repeat the same process with other numbers in the 5-times table, for example: 26 ÷ 5 = 5 r1 or 5 and 1/5; 43 ÷ 5 = 8 r3, or 8 and 3/5. Revise how we can write 1/5 as a decimal (0.2), and that 5 and 1/5 would be 5.2 and 8 and 3/5 would be 8.6.

Now write 36 ÷ 10 on the board and ask for alternative answers. Children should provide 3 r6 or 3 and 6/10. Point out that 1/10 is written as 0.1, so the answer could be written as 3.6.

Finally, write 19 ÷ 2. Answers provided should be 9 r1 or 9 1/2. Point out that when dividing by 2 the only remainder can be 1. We write a half as 0.5, so 19 ÷ 2 = 9.5.

Paired work: In pairs, children choose numbers to divide by 2, 5 and 10 and give their answers in fraction and decimal form. Pairs of ten-sided dice can be used to generate numbers. Draw up a table and do the first two rows together (see margin).

Digits chosen	÷ 2	÷ 5	÷ 10
32	16	6 r 2	3.2
47	23 1/2	9 r 2	4.7

Differentiation

Less able: It may be better to begin with dividing by 10, where the remainder automatically becomes a decimal number. Fifths and halves can then be introduced later.

More able: Work with this group and extend the activity to include dividing by 4. Revise with the children that 1/4 is 0.25 as a decimal, 2/4 or 1/2 is 0.5 and 3/4 is 1/2 + 1/4, ie 0.5 + 0.25 = 0.75. So 17 ÷ 4 = 4 r 1, or 4.25; 22 ÷ 4 = 5 r 2, or 5.5; 27 ÷ 4 = 6 r 3 or 6.75. Then try the same method with three-digit numbers.

Plenary & assessment

Again use a 'hit the target' type game. Ask children to provide division calculations that will give a whole number and a remainder equivalent to 0.3, 0.7, (divide by 10, eg 23 ÷ 10 = 2.3; 57 ÷ 10 = 5.7), 0.5, (divide by 2, eg 17 ÷ 2 = 8.5) 0.2, 0.4, 0.6 and 0.8 (divide by 5, eg 16 ÷ 5 = 3.2; 32 ÷ 5 = 7.4; 43 ÷ 5 = 8.6; 69 ÷ 5 = 13.8). Check with the more able group to see how they divided by 4 and converted remainders into decimal numbers.

Lesson

Starter

Revise dividing decimal numbers by 10 and 100. Work through some examples to show the movement of digits to the left relative to the decimal point, for example, 3.8 ÷ 10 = 0.38 and 3.8 ÷ 100 = 0.038. Try other examples: 6.2, 9.7, 13.5. Then introduce numbers to two decimal places, for example, 16.57 ÷ 10 = 1.657 and 16.57 ÷ 100 = 0.1657. Use other examples: 9.34, 12.72, 37.54. Extend to dividing integers by 1000.

Main teaching activity

Whole class: Briefly revise the work done in the previous lesson on dividing numbers by 5, 10, 2 and 4 and giving answers in fraction and decimal form. Then go on to look at what happens when the divisor is different from these numbers.

Write 75 ÷ 9 on the whiteboard. Ask the children to provide the answer with a remainder and then show the remainder as a fraction. They should reply with 8 r3 or 8 and 3/9. Ask them how the 3/9 can be written in decimal terms. Ask them to work out 3 ÷ 9 = 0.333333333 using a calculator. Tell them this is called a recurring decimal number because the same digit is repeated or recurs throughout. Then check the solution to the whole calculation on the calculator: 75 ÷ 9 = 8.333333333. Ask: *What is the answer to the nearest whole number?* The answer is 8 because 8.3 is nearer to 8 than it is to 9. Say: *If we rounded to one decimal place the answer would be 8.3.* The 3 in the hundredths column is less than 5, so it would not be big enough to round up the 3 in the tenths column. Try other examples, such as 65 ÷ 6 (11 and 10.8), 123 ÷ 8 (15 and 15.4).

Then move on to calculations where the divisor is a two-digit number. Write 274 ÷ 14 on the whiteboard. Demonstrate a method of long division to get the answer 19 r 8, or 19 and 8/14. Then go through the method on the calculator to find 8/14 as a decimal, i.e. 8 ÷ 14 = 0.571428571. Check the solution to the whole calculation on the calculator 274 ÷ 14 = 19.57142857. Ask: *What would this be to the nearest whole number? And rounded to one decimal place?* It would be 20 to the nearest whole number because 19.57 is more than a half, and 19.6 rounded to one decimal place because the 7 in the hundredths column is more than 5, so the 5 is put up to a 6. Try other examples, such as 356 ÷ 24 (15 and 14.8) and 475 ÷ 36 (13 and 13.1).

Individual work: Put other examples on the whiteboard for children to calculate. Start with the divisor as a single digit, for example: 32 ÷ 9, 74 ÷ 7, 56 ÷ 5, 98 ÷ 8; then move on to two-digit numbers, for example: 46 ÷ 11, 64 ÷ 12 and 97 ÷ 15. Each time, children should show the remainder, the remainder as a fraction, the answer to the nearest whole number and then the answer rounded to one decimal place.

Differentiation

Less able: Restrict the divisor to a single-digit number until the children are able to work out these calculations confidently.

More able: Continue to encourage children to use the inverse operation – in this case multiplication – to check the answers to division calculations, for example: if 426 ÷ 16 = 26 r 10, then 26 × 16 + 10 = 426.

Plenary & assessment

Mark the work the children have produced and clarify any points that have arisen. Children should be able to give a quotient as a decimal rounded off to at least one decimal place. Remind children that the quotient is the answer to a division calculation. Ask: *How many different ways do you now know of showing the remainder in a division calculation? When rounding remainders to one decimal place, what rules govern changes to digits in the tenths column?*

Lesson ⑤

Starter

Write some one-place decimal numbers less than one on the whiteboard and discuss ways of doubling them. Suggest that numbers are treated as whole numbers, doubled and then the decimal point reinstated, for example: 0.8, double 8 is 16, replace decimal point, 1.6, the decimal point being positioned one place in from the right-hand side. Try other examples, such as 0.4, 0.6 and 0.9. Extend to numbers less than one with two decimal places, for example, 0.28. Suggest the same method, for example, double 28 becomes 56, replace decimal point, 0.56. The decimal point is now two places in from the right-hand side. Work through other examples, such as 0.18, 0.32, 0.54 and 0.63. Repeat the process with halving. Work with one-place decimal numbers less than one first, then move to two-place decimal numbers, for example, half of 0.6 = 0.3 and half of 0.64 = 0.32.

Main teaching activity

Whole class: Explain to the children that in this lesson they will learn how to divide pounds and pence by a two-digit number to get £ and p. Give them this problem: *Twelve people went out for a meal in a restaurant. The bill came to £110.40. How much did they need to pay each?* Working in pairs with a calculator, children find the answer: 110.40 ÷ 12 = 9.2. Point out that as it is a money calculation the .2 has to be written in money terms, so it becomes 20p. Each person has to pay £9.20. Tell children to check the answer using the inverse operation, ie £9.20 × 12 = £110.40. Try another example: 16 people sharing a food bill of £135.68. Tell children they will return to some of these questions later.

Move to 'real life' division calculations that require rounding up or rounding down. Write this problem on the whiteboard: *The football club organiser has £100. Tickets for the match are £7 each. How many children can she take?* Do the calculation £100 ÷ 7 = 14 remainder 2. Point out that you cannot buy two-sevenths of a ticket, so the answer is rounded down. Only 14 tickets can be bought and £2 will be left over. Write up a second problem: *There are 127 adults going on a trip. Only 20-seater minibuses can be hired. How many minibuses are needed?* (127 ÷ 20 = 6 remainder 7) Seven people cannot be left behind, so the answer has to be rounded up. Seven mini-buses will be needed, even though one of them will not be full.

Individual work: Return to the division tasks carried out in the first part of the lesson. Continue the eating out theme with groups of children working in ability pairs from the differentiated 'Eating out' activity sheets.

Differentiation

Less able: This group will work on the activity sheet with simpler calculations. Make sure they are able to interpret the calculator display correctly, especially £15.2 being read as £15.20.
More able: This group will work on the activity sheet with more complex calculations. Working out should be shown, but calculators should only be used for checking answers.

Plenary & assessment

Ask quick-fire questions in which 'read outs' from the calculator have to be converted into £ and p., for example, 14.3 becomes £14.30, 27.5 becomes £27.50 and 49.9 becomes £49.90. Check the individual work carried out in the lesson on restaurant bills.

Name		Date

Speed check

- **You will need a stopwatch or the classroom clock to do this speed check.**
- Work through the questions using your calculator. Record how long it took to answer the questions. Check how many you got right.
- Cover your answers. Work through the questions again, **without** using your calculator this time, and record how long it took.
- Did you beat the calculator? How did your marks compare?

1.	0.2 x 3			**11.**	1.46 x 10		
2.	0.5 x 4			**12.**	2.62 x 5		
3.	0.6 x 5			**13.**	5.02 x 3		
4.	0.3 x 8			**14.**	3.68 x 10		
5.	0.7 x 6			**15.**	2.25 x 4		
6.	0.9 x 7			**16.**	7.14 x 2		
7.	0.4 x 9			**17.**	£2.15 x 3		
8.	0.5 x 10			**18.**	£3.40 x 4		
9.	0.3 x 9			**19.**	£4.15 x 5		
10.	0.5 x 7			**20.**	£5.63 x 10		

Times:

SCHOLASTIC

photocopiable

Multiplication and division 2

Lessons 1 and 2 look at the use of brackets in multiplication and division, and the importance of factors in multiplication. Lessons 3 to 5 examine in detail formal written methods for long multiplication (HTU x TU) and division (HTU ÷ U, HTU ÷ TU and TU ÷ U). Examples are given of how these methods should be recorded on paper.

LEARNING OBJECTIVES

		Topics	Starter	Main teaching activity
Lesson	1	Understanding multiplication and division	● **Derive quickly: division facts corresponding to tables up to 10 x 10.**	● Use brackets. ● Understand and use the relationships between the four operations, and the principles of the arithmetic laws.
Lesson	2	Mental calculation strategies (x and ÷)	● Use factors (eg 35 x 18 = 35 x 6 x 3).	● Use closely related facts. ● Use factors (eg 35 x 18 = 35 x 6 x 3).
Lesson	3	Pencil and paper procedures (x and ÷)	● Use related facts and doubling or halving. For example: to multiply by 25, multiply by 100 then divide by 4.	● **Extend written methods to: long multiplication of a three-digit by a two-digit integer.**
Lesson	4	As for Lesson 3.	As for Lesson 3.	● **Extend written methods to:** short division of HTU by U (mixed-number answer).
Lesson	5	As for Lesson 3.	● Use closely related facts, for example: multiply by 49 or 51 by multiplying by 50 and adjusting.	● **Extend written methods to:** division of HTU by TU (long division, whole number answer); **short division of numbers involving decimals.**

Lessons   overview

Preparation
Prepare your own version of the 'Division time' and 'Division time 2' activity sheets from the templates if desired.

Learning objectives
Starters
● **Derive quickly: division facts corresponding to tables up to 10 x 10.**
● Use factors (eg 35 x 18 = 35 x 6 x 3).
● Use related facts and doubling or halving. For example: to multiply by 25, multiply by 100 then divide by 4.
● Use closely related facts, for example: multiply by 49 or 51 by multiplying by 50 and adjusting.
Main teaching activities
● Use brackets.
● Use factors (eg 35 x 18 = 35 x 6 x 3).
● **Extend written methods to: long multiplication of a three-digit by a two-digit integer;** short division of HTU by U; division of HTU by TU (long division, whole-number answer); **short division of numbers involving decimals.**

Vocabulary
operation, brackets, inverse, mixed number, times, multiply, multiplied by, product, multiple, inverse, factor, prime number, estimate, approximate, integer, remainder, mixed number, adjust, adjusting, double, quotient, repeated addition, long division

You will need:
Photocopiable pages
A copy of 'Brackets first' (page 96) and, 'Starting grid' (page 97) for each child.

CD pages
A set of 1–9 digit cards (which can be made from 'Digit (+ and –) and decimal point cards'); copies of 'Division time' and 'Division time 2' for each child differentiated copies of 'Brackets first', 'Starting grid' 'Division time' and 'Division time 2' for each less able and more able child and a copy of the 'Division time 2' template (see General resources).

Equipment
Table squares; large-squared paper (5cm); rulers; calculators.

Lesson

Starter

Explain that you would like the children to use multiplication table facts to derive the answers to division questions. Say, for example: *I have 36 apples to share between 6 children. How many do they each receive? The total cost of tickets for a pop concert was £72. If there are 8 tickets, how much did each cost?* Ask other division questions set in context.

Main teaching activity

Whole class: Explain to the children that they are going to investigate how brackets are used in calculations. Put an example on the whiteboard to illustrate how calculations can provide different solutions depending on the order in which operations are carried out. For example, 10 x 3 + 6 can produce either 36 or 90. Show the children how the use of brackets can tell us which operation to carry out first, ie (10 x 3) + 6 = 36 and 10 x (3 + 6) = 90. Show other examples, incorporating each of the four main operations signs. Ask children to work out which answers are possible and then indicate where brackets have to be positioned to produce these answers. Another example could be 90 ÷ 10 + 5, which can produce (90 ÷ 10) + 5 = 14 or 90 ÷ (10 + 5) = 6.

Group work: Children work through the 'Brackets first' activity sheet.

Differentiation

Less able: This group should work on the 'Brackets first' activity sheet with only one set of questions. Provide table squares if necessary, so multiplication and division problems can be solved quickly.

More able: Provide this group with the more demanding 'Brackets first' activity sheet. In the second section children, working in pairs, can devise their own problems involving brackets, where the answers are given and they have to provide the variables. How many different solutions for each can they find? For example, find suitable figures for the empty boxes in ☐ + ☐ x ☐ = 24, ☐ – ☐ ÷ ☐ = 6 and ☐ x ☐ – ☐ = 18. Possible answers might include (7 + 1) x 3 = 24, (20 – 2) ÷ 3 = 6 and (5 x 4) – 2 = 18.

Plenary & assessment

Go through the activity sheets, marking them with the children. Reinforce that operations in brackets must be carried out first. Tell the children that if brackets are not shown, there is an agreed order in which operations should be carried out. This can be shortened to BODMAS (brackets, of (x), division, multiplication, addition and subtraction) to help them remember. Ask for some examples to test this out.

Lesson

Starter

Revise with the children what a factor is (a number that goes into another number exactly without leaving a remainder). Then write numbers on the whiteboard and ask children to give you a pair of its factors. For example, 12 would produce 6 and 2, 4 and 3, 12 and 1; 18 would produce 1 and 18, 2 and 9, 3 and 6; 20 would produce 2 and 10, 1 and 20, 5 and 4. Include some square numbers like 16 that produces 2 and 8, 1 and 16 and 4 and 4.

Main teaching activity

Whole class: Write the calculation 16 x 12 on the whiteboard. Ask: *How can factors be used to help make this multiplication easier?* Start with the 12 first. It could be broken down into 16 x 2 x 6 or 16 x 3 x 4. Ask children to work out the answers and then suggest which way they found most

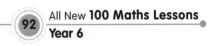

straightforward. Then look at ways of factorising 16 as well. Try 8 x 2 x 3 x 4 or 4 x 4 x 2 x 6. Discuss the most efficient method. Then show the children how factors can be used in the division process, for example, 288 ÷ 18. Since 2 x 9 = 18, this division can be calculated as 288 ÷ 2 = 144; then 144 ÷ 9 = 16.

Individual work: On the whiteboard write ten examples showing the use of factors in multiplication and division calculations. Children should work these out individually. Tell them they should use the factors they feel are most suitable. Examples might include: 16 x 8, 19 x 12, 20 x 24, 28 x 14, 36 x 18, 45 x 30, 112 ÷ 14, 324 ÷ 36, 432 ÷ 18, 456 ÷ 24.

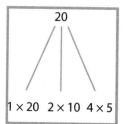

Differentiation

Less able: Work with this group to ensure numbers are being factorised correctly. Table squares or charts showing factors of numbers may be needed by some children for reference purposes.

More able: Invite children to make their own factor trees – that is, splitting up numbers into multiplication facts. A factor tree of 20, for example, would include the branches 1 x 20, 2 x 10 and 4 x 5 (see margin).

Plenary & assessment

Play a game in which the children have to spot the odd one out in a list of factors. For example, if the factors of 21 were given as 1, 3, 4, 7 and 21, then 4 would be the odd one out because 21 does not come in the four times table. Or leave out a factor and ask children to tell you what is missing. For example if the factors of 24 were given as 1, 2, 3, 4, 6, 12 and 24, 8 would be the missing number. Ensure that children understand the difference between the terms 'multiple' and 'factor'. The multiples of 9 are 9, 18, 27, 36…, while the factors of 9 are 1, 3 and 9.

Lesson ③

Starter

Ask: *How many 25s are there in 100?* Explain to the children that to multiply by 25 they can multiply by 100 and divide by 4. Ask questions such as: *What is 40 multiplied by 25? … 30×25? So what would 31 multiplied by 25 be? How could you work that out?* Repeat for other multiples of 25, using multiples of 10 or near multiples of 10.

×	200	40	8	Totals
50	10,000	2000	400	= 12,400
3	600	120	24	= 744
				13,144

Grid method

Main teaching activity

Whole class: Tell the children you are going to show them how to multiply a three-digit number by a two-digit integer using the grid method (see margin). Use 248 x 53 as an example. Estimate first: 250 x 50 = 12 500.

Then write the following on the board. Explain the steps being taken and how they link to the grid method.

```
    248
  × 53
  10000   200  x 50
   2000    40  x 50
    400     8  x 50
+   600   200  x  3
    120    40  x  3
     24     8  x  3
  13144
      1
```

Finally, demonstrate the compact method to show how 248 x 50 and 248 x 3 can be calculated the least number of steps.

```
    248
  × 53
  12400   248 x 50
+  744   248 x  3
  13144
     1
```

Group work: Provide groups of children with the 'Starting grid' activity sheet. Emphasise that they should estimate answers first, that they must use the methods outlined in the lesson and should show all their working out.

Differentiation

Less able: Provide this group with the less demanding 'Starting grid' activity sheet. Make sure children are comfortable with multiplying a three-digit number by a single digit using the grid method before progressing to the type of calculations shown above.

More able: This group should work on the 'Starting grid' activity sheet in which multiplication problems are given as word problems. There is also scope for them to make up similar problems of their own for friends to work out.

Plenary & assessment

Work selected examples on the board to ensure the methods used by children are secure. Ask volunteers to come out to the front of the class and show others on the whiteboard each stage in the working out process. Which part of the processes did they find most difficult? Can they come up with a set of instructions or rules to help them follow the various procedures? If time is available, look at the word problems set by the more able group. Pick out the key vocabulary used in the questions. Ask: *Which calculation methods would you use to solve these problems?*

Lesson 4

Starter
Repeat the starter for Lesson 3. Include examples such as 42×25 and 19×25.

$$
\begin{array}{r}
6\overline{)158} \\
-\quad 60 \quad 10 \times 6 \\
\hline
98 \\
-\quad 60 \quad 10 \times 6 \\
\hline
38 \\
-\quad 36 \quad 6 \times 6 \\
\hline
02 \quad 26
\end{array}
$$

Answer: 26 r2
Show that the answer can also be written like this:

$$
6\overline{)158}^{\,26\quad r2}
$$

Main teaching activity

Whole class: Revise dividing HTU by U by setting the children the following practical problem. *Toy trains are packed in boxes of six. If 158 toy trains have been made during the day, how many boxes are needed?* Approximate first: $150 \div 5 = 30$. Then calculate the answer using the 'chunking' method (see the worked example in the margin). Remind children to set out digits in the correct columns – units under units, tens under tens and so on. The answer comes to 26 r2. Compare this with the estimate. Remind the children that as a mixed number this would be 26 2/6 or 26 1/3. Also stress that the answer would need to be rounded up, and that 27 boxes would be needed.

Individual work: Children practise examples using the 'Division time' activity sheet. Ask them to show their working out and to write their answers as mixed numbers, eg 26 1/3 flowers.

Differentiation

Less able: Provide these children with the version of the sheet that includes some less demanding examples. You might also wish to limit the children to using integer remainders, eg 26 r2, or adapt the template provided as desired.

More able: Provide these children with the version of the sheet that includes some more demanding examples (including HTU $\div$ TU). You might also require the children to show evidence in their calculations that they have checked answers by using the inverse operation – multiplication in this case.

Plenary and assessment

Review the 'Division time' answers. Discuss whether all the examples are 'sensible'. For example, the balloon seller would not be given 2/7 of a balloon because it would burst! Ask the children to decide whether to round up or round down these answers, based on the context. Invite children to model examples on the board using the short division method. Collect answers and correct any misconceptions. Provide some additional examples if necessary, for example: *'There are 374 children divided equally in 13 classes. How many children in each class? What fraction of a class would be left?'* (28 children in each of 13 classes with 10 children (10/13) left).

Lesson ⑤

Starter

Ask: *What is 20 multiplied by 5? So what is 20 multiplied by 50? How could we calculate 20 multiplied by 49…51?* Elicit the response that you can multiply by 50 and adjust by subtracting or adding 20. Repeat for other examples, such as $30 \times 51, 30 \times 41$.

```
          35
     28)980
    -   560    20 x 28
        420
    -   280    10 x 28
        140
    -   140     5 x 28
        000
```

```
          12.3
      8)98.4
    -  80.0    10 x 28
       18.4
    -  16.0     2 x 8
        2.4
    -   2.4    0.3 x 8
        0.0
```

Main teaching activity

Whole class: Review work from the previous lesson. Then consider division where HTU is divided by TU. Look at the example 980 ÷ 28. Approximate first (990 ÷ 30 = 33), then explain orally (see workings on left). The answer would be 35. Compare this with the estimate.

Finally, demonstrate an example of the short division method involving the use of decimal numbers. Remind children that when setting this down it is important that the decimal points are lined up underneath each other. Use the example 98.4 ÷ 8. Approximate first (96 ÷ 8 = 12), then explain orally (see workings on left). The answer is 12.3.

Individual work: Children practise examples of these calculations individually, using the 'Division time 2' activity sheet. Stress the importance of estimating first and showing each stage of the working-out process.

Differentiation

Less able: This group should work on the less demanding 'Division time 2' activity sheet, where they have the opportunity to build up confidence by dividing three-digit numbers by a single digit first. A blank version of the activity sheet is also provided for this group for the teacher to fill in with suitable smaller numbers if necessary.

More able: Children in this group should be provided with the more demanding version of the 'Division time 2' activity sheet. Children should also show evidence in their calculations that they are checking answers by using the inverse operation – multiplication in this case.

Plenary & assessment

Invite children to demonstrate each of the three types of division covered during the last two lessons. Look at some examples of division calculations that have been checked by using the inverse operation. What do the methods demonstrate about the relationship between multiplication and division?

Name	Date

Brackets first

Copy and complete these calculations. Remember to work out the brackets first.

1. (6 x 3) + 7 _____

2. 9 + (5 x 4) _____

3. (7 x 5) + 6 _____

4. 34 – (18 ÷ 2) _____

5. (17 + 8) ÷ 5 _____

6. 12 + (19 – 7) _____

7. (16 + 12) ÷ (19 – 12) _____

8. (5 x 4) x (28 – 25) _____

Write true or false after these number statements.

1. (3 + 7) x 2 = 3 + (7 x 2) _____

2. (5 x 5) + 4 = 5 x (5 + 4) _____

3. (12 – 10) ÷ 2 = 10 – (27 ÷ 3) _____

4. (15 ÷ 3) + 5 = 15 – (10 ÷ 2) _____

5. (4 x 7) – 6 = 4 x (7 – 6) _____

| Name | Date |

Starting grid

- **Work out the area (length × width) of the tops of these worktables used in school.**
- Estimate your answers first, then use the methods you have been shown in the lesson. Show all your working out.

1. 212cm by 35cm

2. 326cm by 28cm

3. 198cm by 42cm

4. 234cm by 46cm

5. 157cm by 59cm

Which table has the biggest surface area to work on?

_____

_____

Problem solving

Children have to choose and use appropriate number operations to solve problems. They give reasons for their choice, explain the methods they use and demonstrate several methods of checking their calculations. A step by step approach is provided for children who need a structured approach to problem solving.

LEARNING OBJECTIVES

		Topics	Starter	Main teaching activity
Lesson	1	Making decisions Problems involving 'real life', money and measures	● Order fractions such as 2/3, 3/4 and 5/6 by converting them to fractions with a common denominator, and position them on a number line.	● Choose and use appropriate number operations to solve problems, and appropriate ways of calculating. **● Explain methods and reasoning.**
Lesson	2	As for Lesson 1.	● Know what each digit represents in a number with up to three decimal places.	● As for Lesson 1.
Lesson	3	As for Lesson 1.	**● Order a mixed set of numbers or measurements with up to three decimal places.**	● As for Lesson 1.
Lesson	4	As for Lesson 1.	As for Lesson 3.	**● Identify and use appropriate operations to solve word problems involving** converting numbers and quantities based on ' real life', money… including pounds to foreign currency and vice versa.
Lesson	5	Checking results of calculations	● Round a number with two decimal places to the nearest tenth or to the nearest whole number.	● Check the sum of several numbers by adding in reverse order. ● Check with an equivalent calculation.

Lessons overview

Preparation
Assemble the materials to make the operation cards needed for Lesson 1. The children can make these from scrap paper at the start of the lesson (or in registration time). Prepare OHTs of 'Five steps to successful problem solving', 'Football factsheet questions' and 'Check it out'. Prepare your own version of the 'Step by step' activity sheet from the template if desired.

Learning objectives
Starters
● Order fractions such as 2/3, 3/4 and 5/6 by converting them to fractions with a common denominator, and position them on a number line.
● Know what each digit represents in a number with up to three decimal places.
● **Order a mixed set of numbers or measurements with up to three decimal places.**
● Round a number with two decimal places to the nearest tenth or to the nearest whole number.
Main teaching activities
● Choose and use appropriate number operations to solve problems and appropriate ways of calculating, mental, mental with jottings, written methods, calculator.
● **Explain methods and reasoning.**
● **Identify and use appropriate operations to solve word problems involving** converting numbers and quantities based on ' real life', money… including pounds to foreign currency and vice versa.
● Check the sum of several numbers by adding in reverse order.
● Check with an equivalent calculation.

Vocabulary
ten thousand, hundred thousand, million, four-digit, five-digit, six-digit numbers, place value, order, plus, increase, sum, total, altogether, subtract, minus, decrease, difference between, Euros ( ) , exchange (times, product, multiply, repeated addition, divide, equal groups of, share equally, remainder, quotient, calculation, method, strategy, jotting, answer, right, correct, wrong, what could we try next?, how did you work it out?, number sentence, sign, operation, symbol

You will need:
Photocopiable pages
A copy of 'Step by step' (page 102) for each child

CD pages
OHTs of 'Five steps to successful problem solving', 'Football factsheets questions' and 'Check it out', a copy of 'Five steps to successful problem solving' for each less able child, a copy of 'Football factsheets' for each group; differentiated versions of 'Step by step' for each more able and less able child, 'Step by step' template (see General resources), Foreign currency' for each pair (core, less able, more able and template versions).

Equipment
Materials for each child to make a set of operation cards (+, −, x and ÷); an OHP calculator; an OHP.

Lesson

Starter

Write on the board the following fractions: 1/4, 1/2, 3/8, 5/8. Ask: *How can we order these fractions?* Encourage the children to find the common denominator, and then to order the fractions. Draw an empty number line labelled 0 at one end and 1 at the other. Invite children to place each fraction where they estimate it belongs. Repeat this for another family of fractions, such as 1/3, 3/5, 5/6, 4/5.

Main teaching activity

Whole class: Write two simple word problems on the whiteboard – the first involving a one-step process only and the second incorporating at least two steps. Examples might be as follows: *Tom, Sanjay and Alison have 72 stickers. They share them out equally. How many do they have each?* (one -step) *My reading book has 224 pages. I have read a quarter of it. How many pages are still left to read?* (two-steps) Work through the examples with the children using a five-step strategy (see 'Five steps to successful problem solving', which you can display as an OHT). Discuss the different approaches they suggest.

Individual/group work: Children work on the 'Step by step' activity sheet. They can either work individually or in pairs. Stress that they should work through the sheet very carefully, as being able to explain their method and reasoning, and showing their working out, are as important on this occasion as producing the correct answer.

Differentiation

Less able: This group should use the 'Step by step' activity sheet that uses simpler numbers. Provide verbal support with the use of vocabulary and the way in which working out is shown and explanations are written down.

More able: This group should work on the 'Step by step' activity sheet. Children can make up their own two-step problems on the back of the sheet, for each of the four main operations.

Plenary & assessment

Take feedback from each of the groups and discuss with them decisions that were taken about picking out key words and numbers, deciding on operations to use, estimating answers, choosing methods and checking solutions. Sum up with the following questions: *Has the question been answered? Does the answer make sense? How does this question help to answer similar word problems?*

Lesson

Starter

Write 2.5 on the board and ask: What does the 2 represent? What does the 5 represent? Now write a number with two decimal places, such as 4.56. Ask what each digit represents. Repeat for other similar numbers. Extend this to numbers with three decimal places, such as 6.254. Invite the children to use the digits, re-order them to make a new number, and to say what each digit is now worth.

Main teaching activity

Whole class: Tell the children that during the next three lessons they are going to work on choosing and using appropriate number operations to solve problems. Explain that they will also need to choose appropriate ways of calculating, such as mental, mental with jottings, written and calculator. Revise these terms to make sure children understand what they mean. Explain that calculators will not be an option on this occasion. Tell the children that the problems will involve football matches played in the Premiership. Point out that they will be working in this lesson on attendance figures (shown on the first sheet) and ground capacities (shown on the second sheet). Remind children of the step-by-step approach used during Lesson 1. Some children may benefit from using the 'Five steps to successful problem solving' resource sheet. Stress that they should use this method, estimating answers first, showing their working out and checking their answers. Say that they will be asked to explain their methods and reasoning. Split the class into mixed-ability pairs or groups of three for these activities.

Group work: Distribute copies of 'Football factsheets' to each group. These contain the information that the children will need. Then display the 'Football factsheets questions' as an OHT or on the whiteboard. Children work through the 'Attendance figures' questions.

Differentiation

Less able: Ensure that children receive support in the mixed-ability groups, especially with place value and ordering attendance figures. Tell children to focus particularly on one-step questions. Stress that they should refer back to and follow the five-step guide used in Lesson 1.

More able: Encourage this group to focus on the multi-step questions. They can then make up their own questions using the information provided.

Plenary & assessment

Review the problems the groups of children have been working on. Discuss which parts of solving problems they found most difficult and which they found easiest. Assess how helpful the five-step guide was.

Lesson ③

Starter

Write on the board a list of numbers such as 4.25, 18.7, 6.39, 8.25, 5.3. Invite the children to order the numbers from smallest to largest. Repeat with a set such as 4.25, 9.72, 4.52, 9.27. Repeat, extending the number range to include some numbers with three places of decimals.

Main teaching activity

Whole class: Review the work on attendance figures from the previous lesson. Tell the children that in this lesson they will be looking at the number of goals scored in a particular week and the time in which they were scored (shown on the first sheet beside the name of the scorer). They will also look at the difference between goals scored and conceded (shown in bold on the first sheet) by each side. Check that the children understand the naming of the column letters and the points system on the second sheet. Remind them that although mathematically a difference cannot be negative, in football terms 17 goals for and 23 goals against would give a 'difference' of −6. Work through an example of each type of question.

Group work: Again, split the class into mixed ability pairs or groups of three. Distribute copies of the 'Football factsheets' to the children and a set of 'Football factsheets questions', or display them on OHT. They should now work through the second and third sets of questions.

Differentiation

Less able: Provide support in the mixed-ability groups. If necessary, work with less confident children on similar examples, particularly related to the 'Goal difference and points' questions, for example: *A team that has played 14 games, won 7, drawn 5 and lost 2, has 26 points.* Demonstrate that the 3-times table could be used to calculate the points scored from wins: $7 \times 3 + 5 = 26$.

More able: Once this group has answered all the questions encourage them to make up their own questions using the information provided on the 'Football factsheets'.

Plenary and assessment

Examine the methods children have used to find solutions. Try out further examples: *What is the time difference between goals scored at 16 minutes and 83 minutes? Did you find it easier to add or subtract in these examples?* Review the use of negative numbers for goal difference (for example, 26 goals scored, 31 conceded gives a goal difference of −5 or 5 less goals scored than conceded) and checking total points (for example, P20, W14, D4, L2 = 14 × 3 + 4 = 46). Allow additional time for children to complete all the factsheet questions and set as homework if necessary.

Lesson 4

Repeat the Starter for Lesson 3, this time asking the children to order sets of decimals for measurements. For example, ask then to order 3.5 km, 5.27km.

In the **Main teaching activity** remind children about previous work on converting pounds to foreign currencies. Talk about exchange rates and why they are needed. Demonstrate, using an OHP calculator, how to change from pounds Euros to pounds by dividing or multiplying by the exchange rate, eg 144 Euros can be bought for £100. Ask questions for the children to work on in pairs using written methods or calculators, for example: *'I have £50. How much is that in Euros? A CD costs 20 Euros. How much is that is pounds?*

Give each pair a copy of the 'Foreign currency' sheet. Ask the children to discuss methods of calculation and to work out each answer. There are differentiated versions of the sheet for more able and less able children.

In the **Plenary,** collect answers, discuss the children's methods and correct errors. Ask further questions based on exchange rates and challenge the children to ask and answer their own exchange rate questions. Supply the current exchange rates from the Internet.

Lesson 5

Starter

Explain that you would like the children to round numbers with two or more decimal places to the nearest tenth. Write some numbers on the board, such as 5.27, 3.82, 9.05, 8.03. Invite children to explain their rounding.

Examples
Reverse order:
652 + 198 + 354 = 1204 and
354 + 198 + 652 = 1204.
Equivalent calculations:
1900 + 4725 = 5000 + 1625 or
2625 + 4000 = 6625
36.5 − 9.25 = 27 + 0.5 − 0.25 or
36.5 − 9.5 + 0.25 = 27.25
536 x 9 = 536 x 10 − 536 or
536 x 5 + 536 x 4 = 4824

Main teaching activity
Whole class: Explain that in this lesson the class will look at two ways of checking calculations (adding lists of numbers in reverse order and using an equivalent calculation). On the whiteboard, work through the examples in the margin, explaining each step of the process. Estimate answers first. Focus particularly on +, − and x calculations and include some decimal numbers.
Paired work: Write the calculations from 'Check it out' on the whiteboard or display as an OHT. Ask children, working in pairs, to estimate each answer. They should then calculate answers, first using the usual written methods and then checking solutions using strategies outlined above. Stress that they should show clearly their working out. Questions 1–4 are easiest to check by adding in another order, questions 5–8 by using an equivalent calculation.

Differentiation
Less able: Encourage this group to focus on the reverse order (questions 1–4) particularly. It may be necessary to simplify the numbers used in the later questions and limit them to finding one equivalent calculation only. Assist with methods of recording.
More able: Expect this group to be able to explain to other children in the class the exact method they are using. Children can generate their own calculations using larger numbers.

Plenary & assessment
Ask for volunteers to show the rest of the class how they checked solutions for each of the given questions. Ask: *What rule can you apply to adding numbers?* (Numbers can be added in any order and will always produce the same answer.) *What other operation does this apply to?* (multiplication). *For which operation did you find the 'equivalent calculation' method most suitable, +, − or x?*

Name	Date

Step by step

Solve this problem. Show your working out in the box.

Two thousand six hundred and fifty-six people queue up to see a pop concert. Seven hundred and ninety-eight give up and leave the queue before it starts. How many are still left to see the concert?

Explain in words how you solved the problem by answering these questions.

● What were the key words in the question and the important numbers you needed?

_____

● What operations did you need to use?

_____

● How did you estimate the answer?

_____

● What method did you use to calculate the answer?

_____

● How did you check the answer? Did it make sense? Show in the box below.

Fractions, decimals and percentages

Topics covered include ordering fractions, and finding fractional amounts of numbers and quantities. The unit also looks at converting fractions into decimals using division, and finding simple whole numbers. Children are shown how to calculate more difficult percentage problems using a calculator.

LEARNING OBJECTIVES

		Topics	Starter	Main teaching activity
Lesson	1	Fractions, decimals and percentages	● **Understand percentage the number of parts in every 100.** ● Express simple fractions as percentages.	● Order fractions such as 2/3, 3/4 and 5/8 by converting them into fractions with a common denominator, and position them on a number line.
Lesson	2	Fractions, decimals and percentages	● **Derive quickly** squares of multiples of 10 to 100 (eg 60 × 60).	● **Use a fraction as an 'operator' to find fractions of numbers or quantities.**
Lesson	3	Fractions, decimals and percentages	● Order a set of positive and negative integers.	● Begin to convert a fraction to a decimal using division.
Lesson	4	Fractions, decimals and percentages	● **Find simple percentages of small whole-number quantities.**	● **Find simple percentages of small whole-number quantities.**
Lesson	5	Fractions, decimals and percentages. Using a calculator	As for Lesson 4.	As for Lesson 4. ● Develop calculator skills and use a calculator effectively.

Lessons overview

Preparation
Draw horizontal number lines and groups of fractions to order (see Lesson 1). Copy a set of 'Fraction cards' and 'Decimal equivalents' for each child and cut them out. Prepare your own version of the 'Planet Zogtroon' activity sheet from the template if desired.

Learning objectives
Starters
● **Understand percentage as the number of parts in every 100.**
● Express simple fractions as percentages.
● **Derive quickly** squares of multiples of 10 to 100 (eg 60 × 60).
● Order a set of positive and negative integers.
● **Find simple percentages of small whole-number quantities.**
Main teaching activities
● Order fractions such as 2/3, 3/4 and 5/8 by converting them into fractions with a common denominator, and position them on a number line.
● **Use a fraction as an 'operator' to find fractions of numbers or quantities.**
● Begin to convert a fraction into a decimal using division.
● **Find simple percentages of small whole-number quantities.**
● Develop calculator skills and use a calculator effectively.

Vocabulary
proper/improper fraction, mixed number, equivalent, numerator, denominator, reduced to, cancel, factor, third, fifth, eighth, ninth, tenth, twentieth, hundredth, thousandth, half, quarter, percentage, per cent, %

You will need:
Photocopiable pages
A copy of 'Change over' (page 108) and 'Planet Zogtroon' (page 109) for each child.

CD pages
A set of 1–9 digit cards (which can be made from 'Digit (+ and –) and decimal point cards'), a copy of 'Blank number lines' for each child, a set of 'Fraction cards', a copy of 'Decimal equivalents' for each less able child, a copy of 'Percentages' for each child; differentiated copies of 'Smooth operators', 'Change over' and 'Planet Zogtroon' for each less able and more able child, 'Planet Zogtroon' template (see General resources).

Equipment
An OHP calculator; a calculator for each child; table squares for less able children.

Lesson

Starter

Revise the decimal and percentage equivalents of the common fractions half (0.5 and 50%), quarter (0.25 and 25%) and three-quarters (0.75 and 75%). Check that children remember a tenth (0.1 and 10%), a fifth (0.2 and 20%) and a twentieth (0.05 and 5%). Write the number 200 on the whiteboard. Ask questions based on this number, such as: *What is half/fifty per cent of 200? What is a quarter/twenty five per cent of 200?* Repeat the same two-part questions for three-quarters, a tenth, a fifth and a twentieth.

Main teaching activity

Whole class: Explain that the lesson is about ordering fractions. Write the fractions 1/2, 1/4 and 1/3 on the whiteboard. Ask: *How would you put these fractions into order without using a calculator?* Explain that we need to find the lowest common denominator for each one, ie put them into the same fraction family. Ask children to find the lowest number common to all three tables (2×, 4× and 3×). Then show them how to convert 1/2 into 6/12, 1/4 into 3/12 and 1/3 into 4/12. Stress that when converting we must do the same thing to both parts of the fraction, denominator and numerator. Now draw a straight horizontal number line on the whiteboard, divide it into twelve equal sections and ask volunteers to mark the correct position of 1/2 (6/12), 1/4 (3/12) and 1/3 (4/12). Go through the same process with another example, say 1/4, 1/2 and 3/8 using eighths as the lowest common denominator.

Individual work: Give each child a copy of 'Blank number lines', then write the following examples on the whiteboard for them to order in the same way and place in the correct position on a number line. The lowest common denominator is given in brackets – do not provide these for the children. **1** 1/3, 1/2, 5/6 (6); **2** 3/5, 1/2, 7/10 (10); **3** 1/3, 1/4, 5/12 (12); **4** 2/3, 1/2, 7/12 (12); **5** 2/3, 5/6, 1/4 (12) and **6** 9/20, 2/5, 1/4 (20).

Differentiation

Less able: This group may need to start by ordering fractions that are in the same fraction family, for example, 2/6, 1/6 and 5/6. Then move on to pairs of fractions in which the common denominator is easy to find, for example, 1/2 and 1/4, 2/3 and a 1/6.

More able: Extend the ordering activity from three to four fractions or increase the size of the denominator, for example, ordering 2/3, 1/2, 7/10 and 3/5 (lowest common denominator 30). Set word problems requiring children to find the common denominator of groups of fractions, for example: *If Rakesh reads 3/8 of his book one day and 1/4 of the book the next day, what fraction does he still have to read?*

Plenary & assessment

Go through each of the whiteboard examples with the children and check the fractions have been correctly positioned on each of the number lines. Ensure children fully understand each word in the term 'lowest common denominator'. Stress that when converting, both numerator and denominator must be treated in exactly the same way.

Lesson

Starter

Explain that you will ask the children to write down some squares. Say: *Write the square of 5. What is 6 multiplied by 6? What is the product of 9 and 9?* Repeat until all square numbers up to 10 × 10 have been covered. Now ask the children to use their knowledge to derive the squares of multiples of 10, such as 30 × 30, 50 × 50… up to 100 × 100.

Main teaching activity

Whole class: Stress to the children from the outset that the lesson is looking at the close relationship between fractions and division. Remind them that when we find half of a number we divide by 2, and when we find a quarter of a number we divide by 4. Ask: *What happens when we want to find a fifth of a number, or an eighth, or a tenth?* Try out some examples: *Find 1/2 of 24, 1/3 of 30, 1/10 of 50, 1/8 of 32.* Explain that in these cases the fraction is being used as an 'operator', as it tells us what number we need to divide by. Explain that in a fraction where the numerator is greater than 1 we have to multiply after the division has been carried out. Go through examples on the whiteboard. *To find 3/4 of 28 we divide by four and then multiply by three: 28 ÷ 4 × 3 = 7 × 3 = 21. To find 7/10 of 50 we divide by ten and then multiply by seven: 50 ÷ 10 × 7 = 5 × 7 = 35.*

Group work: Groups should work through the 'Smooth operators' activity sheet.

Differentiation

Less able: This group should be provided with the version of 'Smooth operators' where the questions only involve unit fractions, ie fractions that always have 1 as the numerator. Work with children to ensure they understand that the denominator acts as the 'operator', telling us which number we need to divide by. Table squares may be needed to assist with division.

More able: This group should first complete the version of 'Smooth operators' with more difficult fractions. Then extend the task set at the end of Lesson 1, where children have to think up more questions in 'real life' situations. For example: *In a class of 36 children, a third liked apples, three-quarters liked grapes and two-ninths liked pears. How many children were there in each case?*

Plenary & assessment

Play a game of 'Make your mind up', in which children have to decide which fraction of a number of objects they would prefer to have. For example, ask: *Would you prefer two-fifths or one-third of 15 sweets? Would you prefer three-quarters or five-eighths of 32 football stickers?* They will probably go for the larger number each time. Ask them to explain how they made their decisions.

Lesson 3

Starter

Write on the board the following set of numbers: 15, 23, −15, −23. Ask the children to order the numbers, from smallest to largest. Repeat for other sets of positive and negative integers.

Main teaching activity

Whole class: Refer the children to the work carried out in Lesson 1, where fractions were ordered by finding a common denominator. Ask if they know another approach. Elicit the response that suggests the fractions can be turned into decimal numbers by dividing the denominator into the numerator. Practise with some conversions the children will be familiar with first, for example: order 1/4 (0.25), 1/10 (0.1) and 1/5 (0.2) and 3/10 (0.3), 1/2 (0.5) and 4/5 (0.8). Then explain that with more difficult divisions it is better to use a calculator. Show some examples on the OHP calculator: 1/3 is 1 ÷ 3 (0.333333333), 1/8 is 1 ÷ 8 (0.125), 5/6 is 5 ÷ 6 (0.833333333) and 5/8 is 5 ÷ 8 (0.625). Use these examples to explain the difference between a terminating decimal number (0.125), an infinite decimal number (0.833333333) and a recurring decimal number, where the same digit comes in every place (0.333333333). Stress that in the last two cases the display on the calculator shows only part of the decimal representation.

Paired work: Children should work in mixed ability pairs. Provide each pair with the 'Change over' activity sheets, where they are required to sort groups of fractions by changing them into decimal numbers. They should convert tenths and fifths mentally, but use calculators to convert the other fractions.

Differentiation

Less able: Support this group in working on the less demanding activity sheet. A copy of 'Decimal equivalents' may be needed by some to refer to.

More able: This group should work from the more demanding version of the 'Change over' activity sheet. Encourage them to make logical steps from some of the solutions they obtain. For example, if one-third is 0.333333333 recurring, then two-thirds is 0.666666666, and if one-eighth is 0.125, then two-eighths is 0.125 × 2 = 0.25.

Plenary & assessment

Mark the ordering activity with the children, checking any calculator calculations that might have caused trouble. Challenge the more able group to report on any interesting discoveries they have made, for example, 1/9 has a 1 in every place and 2/9 has a 2 in every place. Can they predict the rest of the 'ninths family' from this?

Lesson ④

Starter

Explain that you will say a number and ask the children to find a given percentage of it. Say, for example: *What is 25% of 40? What is 30% of 90? What is 10% of £400? And 20%?*

Main teaching activity

Whole class: Tell the children that in this lesson you are going to explain how many percentage problems can be calculated without using a calculator. Go through the following examples on the whiteboard or using an OHP: *Fifty percent of 24 would be 1/2, so divide by 2: 24 ÷ 2 = 12. Twenty five percent of 32 would be 1/4, so divide by 4: 32 ÷ 4 = 8. 75% of 40 would be 3/4, so divide by 4 and multiply by 3: 40 ÷ 4 = 10 × 3 = 30. Ten percent of 60 would be 1/10, so divide by 10: 60 ÷ 10 = 6.* Also explain that finding 20%, 30%, 40% and so on can be done by finding 10% and then multiplying by 2, 3 or 4, and that 5% can be calculated by finding 10% and then halving the answer, for example, 5% of 40 would be 40 ÷ 10 ÷ 2 = 4 ÷ 2. Demonstrate how 15%, 35%, 45%, and so on, can be calculated in the same way.

Group work: Provide the children with the 'Percentages' resource sheet. They should choose a percentage amount from the square and a number from the triangle and work out the answer either in their heads, by using jottings or by using a written method. No calculators should be allowed.

Differentiation

Less able: Help make selections for this group so that they focus on the more straightforward percentage numbers, for example, 50%, 10% and 20%.

More able: Set this group a time limit to finish ten questions as quickly as they can. Can they find at least two methods of obtaining the same answer?

Plenary & assessment

Go through examples worked by each of the ability groups. Revise the general concept of percentage, ie out of or parts of 100. Discuss the % sign with its one and two zeros as a version of writing hundredths.

Lesson ⑤

Starter

Repeat the Starter for Lesson 4, this time asking the children to find 10%, 20%, 40% 80% of £200, by using their previous answer and doubling. Repeat for another example.

Main teaching activity

Whole class: Review work on percentages from previous lessons. Demonstrate on the OHP calculator two methods that can be used to find percentages of numbers and amounts when the problem is more difficult and a calculator needs to be used. Set the problem: *Find 16% of 50.* Using the first method, change the 16% to 16/100 and multiply by 50 0.16 x 50 = 8. Using the second method, use the percentage facility found on most calculators: enter [50] [×] [16] [%] to get the answer 8.

Group work: Provide the children groups with the 'Planet Zogtroon' activity sheet.

Differentiation

Less able: Provide this group with the version of the activity sheet with simpler data (or use the template to prepare your own versions of the sheet if desired).

More able: Provide this group with the more demanding version of the activity sheet.

Plenary & assessment

Check children's responses to the sheet and go through any common misunderstandings. Also, discuss mental methods of finding some percentages (for example, 50%, 25% or 10%) and the use of calculator methods when questions become more difficult. Review how to use the percentage key facility on the calculator.

Name	Date

Change over

- **Change these fractions to decimal numbers by dividing. Use a calculator for the more difficult ones.**
- In the third column, comment on any interesting discoveries you make.

Fraction	Decimal number	Comments
$\frac{1}{2}$		
$\frac{1}{4}$		
$\frac{3}{4}$		
$\frac{1}{10}$		
$\frac{3}{10}$		
$\frac{7}{10}$		
$\frac{9}{10}$		
$\frac{1}{5}$		
$\frac{3}{5}$		
$\frac{1}{3}$		
$\frac{2}{3}$		
$\frac{1}{8}$		

Name		Date	

Planet Zogtroon

- The four main towns and cities on the planet Zogtroon and their populations are listed below, with some interesting details about each place.

- Calculate the actual number of people for each fact by solving the percentage problems.

Town	Population	Information	Answer
Rankin	150	20% are men 10% are women 30% are girls	
Davron	500	15% play armball 40% play ricket 10% play sockey	
Skelab	800	45% work on farms 25% work in mines 20% work in factories	
Thorit	1200	30% holiday at the lakes 55% holiday in the mountains 5% holiday in the desert	

Rotation and reflection

These three highly practical lessons include: recognising where a shape will be after a rotation through 90 degrees, and where a shape will be after reflection. Children are given plenty of practice in learning how to draw symmetrical shapes accurately.

LEARNING OBJECTIVES

	Topics	Starter	Main teaching activity
Lesson 1	Shape and space	● Use, read and write standard metric units (km, m, cm, mm …) including their abbreviations, and relationships between them.	● Recognise where a shape will be after a rotation through 90° about one of its vertices.
Lesson 2	As for Lesson 1	As for Lesson 1.	● Recognise where a shape will be after reflection: in a mirror line touching the shape at a point (sides of the shape nor necessarily parallel or perpendicular to the mirror line).
Lesson 3	As for Lesson 1	● Count on in steps of 0.1, 0.2, 0.25, 0.5, and then back.	● Recognise where a shape will be after reflection: in two mirror lines at right angles, sides of shape all parallel or perpendicular to the mirror line.

Lessons   overview

Preparation
Prepare cardboard/plastic 2-D shapes, felt pens, plastic sheets, wiper, etc for demonstrations on the OHP. If desired, draw your own 2-D shapes on the 'Shape up' template for less able children.

Learning objectives
Starters
● Use, read and write standard metric units (km, m, cm, mm …) including their abbreviations, and relationships between them.
● Count on in steps of 0.1, 0.2, 0.25, 0.5, and then back.
Main teaching activities
● Recognise where a shape will be after a rotation through 90° about one of its vertices.
● Recognise where a shape will be after reflection:
 ● in a mirror line touching the shape at a point (sides of the shape not
 ● necessarily parallel or perpendicular to the mirror line); in two mirror lines at right angles (sides of shape all parallel or perpendicular to mirror line).

Vocabulary
two-dimensional, 2-D, shape, symmetrical, line of symmetry, axis of symmetry, mirror line, reflective symmetry, fold, match, reflection, reflect, translation, pattern, repeating pattern, diagonal, angle, right-angled, co-ordinates, clockwise, anti-clockwise, congruent

You will need:
Photocopiable pages
A copy of 'Shape up' (page 113), 'On reflection' (page 114) for each child.

CD pages
Prepared copies of the 'Shape up' template for less able children if necessary, a copy of the 'On reflection' template for each more able child (see General resources).

Equipment
Large cardboard/plastic 2-D shapes; an OHP; felt pens; clear plastic sheets and a wiper; protractors; plastic mirrors; tracing paper; squared grid paper; counting stick.

Lesson

Starter

Invite children to write on the board the full word for the abbreviations for measurements of length, such as mm, cm and m. Now ask the children to write the equivalent measurement as follows: *Write 4.268km in metres; 9.65m in centimetres.*

Main teaching activity

Whole class: Revise briefly with the children the work done during the Autumn Term on plotting co-ordinates in all four quadrants, and recognising where shapes will be after two translations. Explain that the purpose of the lesson is to investigate rotating a simple two-dimensional shape through 90°. Discuss the meaning of the word 'rotate'. Show the class a large cardboard or plastic equilateral triangle on the OHP and demonstrate how it can be rotated about one of its vertices or corners through 90°. Draw round the shape first in its starting position and mark the centre of rotation R. Then rotate the shape through 90° anti-clockwise. Stress that all the sides of the triangle need to move through 90°. Mark its new position with a dotted line. Tell children this new position is called the image. Return it to its original position and ask one of the children to demonstrate the same procedure. Ask for a volunteer to turn the triangle through 90° clockwise, this time with the centre of rotation marked S. Again mark the new position. Ask: *How can we check that the rotations are accurate?* Elicit the answer that a protractor can be used to check the 90° angle. Show how to do this on the OHP.

Paired work: Children should work in mixed-ability pairs. Provide them with the 'Shape up' activity sheet, on which there are a series of two-dimensional shapes that have to be rotated through 90°. Children have to rotate the shape through 90° anti-clockwise, 90° clockwise, draw in the new positions of the shape and give the new co-ordinates for the lettered points. Teachers can also use the 'Shape up' template to add their own shapes as and when required.

Differentiation

Less able: This group should focus on simple shapes like the first two on the activity sheet. Work with this group. They may benefit from using cardboard templates of the shapes given, and tracing paper.

More able: Encourage this group to think about the fact that 90° anti-clockwise is the same as 270° clockwise. Ask them also to investigate 180° rotations of the shapes.

Plenary & assessment

Look at and discuss examples of the images that children have produced. Check the co-ordinates the children have recorded for each shape and look for any similarities, patterns and changes in sign that occur. Discuss how many rotations of 90° might be needed before the shape returns to its original position.

Lesson

Starter

Repeat the Starter for Lesson 1, this time for units for mass, such as kg, g. Ask the children to write 7.45 kg in grams and 10.6kg in grams. Repeat this for capacity, such as l, ml and cl. Ask the children to write: *1.36l in ml…*

Main teaching activity

Whole class: Explain to the children that in this lesson they are going to reflect shapes in a mirror line but without the use of a grid. Go through some important rules. Stress that the reflected shape must be identical to the original, and that the distance of the shape from the mirror line stays the same. Discuss the meaning of the word 'congruent' (plane figures that are identical in shape and size). Then use a prepared shape on the OHP and demonstrate how it is reflected, asking the children to offer advice and assistance. Ask them to explain step by step how the process is carried out.

Group work: Provide children with copies of 'On reflection'. In this lesson focus on those tasks involving a single mirror line (children will complete the sheet in the next lesson).

Differentiation

Less able: This group will receive support by working in mixed-ability pairs. Provide mirrors, tracing paper and card templates when needed. Focus on single mirror line activities. Discuss the sketches produced by the children.

More able: Encourage this group to move on to the examples with two mirror lines as soon as they can.

Plenary & assessment

Discuss a selection of reflections the children have produced. What strategies were used? Which proved to be the most successful?

Lesson ③

Starter

Label one end of the counting stick 0 and the other end 1. Count in steps of 0.1 along and back on the stick. Point to any point on the stick and ask the children to say what decimal fits there. Repeat, labelling the stick in steps of 0.2 then 0.25 and so on.

Main teaching activity

Whole class: Review work from the previous lesson and extend to reflections in two mirror lines. Provide an example such as the one on the left. Discuss the positioning of the reflection and reinforce the fact that the distance the shape is away from the mirror line stays the same. Also, make sure that children understand that each point on the original shape reflects at right angles to the mirror line. Demonstrate how the shape is reflected in two mirror lines.

Group work: Ask the children to complete their 'On reflection' activity sheets, doing the examples involving reflection in two mirror lines. If time is available, ask the children to practise drawing their own mirror lines on squared paper.

Differentiation

Less able: Work with these groups and check children's understanding of the correct procedures to reflect a shape in two mirror lines.

More able: Provide children with the 'On reflection' template to produce their own shapes for a partner to reflect. Challenge them to use different shapes, including a range of quadrilaterals and pentagons.

Plenary & assessment

Emphasise and consolidate the fact that reflection does not change the shape and size of the object, only its position. Ask: *How can you be sure that the reflection you have drawn is correct?* Discuss suggestions from the children as to how they can check their work, including the use of mirrors and tracing paper.

| Name | | Date | |

Shape up

On the grids provided:

a) rotate the shape 90° anti-clockwise, at point A

b) rotate the shape 90° clockwise, at point A

c) draw in the new positions of the shape

d) write the new coordinates for the letter points.

1.

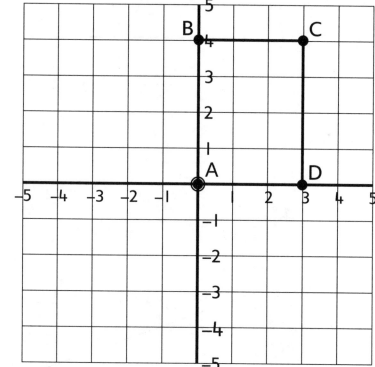

2.

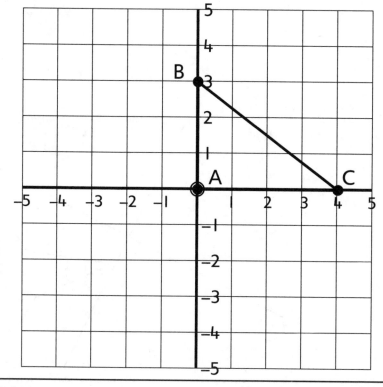

Name   Date

On reflection

Draw reflections of the following shapes.

1.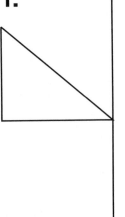

2.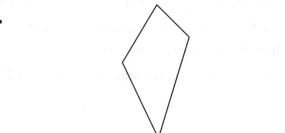

3.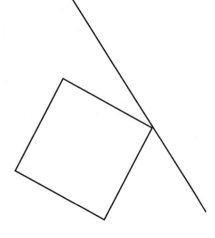

4.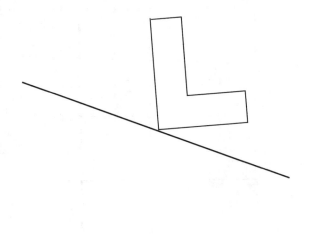

5.

6.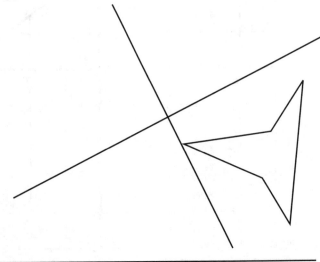

Addition and subtraction

Written methods for column addition and subtraction are examined, including the use of decimal numbers. There are further 'real life' problem-solving activities, including the conversion of sterling to foreign currency and calculating percentages like VAT. Children not only have to find solutions but also explain their methods and reasoning.

LEARNING OBJECTIVES

	Topics	Starter	Main teaching activity
Lesson 1 / Lesson 2	Pencil and paper procedures (+ and –)	● Consolidate all strategies from previous year, including: add several numbers. ● Use known number facts and place value to consolidate mental addition and subtraction.	● **Extend written methods to column addition and subtraction of numbers involving decimals.**
Lesson 3 / Lesson 4	Problems involving 'real life', money and measures	● Consolidate all strategies from previous year, including: find a difference by counting up; use the relationship between addition and subtraction.	● **Identify and use appropriate operations (including combinations of operations) to solve word problems involving numbers and quantities.** ● **Explain methods and reasoning.**
Lesson 5	Using a calculator	● Use known number facts and place value to consolidate mental addition and subtraction.	● **Identify and use appropriate operations to solve word problems,** including converting pounds to foreign currency and calculating percentages such as VAT.

Lessons   overview

Preparation
Write a set of number statements on the board for pairs of more able children (see Lesson 3). Also write up questions on the whiteboard for Lesson 5 group work, and check the exchange rate for £ sterling to Euros and vice versa.

Learning objectives
Starters
● Consolidate all strategies from previous year, including:
   ● add several numbers;
   ● find a difference by counting up;
   ● use the relationship between addition and subtraction.
● Use all known number facts and place value to consolidate mental addition and subtraction.

Main teaching activities
● **Extend written methods to column addition and subtraction of numbers involving decimals.**
● **Identify and use appropriate operations (including combinations of operations) to solve word problems involving numbers and quantities,** including converting pounds to foreign currency and calculating percentages such as VAT.
● **Explain methods and reasoning.**

Vocabulary
plus, increase, sum, total, altogether, take away, minus, decrease, leave, how much more/less is…, halve, difference between, equals, sign, operation, symbol, equation, number sentence, inverse, estimate, approximate, calculate, calculation, method, strategy, jotting, answer, solution, calculator, display, operation key, enter, clear, currency, percentage

You will need:
Photocopiable pages
A copy of 'In the swim (factsheet)' (page 120) and 'In the swim (problems)' (page 121) for each child.

CD pages
A copy of 'Quick thinker' and set of 'Digit (+ and –) and decimal point cards' or a copy of 'Make your choice' for each child (see General resources).

Equipment
An OHP; marker pens and wiper; an OHP calculator; calculators for children.

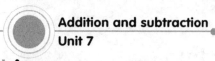

Lesson ①

Starter

Practise quick-fire questions where children total three and then four multiples of 10, for example, 40 + 20 + 50 and 50 + 70 + 30 + 10. Then work on groups of three or four numbers, where children create multiples of 10 first to make the calculation more straightforward, for example: 12 + 19 + 8 = 12 + 8 + 19 = 39; 27 + 38 + 13 = 27 + 13 + 38 = 78 and 24 + 15 + 17 + 35 = 15 + 35 (50) + 24 + 17 = 91.

Main teaching activity

Whole class: Tell the children they are going to focus on formal written methods of column addition, including using decimal numbers. Revise briefly informal methods (like adding the most significant digits first), before concentrating on the use of 'carrying'. Use the OHP to demonstrate how to add numbers by transferring them from a horizontal position into vertical columns, ensuring digits are correctly positioned. See the first example below. Show how digits being carried are written underneath the lower line of the answer box. Then try a further calculation, like example 2, again stressing that each digit must come in the correct column. Extend to consider decimal numbers, pointing out that decimal points should line up under each other (see examples 3 and 4). Also include examples of what happens when adding mixed amounts (see example 5).

Example 1
236 + 198 + 6409
becomes   236
        + 198
          6409
          6843
           1 2

Example 2
945 + 19 + 6 + 3492
becomes   945
        +   19
             6
          3492
          4462
          1 1 2

Example 3
513.6 + 17.9
becomes 513.6
       + 17.9
         531.5
          1 1

Example 4
74.27 + 3.94 + 105.6
becomes 74.27
       + 3.94
         105.60
         183.81
          1 1 1

Example 5
1.275kg + 845g
becomes   1.275
        + 0.845
           2.120 kg
            1 1 1

Group work: Children should practise adding numbers using the column methods shown during the lesson. They could generate their own numbers to work with using digit cards and a decimal point card, or use the quantities provided in the first section of 'Make your choice'. Remind children to show their working out in full.

Differentiation

Less able: Work with this group and restrict questions to three-digit whole numbers and numbers to one decimal place.
More able: Encourage this group to move on as quickly as possible to examples in which numbers have a different number of digits, including decimal numbers, and where a range of mixed amounts have to be added, for example, 4.275kg + 84g + 1kg 257g.

Plenary & assessment

Mark and check the children's work with them, covering a range of different examples. Ask children to compare written methods of addition and express their preferences. Encourage them to give reasons.

Lesson ②

Starter

Concentrate this time on decimal numbers. Ask: *What do you need to add to 2.63 to make 2.7?* (0.07) *What do you need to add to 5.27 to make 5.3?* (0.03) *What do you need to add to 7.49 to make 7.5?* (0.01) Extend to considering numbers with two decimal places. *What do you need to add to 8.37 to make 9?* (0.63) *What do you need to add to 12.94 to make 13?* (0.06) *What is the difference between 6.6 and 3.7?* (2.9).

Main teaching activity

Whole class: Tell children that the focus of this lesson will be written methods of subtraction. Briefly revise other methods they should be familiar with, like counting up and compensation, but put the emphasis on revising the 'decomposition' method. Look at four-digit numbers first, for example: *find the difference between 9576 and 4092* (see example 6, below), again transferring from the horizontal position to vertical columns, and demonstrate the method using the OHP. Show examples with different numbers of digits (see example 7) and decimal numbers with a different number of digits (see examples 8 and 9). As before, include examples of subtraction involving mixed amounts (see example 10). Remind children that decimal points should always line up under each other.

Example 6	Example 7	Example 8	Example 9	Example 10
9576– 4092	45264 – 3107	34.72 – 9.6	427.3 – 19.7	1.412l – 98ml
becomes	becomes	becomes	becomes	becomes

$$\begin{array}{r} {}^{4}{}_{1} \\ 9\cancel{5}76 \\ -\ 4092 \\ \hline 5484 \end{array} \qquad \begin{array}{r} {}^{5}{}_{1} \\ 452\cancel{6}4 \\ -\ \ 3107 \\ \hline 42157 \end{array} \qquad \begin{array}{r} {}^{2}{}_{1} \\ \cancel{3}4.72 \\ -\ \ 9.60 \\ \hline 25.12 \end{array} \qquad \begin{array}{r} {}^{1}{}^{6}{}_{1} \\ 4\cancel{2}7.30 \\ -\ \ 19.70 \\ \hline 407.60 \end{array} \qquad \begin{array}{r} {}_{3}{}^{10}{}_{1} \\ 1.4\cancel{1}2 \\ -\ 0.098 \\ \hline 1.314 \end{array}$$

Group work: Children now practise subtracting numbers using the column methods shown during the lesson. Again, they could generate their own numbers or use the subtraction questions provided on 'Make your choice'. Working out should always be shown in full.

Differentiation

Less able: Ensure children are proficient at using the decomposition method with three-digit numbers before progressing to four-digit numbers. Provide assistance with setting down questions in columns.

More able: Encourage this group to move as soon as possible to working with metric measures where amounts are given in a variety of ways, for example: 5kg – 3kg 259g; 6.420km – 745m; 10l 960ml – 6.544l.

Plenary & assessment

Check a selection of the questions the children worked through. Ask for volunteers to explain the stages of the 'decomposition' method to the others. Which parts of the process caused the most difficulty? Revise these parts if necessary.

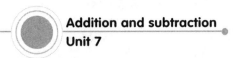

Lesson ③

Starter

Revise counting up from a smaller to a larger number. Look at numbers that are close together first, for example, 2000 – 1993 and 4000 – 1989. Then widen the gap and ask children to explain orally how they are calculating the difference, for example, 5000 – 4972 = 8 + 20 = 28 and 9000 – 8827 = 3 + 70 + 100 = 173.

Main teaching activity

Whole class: Explain to the children that in this lesson they are going to choose and use suitable operations to solve word problems involving numbers and quantities. Discuss with them key words and phrases that might come up, such as total, altogether, difference, average, range, how much more?, highest, lowest, quickest. Also consider strategies to be used. Ask: *Can you calculate answers mentally? Do you need the help of jottings? Are formal written calculations like adding and subtracting in columns necessary?* Stress that, where possible, answers should be approximated first and checked at the end, but that calculators should not be used for these activities.

Paired work: Children should work through the lesson in mixed ability pairs so that they can discuss operations and strategies. Provide each pair with a copy of 'In the swim (factsheet)' and 'In the swim (problems)'. In this lesson, focus on the single-step operations on the problem sheet.

Differentiation

Less able: Encourage this group to write down all working out in order to analyse the strategies they are using. Provide particular support with vocabulary and questions involving numbers to two decimal places.

More able: This group should be able to provide their own one-step problems from the information contained on the factsheet. You could also provide them with a set of number statements (eg 108, 15, 32; £50, 1/2, 10%) and then ask them to make up their own 'real life' problems from them, for example: *108 runners enter a long-distance race. If 15 fail to start and 32 drop out during the race, how many complete the course? Paul is given £50 for his birthday. If he puts half of it into a Building Society account and spends 10%, how much money will he have left?* (saves £25, spends £5, £20 left)

Plenary & assessment

At the end of the session, check through solutions with the children. Discuss the strategies they have used. What alternative approaches were there? Did working out estimated answers first prove to be helpful?

Lesson ④

During the **Starter**, look at the relationship between addition and subtraction. For example, if 2.74 + 6.29 = 9.03, then what is 9.03 – 2.74 and 9.03 – 6.29? Investigate closely related calculations, for example, if 5279 – 1740 is 3539, what is 5280 – 1740 and 5279 – 1737?

For the **Main activity** concentrate this time on the multi-step problems on 'In the swim' with the children again working in mixed-ability pairs. When the problems have been completed, some children may be able to make up their own questions from the information provided. In the **Plenary**, check the solutions of the problems tackled and the types of methods used for checking answers, such as reverse order, equivalent calculations and inverse operations.

Lesson ⑤

Starter

Use a twenty-question timed test with the children, featuring addition and subtraction, so they get used to listening to questions carefully, interpreting key mathematical words and phrases and calculating solutions quickly within a given time span. Twenty possible questions are provided on 'Quick thinker'. Number prompts could be given for some questions if they are thought to be necessary.

Main teaching activity

Whole class: Inform the children that the purpose of this lesson is twofold. It will provide the opportunity to continue with the work on solving problems involving numbers in 'real life' situations, and to practise calculator skills. Remind the children about work in Unit 4 on converting pounds to Euros and vice versa. Show examples on the OHP using £1 = 1.6 Euros and a Euro = £0.62. (Again, check current exchange rates.) So, £5 can be converted by 5 x 1.6 = 8 Euros and 5 Euros would by 5 x 0.62 = £3.10.

Also revise with the children how the calculator can be used to work out percentage problems including VAT. Start by revising some easy examples on the OHP calculator, like 10% of £12 (0.10 x 12 = £1.20) and 15% of £50 (0.15 x 50 = £7.50). Remind children that when the calculator shows 1.2 as an answer a zero needs to be placed on the end of the number to make sense in money terms.

Then look at more difficult percentage questions like how much VAT (17½%) would be paid on an item costing £19.99. The calculation would be 0.175 x 19.99 = £3.49825. Show children how in money terms and to two decimal places this would become £3.50.

Group work: Write the following questions on the whiteboard or the OHP for children to work through using a calculator. They are graded so that they gradually become more difficult. *Converting £ to Euros: £2, £4, £8, £10, £15, £35, £58, £175, £250, £625. Converting Euros into £: 4 Euros, 10 Euros, 18 Euros, 24 Euros, 40 Euros, 96 Euros, 120 Euros, 195 Euros, 270 Euros, 550 Euros. Work out the following percentages: 10% of £15, 15% of £24, 5% of £30, 25% of £75, 70% of £120, 12% of £12.50, 34% of £25.75, 17½% of £20, 17½% of £49.99 and 17 1/2% of £107.98.*

Differentiation

Less able: Work with this group, focusing on the earlier questions in each section. Check that the correct method is being used on the calculator and that children can convert readings into money amounts and round off numbers to two decimal places where necessary.

More able: This group can go on to make up their own questions if time allows. Also encourage them to develop a formula for use with the conversion questions, for example: *If P represents pounds and E stands for Euros, then changing pounds to Euros would be E = 1.6 x P and changing Euros into pounds would be P = E ÷ 1.6 rounded to the nearest penny.*

Plenary & assessment

Mark the three types of questions featured in the lesson. Invite children out to the OHP calculator to demonstrate how solutions were calculated. Revise converting calculator read-outs into money amounts, for example: *What does 1.4 represent?* (£1.40) *What does 16.7 represent?* (£16.70) Also revise rounding money answers to two decimal places: *What would £5.72964 become?* (£5.73) *What would £12.04327 become?* (£12.04)

Name	Date

In the swim (factsheet)

- Some of the Year 6 children at Copthorne Primary School hold a swimming day. They take part in a sponsored swim first to raise money for the school's computer suite, and then some of them compete in races.

- The results of the sponsored swim and the races are given in the charts below.

Sponsored event:

Name	Height (m)	Lengths completed (max 20)	Sponsorship for each length	Total money raised
Anya Allen	1.24	18	50p	
Ben Bridge	1.16	12	£1.00	
Carla Chase	1.15	4	£2.00	
Daniel Dunn	1.23	7	£2.50	
Eva Evans	1.25	6	£0.40	
Fiona French	1.19	10	£1.25	
Gary Green	1.17	14	£3.00	
Helen Harris	1.31	20	£1.60	
Ian Inch	1.29	9	60p	
Jamil Jones	1.18	20	£2.30	
Kumar Khan	1.26	16	£1.30	
Leroy Lovell	1.29	12	40p	

Race results: All times are given in seconds.

Scoring system: 1st = 10 points, 2nd = 7 points, 3rd = 5 points, 4th = 2 points

Name	Race 1	Race 2	Race 3	Race 4	Race 5	Points
Anya	32.3	19.0	20.2	18.32	54.36	
Daniel	29.7	21.3	20.1	22.08	58.20	
Gary	33.4	22.1	21.6	20.27	49.74	
Fiona	28.4	17.8	24.6	19.91	45.78	
Helen	31.2	20.2	17.9	19.56	50.06	
Jamil	40.6	16.5	18.0	18.27	47.29	
Leroy	39.2	23.7	22.1	18.57	55.72	
Carla	30.7	18.7	23.2	20.45	52.45	

☞

Name	Date

In the swim (problems)

You will need a copy of 'In the swim (factsheet)' to answer these word problems.

One-step problems

1. Calculate the money raised by each child in the sponsored swim.

2. Find the total number of lengths swum in the sponsored swim. _____

3. How much taller is Helen than Jamil? _____

4. What is the difference in height between Anya and Fiona? _____

5. What is the average number of lengths swum by each child?
   Give your answer to the nearest whole number. _____

6. How much more does Helen raise than Ian? _____

7. Find the difference between the shortest and the tallest child. _____

8. In Race 1, how much quicker is Fiona than Gary? _____

9. Work out the total time taken by Daniel, Helen and Carla in Race 4. _____

10. If a third of Year 6 took part in the sponsored swim, how many children are there in
    Year 6 altogether? _____

Multi-step problems

1. Work out the positions taken by each child in the five races and then calculate the number
   of points they have scored.

2. Which child scored the highest points total? _____

3. What margin did he win by? _____

4. The school requires £1000 for improvements to the computer suite.
   How much more money do they need to raise after the sponsored swim? _____

5. Find the average height of the children who took part in the races. _____

6. The rest of the school, 235 pupils and 11 staff, travel to the baths to watch.
   How many 38-seater coaches are needed to transport them? _____

7. If 152 adults paying £3.00 each, and 48 children paying £1.50 were
   spectators, how much money did the baths collect? _____

8. If 15 rows of chairs are put out with 12 chairs in each row,
   how many spectators have to stand? _____

9. In the car park, 36 cars can fit into each of the 15 bays.
   How many car parking spaces are provided? _____

10. What was the total time taken by Leroy in all his five races? _____

Angles, 2-D and 3-D shapes, perimeter and area

The first four lessons in this unit deal with the properties of 2-D and 3-D shapes and using a protractor to draw and measure angles. There is also a practical activity to demonstrate the three angles of a triangle always total 180°. The final lesson deals with finding the area and perimeter of compound shapes by splitting them into rectangles.

LEARNING OBJECTIVES

		Topics	Starter	Main teaching activity
Lesson	1	Shape and space	● Consolidate knowing by heart multiplication facts up to 10 x 10. ● **Derive quickly: division facts corresponding to tables up to 10 x 10.**	● Recognise and estimate angles. ● **Use a protractor to measure and draw acute and obtuse angles to the nearest degree.** ● Check that the sum of the angles of a triangle is 180°, for example, by measuring or paper folding.
Lesson	2			
Lesson	3	Shape and space	● **Derive quickly:** doubles of two-digit numbers; 10 to 1000 and the corresponding halves.	● Describe and visualise properties of solid shapes such as parallel or perpendicular faces or edges. ● Visualise 3-D shapes from 2-D drawings and identify different nets for a closed cube.
Lesson	4			
Lesson	5	Measures	● Develop the ×17 table by adding facts from the ×10 and ×7 tables.	● **Calculate the perimeter and area of simple compound shapes that can be split into rectangles.**

Lessons   overview

Preparation
Prepare a large card or stiff paper triangle (Lesson 2), examples of angles on large flashcards (Lessons 1 and 2), and examples of compound shapes on the whiteboard for finding areas (Lesson 5).

Learning objectives
Starters
● Consolidate knowing by heart multiplication facts up to 10 x 10.
● **Derive quickly division facts corresponding to tables up to 10 x 10.**
● **Derive quickly:** doubles of two-digit numbers; 10 to 1000 and the corresponding halves.
Main teaching activities
● Recognise and estimate angles.
● Use a protractor to measure and draw acute and obtuse angles to the nearest degree.
● Check that the sum of the angles of a triangle is 180°, for example, by measuring or paper folding.
● Describe and visualise properties of solid shapes such as parallel or perpendicular faces or edges.
● Visualise 3-D shapes from 2-D drawings and identify different nets for a closed cube.
● Calculate the perimeter and area of simple compound shapes that can be split into rectangles.

Vocabulary
curved, straight, hollow, solid, corner, vertex, vertices, edge, face, side, end, make, build, construct, net, intersecting, intersection, 3-D, three-dimensional, polyhedron, cube, cuboid, cylinder, cylindrical, sphere, prism, pyramid, tetrahedron, polyhedron, octahedron, dodecahedron, square-based, triangular, degree, reflex, protractor, angle measurer, area, surface, square centimetre (cm²), square metre (m²) square millimetre (mm²), formula, base, height

You will need:
Photocopiable pages
A copy of 'Hit out' (page 127), 'Best of three' (page 128) and 'Country gardens' (page 129) for each child.

Equipment
Models of 3-D shapes (including a cube, cuboid, a selection of prisms and pyramids, sphere, cylinder, cone); real life examples of 3-D shapes; a large poster showing 2-D drawings of 3-D shapes; cardboard boxes to demonstrate nets; OHP; art straws, sticky tape, Blu-tack, scissors and rulers; construction equipment (eg Polydron and Clixi); squared paper (1cm, 2cm and 5cm); protractors; board or OHP protractor; a set of angle flashcards, including reflex; thick paper and thin card.

Lesson 1

Starter

In this session, revise multiplication facts up to 10 x 10. Use examples of key vocabulary in questioning, for example, ask: *What is 6 times 5? …8 multiplied 4? …double 9? What is the product of 7 and 4? What is the next multiple of 6 after 24?* Also provide children with numbers and ask them for a pair of its factors, for example, you say 18, they say 6 and 3; you say 32, they say 8 and 4.

Main teaching activity

Whole class: Explain to the children that you will be showing them how to draw and measure angles using a protractor or angle measurer. Revise work done previously on angles by seeing how much the children remember. Ask: *What is an angle? How are angles measured? What types of angles do you know?* Check children's understanding of the terms 'acute angle' (less than 90°), 'right angle' (90°), 'obtuse angle' (between 90° and 180°) and 'straight angle' (180°). Also introduce the term 'reflex' (an angle 'between 180° and 360°), and remind children that 360° is a complete turn. On the OHP, show children some large examples of angles. Ask them to name each angle and to estimate its size. They should explain their reasoning, for example: *The angle is about halfway between a right angle and a straight angle, so it is roughly 140-150°.* Then demonstrate how to measure an angle using the OHP protractor, or use a large board protractor on the whiteboard. Stress the importance of placing the protractor on the correct line and reading the correct scale. Make sure that not all lines are horizontal. How accurate was the estimated answer? Also demonstrate how angles can be drawn using a protractor. Include a selection of acute and obtuse angles. Show how lines should be turned into the horizontal position to make the angle-drawing task easier. Point out that at this level, angles should be accurate to within one degree.

Paired work: Provide children with copies of 'Hit out', which provides practice in measuring and naming angles. For practice drawing angles, write the following on the whiteboard: 55°, 140°, 25°, 84°, 127°, 14°, 108°, 182°. Then say: *Using a protractor, draw these angles carefully. Name and label them. Remember, they will be checked for their accuracy and should be within one degree of the number given.* Children should work in mixed-ability pairs, taking it in turns to check their partner's measurements.

Differentiation

Less able: Work with this group as much as possible and provide extra practice with the protractor, both drawing and measuring angles. Pay particular attention to inaccurate use of the inner and outer scales. Encourage double-checking of measurements, for example, if an angle is acute it cannot have a measurement of 150°.

More able: Challenge this group to draw pairs of intersecting lines and to measure the angles they form. What do they notice?

Plenary & assessment

Revise the names of angles, including 'reflex', by showing the children a series of angles on flashcards. Check and discuss the results produced on the activity sheets. List the steps used to measure and/or draw angles with a protractor.

Lesson 2

Starter

Revise tables up to 10 × 10 this time using division facts. Again use important vocabulary, for example, ask: *How many 7s in 35? Divide 45 by 9. What is the quotient of 42 and 7? Halve 36. What is 72 divided by 8?* Provide quotients and ask for pairs of numbers that will produce it, for example, you say 10, they say 50 divided by 5; you say 6, they say how many 4s in 24.

Main teaching activity

Whole class: Tell the children that in this lesson they are going to focus on the angles in a triangle. Remind them that a straight line is made up of two right angles, ie 180°. Show them a large triangle made from sugar paper or thin card. Demonstrate how the three angles can be cut or torn off and arranged into a straight line to show that the angles in a triangle add up to 180°. Also provide examples of calculations to find the angles in a triangle. For example: *If two angles in a triangle are known to be 120° and 40°, the third angle will be 180° – 160° = 20°.* Also show examples of calculating angles involving a straight line and angles around a point.

Paired work: Children should again work in pairs. Ask them to make their own large triangles from thick paper or card and carry out the experiment showing how the three angles produce a straight line (180°). Then give out copies of 'Best of three' to provide practice measuring the angles in a triangle and calculating angles in a triangle (total 180°), on a straight line (180°) and around a point (360°).

Differentiation

Less able: Again, provide plenty of practice and support with the use of a protractor in measuring activities. Check that angle calculation tasks are carried out accurately.

More able: Encourage children to experiment with several different triangles to prove that the same result is always produced. Challenge them to carry out an investigation of the four angles in a quadrilateral to prove that they always total 360°.

Plenary & assessment

Ask the children some quick-fire calculation questions involving the angles in a triangle. Provide them with two angles and they calculate the third. For example, 40° and 75° (65°), 115° and 30° (35°). Also work with the more able group on quadrilaterals. Give three angles and ask them to calculate the fourth, for example, 70°, 45° and 90° (155°).

Lesson ③

Starter

Begin by revising doubling and halving two-digit numbers. This should include whole numbers and decimals. Also include some odd numbers in the halving process, even though they will produce a half. Examples might include: *Double and halve 45.* (90 and 22 1/2) …*56* (112 and 28) …*72* (144 and 36) …*88* (176 and 44) …*3.4* (6.8 and 1.7) …*7.8* (15.6 and 3.9) …*9.6* (19.2 and 4.8). With decimal numbers, some children find it easier to treat them as whole numbers and reinstate the decimal point at the end.

Main teaching activity

Whole class: Start with a display of 3-D shapes, including a cube, cuboid, a selection of prisms and pyramids, sphere, cylinder, cone and so on. Show the children plastic, wooden or cardboard models of the shapes, but also try to have examples of these shapes as they occur in everyday situations, for example: cylinder (drinks can), sphere (ball), cuboid (cereal packet), triangular prism (chocolate bar). Discuss key words like face, edge and vertex, and examine the properties of each shape on display. Ask: *How many faces does it have? What shape(s) are the faces? How many edges are there? How many vertices are there? Which shapes are regular polyhedra?* (ie all their faces are the same shape and size). Also discuss the meaning of the terms 'parallel' and 'perpendicular' when applied to faces and/or edges.

Group work: Children should work in mixed-ability pairs or small groups on the following tasks. Provide the children with art straws, sticky tape or Blu-tack, rulers and scissors and ask them to make skeletal models of some of the straight-sided shapes on display. This will require careful measuring, cutting and fixing. Display the poster showing 2-D drawings of 3-D shapes. Ask the children to identify the shapes and then write a short description of each one. Also make available construction equipment like Polydron and Clixi. Using a colour coding system, such as red face is parallel to blue face, ask them to produce models of polyhedra, noting particular sets of parallel and perpendicular faces for each one.

Differentiation

Less able: Focus particularly on the skeletal models of 3-D shapes and talk through their properties, especially for children who have difficulty calculating the number of edges and vertices of shapes. Edges have to be measured and cut before assembly and vertices become automatic fixing points.

More able: Set this group investigations involving the set of shapes known as the Five Platonic Polyhedra because all their faces are the same shape and size. These are: the cube (six square faces), the tetrahedron (four triangular faces), the octahedron (eight triangular faces), the icosahedron (twenty triangular faces) and the dodecahedron (twenty pentagonal faces).

Plenary & assessment

Play a game of 'Back-to-back', where a child sits back-to-back with a partner, chooses a shape and describes it to the other to guess. Display the large poster to check that children can recognise 3-D shapes from 2-D drawings.

Lesson

Starter

This time, work on doubles and corresponding halves of multiples of 10 up to 1000. For example, say: *Double and halve 40.* (80 and 20) …*120* (240 and 60) …*260* (520 and 130) …*510* (1020 and 255).

Main teaching activity

Whole class: Explain that in this lesson children will continue to explore the characteristics and properties of 3-D shapes. Ensure first that the children appreciate the meaning of the word 'net' when applied to 3-D shapes. Revise using several types of cardboard box. Demonstrate how they can be flattened out to show how they were made. Re-assemble the shape to illustrate how it fits together. Then show children a large version of one of the nets of a closed cube on the whiteboard or the OHP. Explain that this shape is called a hexomino because it has an area of six squares. Demonstrate how this shape makes a closed cube.

Group work: Provide children with squared paper (2cm squares are probably best) and ask them to investigate and find all the nets of a cube that will make a closed box. There should be a total of 11 different nets. Remember that if the nets are likely to be fixed permanently, then gluing flaps will need to be included.

Differentiation

Less able: It may be quicker and easier to provide this group with a series of hexominoes already drawn and cut out, so that the children can focus on making them up to see which nets produce a closed cube.

More able: Expand the 'net' theme by challenging this group to find successful nets for other well-known 3-D shapes, especially the tetrahedron (triangular-based pyramid), the Egyptian pyramid (square-based) and the triangular prism.

Plenary & assessment

Invite volunteers out to the front of the class to demonstrate how some nets successfully made closed cubes while others did not. Mount a classroom display of the successful ones. Also share the results achieved by the more able group in finding the nets of other 3-D shapes.

Lesson ⑤

Starter

Practise developing the 17x table by adding facts from the 7x and 10x tables. For example, 17 x 6 would be 7 x 6 + 10 x 6 = 42 + 60 = 102 and 17 x 9 would be 7 x 9 + 10 x 9 = 63 + 90 = 153. Work on similar tables, such as 15x and 19x. For example, 15 x 8 would be 5 x 8 + 10 x 8 = 40 + 80 = 120 and 19 x 5 would be 9 x 5 + 10 x 5 = 45 + 50 = 95.

Main teaching activity

Whole class: Revise work done previously on area and perimeter. Discuss with the children the difference between area, a measurement of surface calculated in square units, and perimeter, a measurement of distance calculated in length units. Write on the OHP or whiteboard some simple examples of finding area and perimeter using squares and rectangles. Show how the perimeter of a square will be side x 4 and that the perimeter of a rectangle will be length x 2 + width x 2. Revise that the area of a square or a rectangle can be calculated using the formula length x width. Now show the children some examples of simple compound shapes. Demonstrate how the measurement of these shapes, both area and perimeter, can be found by splitting them into convenient squares or rectangles. Point out that often, additional measurements have to be calculated first.

Group work: Provide the children with copies of 'Country gardens' to work through. The calculations become progressively more difficult and some of the later ones also involve things like working out the area of ponds and flowerbeds. Talk through some of the earlier examples with the children before letting them work on their own.

Differentiation

Less able: Ensure children fully understand the difference between area and perimeter. Provide support with splitting shapes into convenient shapes for calculation purposes, finding missing measurements and multiplying numbers to calculate area.

More able: Ask children to investigate whether different rectangles with the same area will all have the same perimeter, or whether they can draw rectangles with different areas that all have the same perimeter. Introduce the formula for finding the area of a triangle (1/2 base x height or base x height ÷ 2). Include some triangular shapes when finding the area of more complicated compound shapes.

Plenary & assessment

Check that definitions of both area and perimeter are accurate. Check that the correct units have been used in answers. Mark with the children questions from the 'Country gardens' activity sheet. Discuss methods, especially how all the necessary dimensions were calculated and where lines were drawn to split up the compound shapes.

Name   Date

Hit out

These are the angles made by some shots played by a batsman during a cricket match.

- Identify the type of angle first.
- Estimate what you think it will be in degrees.
- Then measure each angle from 0° on the base line using a protractor to see how close you were.

Remember to use the outer scale of the protractor.

Record your three answers for each angle on a different sheet of paper.

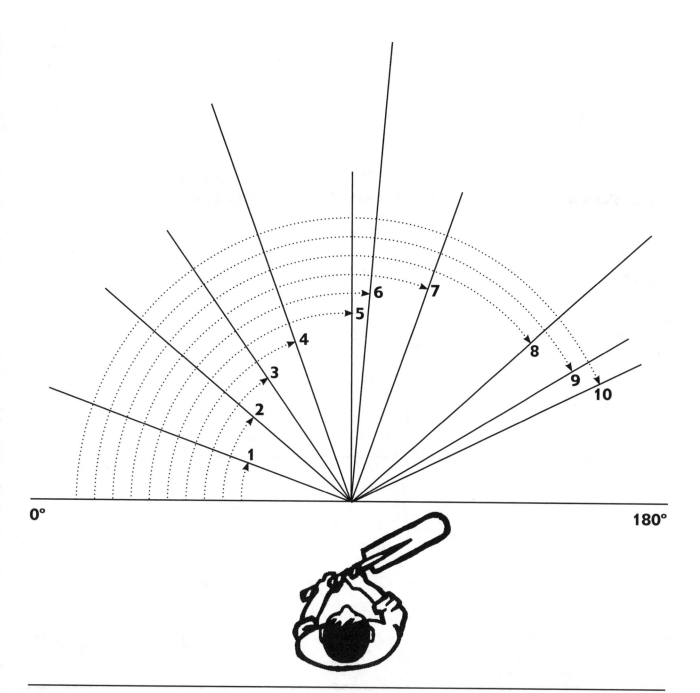

0°   180°

Name	Date

Best of three

Using a protractor, measure the three angles in each of these triangles and then find their total.

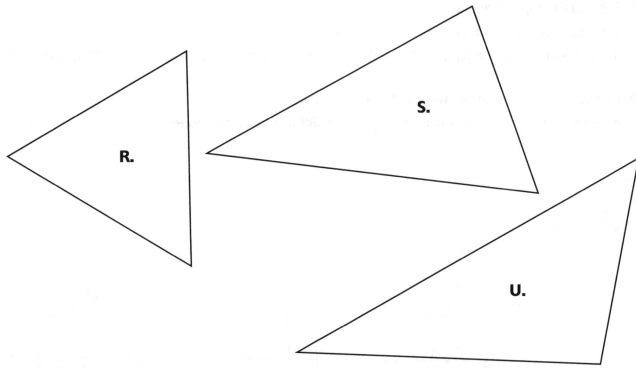

DO NOT measure but calculate each angle marked x in these diagrams.

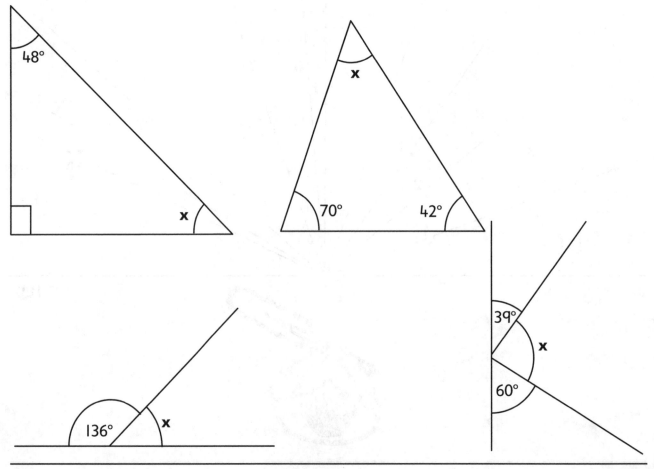

Name   Date

Country gardens

Calculate the area and perimeter of these gardens. They are not drawn to scale.

1.   8m

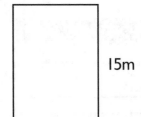

15m

_____

2.

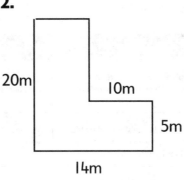

20m
10m
5m
14m

_____

3.   80m

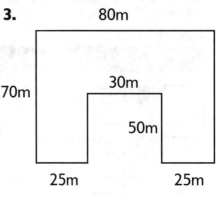

70m
30m
50m
25m   25m

_____

4.   6m

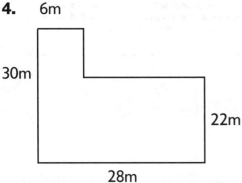

30m
22m
28m

_____

5.   9m

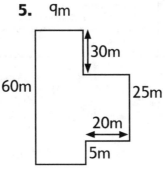

30m
60m
25m
20m
5m

_____

6.   12m

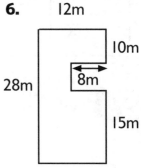

10m
28m
8m
15m

_____

In these gardens, the shading shows the pond sections.
Find the area of each garden that is still lawn and flowerbeds.

7.

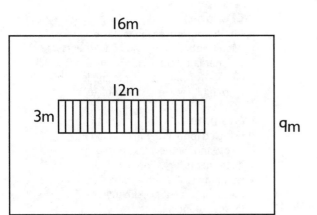

16m
12m
3m
9m

_____

8.

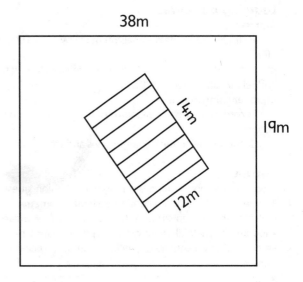

38m
14m
19m
12m

_____

Measures and problem solving

In the first two lessons, children estimate and record reading from the scales of measuring equipment. They also learn how to write metric measurements in several different ways by converting smaller units to larger ones and vice-versa. In Lessons 3 to 5 they solve word problems involving metric measurements and money.

LEARNING OBJECTIVES

		Topics	Starter	Main teaching activity
Lesson	1	Measures	● **Multiply and divide decimals mentally by 10 or 100 and explain the effect.**	● Record estimates and readings from scales to a suitable degree of accuracy.
Lesson	2	As Lesson 1	● Use, read and write standard metric units, including their abbreviations, and relationships between them.	● Convert smaller units to larger units and vice versa.
Lesson	3	As Lesson 1	● Convert smaller units to larger units and vice versa.	● Know imperial units. ● Know rough equivalents of lb and kg, oz and g, miles and km.
Lesson	4	Problems involving 'real life' money or measures	As Lesson 3. ● Know imperial units. ● Know rough equivalents of lb and kg, oz and g, miles and km, litres and pints or gallons.	● **Identify and use appropriate operations (including combinations of operations) to solve word problems involving numbers and quantities** based on 'real life', money or measures.
Lesson	5			

Lessons   overview

Preparation
Copy 'Conversion tables' and 'Metric abbreviations and equivalents' onto acetate.

Learning objectives
Starters
● Multiply and divide decimals mentally by 10 or 1000 and explain the effect.
● Use, read and write standard metric units, including their abbreviations, and relationships between them.
Main teaching activities
● Record estimates and readings from scales to a suitable degree of accuracy.
● Convert smaller units to larger ones and vice versa.

Vocabulary
metric unit, imperial unit, measuring scale, division, guess, estimate, length, kilometre (km), metre (m), centimetre (cm), millimetre (mm), mile, yard, foot, feet, inch, inches, conversion, ruler, metre stick, tape measure, mass, tonne, kilogram (kg), half-kilogram, gram (g), pound, ounce, balance, scales, capacity, litre (l), half-litre, centilitre (cl), millilitre (ml), pint, gallon, container, measuring cylinder

You will need:
Photocopiable pages
A copy of 'On the line' (page 135) and 'All change' (page 136) for each child.

CD Pages
An OHT of 'Conversion tables' and 'Metric abbreviations and equivalents'; differentiated copies of 'On the line' and 'All change' for each more able and less able pair/child (see General resources).

Equipment
Labelled food and drink packaging displaying metric units; measuring instruments including rulers, tapes, weighing scales, spring balances, measuring cylinders; suitable small objects for measuring.

Lesson ①

Starter

Ask the children to multiply the numbers that you write onto the board by 10, 100 and 1000. Write, for example, 56, 92, 103. Repeat this for decimals, this time multiplying by 10 and 100. Write, for example: 6.42, 91.7. Invite the children to explain the effect of the multiplication. Repeat this for division.

Main teaching activity

Whole class: Show children a collection of food packets, containers and so on that are clearly labelled with metric units. Talk about the amounts of grams, litres and millilitres that are shown. Highlight any that have the letter 'e' on them either before or after the weight. Explain that the letter 'e' stands for 'excluding' and means the weight or capacity of the food item inside the packaging but not including the weight of the tin, jar, carton, box or bottle. Also display a variety of measuring instruments used for finding length (rulers, tapes), mass (weighing scales, spring balances) and capacity (measuring cylinders). Look carefully at the scales shown on them and discuss how they are organised. Enlarged versions of some of these should be displayed on the OHP for discussion purposes.

Paired work: Children should work in pairs on 'On the line', where they have to read amounts from a variety of scales showing length, mass and capacity.

Differentiation

Less able: This group should be given the version of 'On the line' with simpler problems. Give them practice filling in scales with some of the numbers missing. Initially measurements can be rounded off, for example to the nearest half-centimetre (length), nearest quarter of a kilogram (mass) and nearest 100 millilitres (capacity).

More able: Start this group with the more demanding version of 'On the line'. Then work with the children while they measure the length, mass and capacity of selected objects in the classroom, using a variety of equipment with a range of different scales.

Plenary & assessment

Ask children from the more able group to make a short presentation to the rest of the class. What objects did they choose? What equipment did they use? Which units were the most suitable? What results did they obtain?

Lesson ②

Starter

Check first that children remember the main fractional parts of 10, 100 and 1000 (one quarter of 10 is 2 1/2, half of 10 is 5, three-quarters of 10 is 7 1/2, one-tenth of 10 is 1; for 100 the fractions would be 25, 50, 75 and 10 and so on). Count on or back in different increments related to metric units including decimal equivalents, for example centimetres to metres (10cm, 20cm, 30cm or 0.1m, 0.2m, 0.3m). Move on to metres to kilometres: counting in hundreds this would be 100m, 200m, 300m or 0.1km, 0.2km, 0.3km; counting in tens this would be 10m, 20m, 30m or 0.01km, 0.02km, 0.03km. Repeat these counting activities using grams to kilograms and millilitres to litres.

Main teaching activity

Whole class: Display the OHT of 'Conversion tables' and go through it with the children, first working from smaller to larger units and then vice versa. Also demonstrate what happens to the position of the decimal point when changing very small units into larger ones. For example, 200ml = 0.2l, 20g = 0.020kg and 2m = 0.002km. Also make sure children are conversant with the facts that 1000kg = 1 tonne, 100 centilitres = 1 litre and 1 centilitre = 10 millilitres.

Individual work: Working individually, children should focus on the 'All change' activity sheet. Length and capacity measurements have to be changed into either smaller or larger units while mass measurements, written in a variety of different ways, have to be ordered from smallest to largest.

Differentiation

Less able: Provide this group with the version of 'All change' where children have to write length, mass and capacity in three different ways. Display the OHT of 'Metric abbreviations and equivalents'.

More able: This group should work from the more demanding version of 'All change'. As an extension, ask children to make up more conversions involving kilograms/tonnes and centilitres/litres, such as 680kg = ? tonne, 4.3 tonne = ? kg, 75cl = ? l and 3.24l = ? cl.

Plenary & assessment

Focus on questions where children have to order a group of measurements, smallest to largest, by putting them into the same family of metric units. Use the following examples: length: 2.45m, 260cm, 2 1/2m, 3/4km, 0.76km, 850m; mass: 1 1/2kg, 1.400kg, 1600g, 1.4800 tonne, 1500kg, 1 tonne, 450kg; capacity: 3.800l, 3l 750ml, 3850ml.

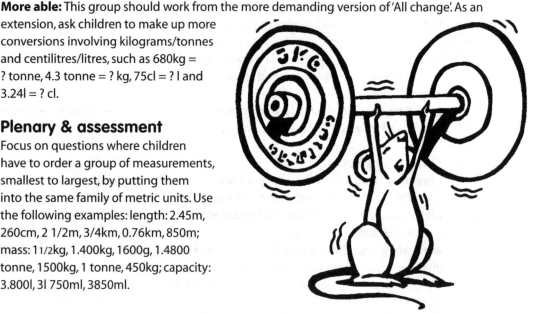

Lessons   overview

Preparation

Display the wall chart of 'Metric abbreviations and equivalents'. Copy 'Kilometres–miles conversion chart' onto acetate.

Learning objectives

Starters
- Convert smaller units to larger units and vice versa.
- Know imperial units.
- Know rough equivalents of lb and kg, oz and g, miles and km, litres and pints or gallons.

Main teaching activities
- Know imperial units.
- Know rough equivalents of lb and kg, oz and g, miles and km.
- **Identify and use appropriate operations (including combinations of operations) to solve word problems involving numbers and quantities** based on 'real life', money or measures.

Vocabulary

as for Lessons 1 and 2, plus: calculate, calculation, mental calculation, method, strategy, jotting, answer, right, correct, wrong, what could we try next?, number sentence, sign, operation, symbol, equation

You will need:

CD Pages
An enlarged version of 'Metric abbreviations and equivalents' to display as a wall chart, an OHT of 'Kilometres–miles conversion chart', a copy of 'Driving distances' for each group, a copy of 'Top six' and 'Weekly shop' for each child and differentiated copies for each less able and more able child (see General resources).

Equipment
Measuring equipment as in Lessons 1 and 2, road atlas, recipe card, (with items in ounces), coins.

Lesson

Starter

Revise the conversion of smaller units into larger units and vice versa from the previous lesson. Work through examples involving length, mass and capacity. Expect children to be able to give measurements in at least one other way, and in most cases push for two alternatives, for example: 57mm = 5cm 7mm = 5.7cm; 1753m = 1km 753m = 1.753km; 2560g = 2kg 560g = 2.560kg; 5004ml = 5l 4ml = 5.004l.

Main teaching activity

Whole class: Remind children that metres, kilometres, litres etc. are units within the metric system, and talk about the relationships between m and km for example. Ask: *What units are used in the imperial system?* Collect responses and record these on the board (check in particular that they know that length is measured in inches, feet, yards and miles).

Write on the board a range of different metric/imperial conversions, for example: 8 kilometres = 5 miles; 1 metre = 3 feet 3 inches; 1 kilogram ≈ 2.2 lb; 30 grams ≈ 1 oz; 4.5 litres ≈ 1 gallon (and 8 pints in 1 gallon). Remind the children about the use of the approximation sign (≈) in these examples. Ask some questions about these conversions, using the OHP calculator to check answers, for example: *How many millilitres in 1 pint?* (570 millilitres) *How many miles in 100 kilometres?* (66 miles).

Focus the children on miles and kilometres and build a conversion chart on the board (use 'Kilometres–miles conversion chart' if required).

Group work: Give each group a copy of the 'Driving distances' activity sheet, which includes distances from channel ports in kilometres. Ask the children to fill in the blank table by converting the distances from kilometres to miles. Allow the groups to use calculators for this purpose. Encourage the groups to approximate their answers before using the calculators.

Differentiation

Less able: Support the children with this activity. Suggest that the children multiply by 0.62 and then round to the nearest mile. For example: *Calais to Cologne is 421 kilometres. 421 x 0.62 is 261.02, so the distance is rounded to 261 miles.*

More able: After completing the activity, provide the children with a road atlas and challenge them to use its distance chart to calculate kilometres to miles or miles to kilometres conversions.

Plenary & assessment

Discuss the conversions the children made and address any difficulties they had with the calculations. Review the other conversions (above) that they will be using in subsequent lessons and extend if necessary, for example: 2.54 cm = 1 ounce. Discuss real-life uses for these imperial units, such as buying petrol and cooking. If you have time, go through a recipe with items in ounces and ask individual children to convert into grams.

Lesson

Starter

Consolidate the work on imperial units. Check that children know that length is measured in inches, feet, yards and miles. Carry out some simple conversions from imperial to metric units based on the following: 1 inch = about 2.5cm; 1 mile = about 1.5km. Ask questions such as: *About how many centimetres are there in 6 inches?* (15cm) *About how many inches are there in 20cm?* (8 inches) *How many kilometres are there in 10 miles?* (15km) *How many miles are there in 50km?* (33 miles)

Main teaching activity

Whole class: In this lesson, the focus switches to length measurement. Some activities are based on long jump results in the 2000 Sydney Olympic Games. Before starting, revise the use of length metric units, especially how distances can be written in a number of different ways, for example: 1m 27cm = 1.27m = 127cm.

Paired work: Again children should work in pairs, this time using the 'Top six' activity sheet. Once the task has been completed, children may be able to collect some of their own long jump results for comparison.

Differentiation

Less able: This group should work on the version of 'Top six' where long jump results are written in a simplified format. Assist with ordering measurements and writing them in different ways.

More able: On the differentiated version of the activity sheet, once the questions have been completed children are required to show the long jump information on a graph.

Plenary & assessment

Check through the results of the length problems given to each of the groups. Ensure that children are conversant with writing this type of measurement in a number of different ways. Ask questions like: *How many centimetres are there in 8.75m?* (875cm) *How would you write 506cm in metres?* (5.06m) *How would you write 698cm in split units?* (6m 98cm) *Put these lengths in order, starting with the smallest first: 755cm, 7m 52cm, 7.25m and 7 1/2m.* (7.25m, 7 1/2m, 7m 52cm, 755cm)

Lesson ⑤

Starter

Concentrate this time on simple conversions between imperial and metric units of mass and capacity. Make sure children know that 1oz ≈ 30g, 2.25lb ≈ 1kg, 1 3/4 pints ≈ 1 litre and that 8 pints (1 gallon) ≈ 4 1/2 litres. Using some rhymes may help, for example: Two and a quarter pounds of jam weighs about a kilogram. A litre of water's a pint and three-quarters.

Main teaching activity

Whole class: Tell the children that in this final problem-solving session the focus is on mass, capacity and money in the context of shopping at the supermarket. Some revision of adding amounts of money may be needed, and also of changing mass and capacity amounts into either larger or smaller units.

Paired work: Children continue to work in pairs as before, this time on the 'Weekly shop' activity sheet.

Differentiation

Less able: Provide this group with their differentiated version of 'Weekly shop'. Give support with fractions of amounts (eg 1/4 kilogram, 1/5 litre) and key words and phrases in questions (eg total weight, least, most, what is the difference?).

More able: Provide this group with the more demanding version of the activity sheet. Encourage children to move on as quickly as possible to the extension task where they need to bring in an old till receipt from home to make up their own questions for friends to answer.

Plenary & assessment

Provide children with number statements involving mass, capacity and money amounts and ask them to make up their own questions from them. For example, provide the statements: *A 400g tin of baked beans costs 64p. A two-litre bottle of lemonade costs £1.05.* Questions might include: *How much would three tins of beans cost?* (£1.92) *What change would there be from a £2 coin after buying both items?* (31p)

Name   Date

On the line

Length: Estimate the lengths shown by the arrows to the nearest millimetre.

Then measure them with your ruler to see if you are correct.

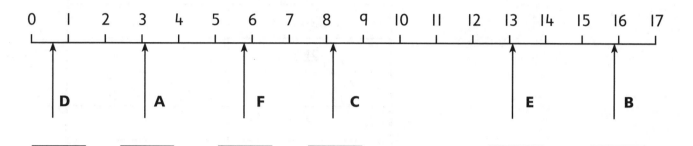

Mass: Give the weights shown by each of the letters.

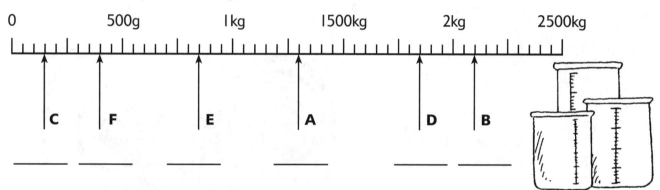

Capacity: Read the levels on the measuring cylinders to the nearest 20ml.

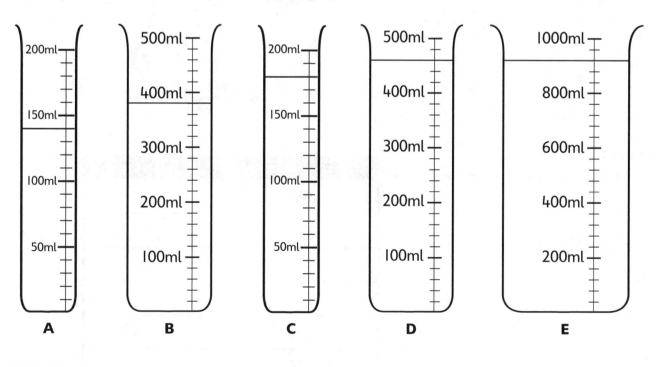

Name	Date

All change

Length

Complete the measurements in the box.

m	km
	1.752
3245	
253	
	3.750
96	
	0.047

Mass

Put these weights in order of size, smallest first.

It may help to put each weight into grams first.

1.

   450g $\frac{1}{2}$ kg   0.405kg

2.

   $1\frac{1}{4}$ kg   1.205kg   1025g

3.

   2.705kg   2570g $2\frac{3}{4}$ kg

4.

   $\frac{3}{4}$ kg   800g   0.705kg

Capacity

Complete the measurements in the box.

ml	l
1950	
400	
	2.375
2050	
	3.515
76	

Name	Date

Weekly shop

Mass

1. Write each of the weights in kilograms.

_____

2. What is the total weight

of the goods in the trolley?

_____

3. Find the difference in weight and in cost

between the fish and the Indian meal.

_____

4. How many 50g weights would it take to

balance the rice? _____

5. Find the total weight of the goods that weigh less than 400g. _____

6. What is the total cost of all the items? How much change would there be from £10.00?

_____

Capacity

1. Find the total capacity of these items in litres.

_____

2. What fraction of a litre is the shampoo? _____

3. Find the largest difference in capacity

between the largest and the smallest amount.

_____

4. Find the difference in cost between the fruit

juice and the kitchen cleaner. _____

5. If all the items were tipped into a 5-litre container,

how much space would be left?

_____

6. Work out the total cost of all the items in the trolley. _____

Fractions, decimals, percentages and handling data

This Unit deals with solving simple problems involving ration and proportion. It includes use of the terms 'mode', 'median', 'mean' and 'range' and contexts in which they may be found. The data-handling tasks involve conversion graphs changing Euros to pounds sterling and miles to kilometres, and pie charts on topics including money and time.

LEARNING OBJECTIVES

	Topics	Starter	Main teaching activity
Lesson 1	Fractions, decimals, percentages, ratio and proportion	● **Understand percentage as the number of parts in every 100.** ● Express simple fractions such as one half, one quarter, three quarters … as percentages.	● **Solve simple problems involving ratio and proportion.**
Lesson 2	Fractions, decimals, percentages, ratio and proportion	● **Find simple percentages of small whole-number quantities.**	● As for Lesson 1.
Lesson 3	Handling data	● Recognise squares of numbers to at least 12 x 12.	● Find the mode and range of a set of data. Begin to find the median and the mean of a set of data.
Lesson 4	Handling data	● Use tests of divisibility.	● **Solve a problem by** representing, **extracting and interpreting data in tables, graphs, charts** and diagrams.
Lesson 5	Handling data	● Count on in steps of 0.1, 0.2, 0.25, 0.5, and then back	● As for Lesson 4.

Lessons overview

Preparation
Prepare marked sticks for Lessons 1 and 2.

Learning objectives
Starters
- ● **Understand percentage as a number of parts in every 100.**
- ● Express simple fractions such as one half, one quarter, three quarters … as percentages.
- ● **Find simple percentages of small whole-number quantities.**
- ● Recognise squares of numbers to at least 12 x 12.
- ● Use tests of divisibility.
- ● Count on in steps of 0.1, 0.2, 0.25, 0.5, and then back

Main teaching activities
- ● **Solve simple problems involving ratio and proportion.**
- ● Find the mode and range of a set of data.
Begin to find the median and the mean of a set of data.
- ● **Solve a problem by** representing, **extracting and interpreting data in tables, graphs, charts** and diagrams.

Vocabulary
percentage, per cent, %, fraction, decimal, proportion, part, one whole, ratio, equal parts, in every, for every, to every, as many as, compare

You will need:
Photocopiable pages
A copy of 'In proportion' (page 143) and 'Ratio time' (page 144) for each child.

CD pages
Differentiated copies of 'In proportion' and 'Ratio time' for each less able and more able child (see General resources).

Equipment
Two sticks, one marked with 4 equal parts, 3 white and one coloured; the other marked with 8 equal parts, 3 white and 5 coloured; table squares for less able children; counting stick.

Lesson

Starter

Revise common fractions as percentages: 1/2 = 50%, 1/4 = 25%, 3/4 = 75%, 1/10 = 10%, 1/5 = 20%, 3/10 = 30%, 4/5 = 80%. Children should also appreciate that 1/3 is about 33% and that 2/3 is about 67%. Reinforce the relationship between percentages, fractions and decimal numbers. Give one version of a family group and ask children to provide the other two, eg, you say 0.36, children respond 36% and 36/100.

Main teaching activity

Whole class: Emphasise to children that proportion is the relationship between a part of something and the whole thing. It compares 'part with whole'. Show the children the stick divided equally into three white parts and one coloured part. Tell them that we can compare the white parts of the whole stick and say the proportion of white parts is 3 out of 4. Show the children this can be written as 3/4 or 0.75 or 75%. Use other examples, for example: *Two parts out of 5 can be written as 2/5 or 0.4 or 40%.* Remind children that, just like fractions, proportional amounts should be cancelled down into their lowest terms even though the amounts remain unchanged. For example, 10 out of 20 = 1/2, 0.5 or 50%, 6 out of 10 = 3/5, 0.6 or 60% and 5 out of 20 = 1/4, 0.25 or 25%. Talk through some practical problems with the children. For example: *An orange drink is made up of 900ml of water and 100ml of orange. What proportion of the drink is water?* Nine-hundred thousandths of the drink is water, which is 9/10, 0.9 or 90%. *Strawberry jam is made from 200g of strawberries and 50g of sugar. What proportion of the jam is strawberries?* Two-hundred over two-hundred and fifty of the jam is strawberries, which is 4/5, 0.8 or 80%.
Individual work: Children work individually on the 'In proportion' activity sheet.

Differentiation

Less able: This group may need table squares to help with the cancelling down operation on their easier version of 'In proportion'. Continue to reinforce the link between proportion, fractions and decimal numbers, for example, one out of four = 1/4 = 0.25 = 25%.
More able: This group should work from the more demanding version of 'In proportion'. Then encourage children to solve proportion problems set in everyday situations. For example, say: *With some times rounded off, what proportion of the day do you spend at school/sleeping/eating?*

Plenary & assessment

Check that children have a secure understanding of the word 'proportion' as the relationship of part of something with the whole thing. Reinforce the fact that proportions may be the same even though figures used may be different, for example, 12/16 and 3/4 are in the same proportion.

Lesson

Starter

Remind children that finding 50% of a number means dividing by 2, 25% means dividing by 4, 10% means dividing by 10 and 20% means dividing by 5. Test these out with questions like the following. *Find 25% of 60, find 50% of 56, find 20% of 80 and find 10% of 130.* Also revise finding 3/4 or 75% of a number by dividing by 4 and then multiplying by 3, for example, 75% of 48 = 36. Then look at multiples of 10 and 20, for example, 30% of 90 = 90 ÷ 10 x 3 = 27 and 80% of 115 = 115 ÷ 5 x 4 = 92.

Main teaching activity

Whole class: Explain that like proportion, the word 'ratio' is used to compare numbers or quantities. Stress, though, that ratio is the relationship between two or more numbers or quantities and that it compares 'part with part'. Use the coloured stick method again, this time showing eight equal parts made up of three white parts and five coloured parts. Compare the white parts with the coloured parts. We say the ratio of the white to coloured is 3 to 5. Explain that this is usually written 3:5. Point out that like proportions, ratios are usually simplified to make them easier to work with, for example, 10:2 would be 5:1, 10:30 would be 1:3 and 100:25 would be 4:1. Use some practical examples of ratio questions, such as: *'Choc-chip' cakes are made from 80g of cake mix and 20g of chocolate. What is the ratio of chocolate to cake mix?* 20:80 is in the ratio 1:4.

Individual work: Children should work individually on the 'Ratio time' activity sheet. First ratios have to be put into the lowest terms and then amounts have to be put into the correct ratio.

Differentiation

Less able: Work with this group as they focus on their version of 'Ratio time'. This reinforces activities started in Unit 5 of the Autumn Term. Ensure the two ratio numbers are added together to give the length of the strip of squared paper overall.

More able: This group should work on the version of 'Ratio time' where problems are linked to measurement and shape.

Plenary & assessment

Once tasks have been checked, revise the last two lessons with more general questions. *What does the word 'proportion' mean? What does the word 'ratio' mean? What is the ratio 21:24 in its lowest terms? Fifteen footballs are in the ratio two white ones for every three yellow ones. How many footballs are white? How many footballs are yellow?*

Lessons   overview

Preparation
Write number data on the whiteboard for Lesson 3 (see lesson notes). Make an enlarged OHT version 'Conversion graphs', and write conversion questions on the whiteboard for Lesson 4 (see lesson notes). Make OHTs of the different types of pie chart grids from the four resources 'Pie charts 1' to 'Pie charts 4'.

Learning objectives
Starters
● Recognise square numbers to at least 12 x 12.
● Use known number facts and place value to consolidate mental multiplication and division.

Main teaching activities
● Find the mode and range of a set of data.
● Begin to find the median and mean of a set of data.
● **Solve a problem by** representing, **extracting and interpreting data in tables, graphs, charts** and diagrams.

Vocabulary
square number, mode, range, mean, average, median, data, database, table, diagram, chart, label, title, axis, axes, statistics, distribution, most popular, most common, least popular, least common, survey, questionnaire, more than, fewer than

You will need:
Photocopiable pages
A copy of 'Numbers sets' (page 145) for each child.

CD pages
An OHT of 'Conversion graphs' and a copy for each pair, copies of 'Pie charts 1', 'Pie charts 2', 'Pie charts 3' and 'Pie charts 4' for pairs of children (see Lesson 5); differentiated copies of 'Numbers sets' for each less able and more able child (see General resources).

Equipment
An OHP; rulers; centimetre-squared graph paper; counting stick.

Lesson

Starter

Revise how to square a number (multiply it by itself) and how to find a square root, for example, ask: *What number squared is equal to 36?* Chant through the square numbers (1 squared is 1, 2 squared is 4) up to 12 squared. Then ask questions at random and in different formats, for example: What is 5 squared? *What is the square of 7? What is 9 to the power of 2? What number multiplied by itself gives 100?* Ask simple questions using children's knowledge of square numbers and involving the four main operations, for example: $3^2 + 5^2$, $10^2 - 6^2$, $2^2 \times 4^2$, $8^2 \div 2^2$.

Main teaching activity

Whole class: Revise the meaning of the words 'mode' and 'range' as applied to sets of data. (See Unit 6 of the Autumn Term). Write a list of statistics on the board, such as the scores achieved by a darts player with his first six darts: 36, 5, 14, 9, 14, 3. Ask: *What is the range of these scores?* It is the difference between the highest and lowest scores, so 36 – 3 = 33. The highest score is 33 more than the lowest score. *What does mode mean?* It is the most frequent value in the list. In this case it is 14. Discuss when knowing the mode of a set of data would be useful, for example, a children's clothing firm knowing which sizes are bought most frequently, and a paint company knowing what colour of paint is the most popular. Then go on to consider 'median' and 'mean'. Again, use a set of data written on the board to explain the meanings. For example, use 10, 2, 7, 9 and 2. Explain that to find the median we put all the numbers in order, smallest to largest, and then find the middle value. The order would be 2, 2, 7, 9 and 10, and the median would be 7. Also explain that to find the mean we divide the total by the number of members in the list. So, 2 + 2 + 7 + 9 + 10 = 30, 30 ÷ 5 = 6. The mean is 6. Explain that if there is no middle value in a set of numbers the median is halfway between the two middle numbers. For example, the median of 5, 9, 11 and 15 is 10, because 10 comes halfway between 9 and 11. Explain that the mean is sometimes referred to as the average, but that this is not technically correct because it is only one type of average. Median and mode are also types of average.

Paired work: Set children to work in pairs on 'Number sets'. Once the sheets have been distributed, quickly revise the processes involved in finding the range, the mode, the median and the mean.

Differentiation

Less able: This group should work from the version of the activity sheet where each of the four terms is dealt with separately. Check at the end of each section that children have carried out the correct processes and calculations.

More able: Children in this group should work on the version of the activity sheet where the problems are more word based. Point out that some of the answers will produce decimal numbers but calculations should not require a calculator. Encourage children to gather their own data for interesting range, mode, median and mean calculations.

Plenary & assessment

Ensure that children fully understand the terms used in the lesson. Ask: *How would you find the range of a set of numbers? What do you understand by the term 'mode'? What do we mean by the term 'median'? What calculations are needed to find the mean of a set of numbers?* Remind them that mode, median and mean are all types of average and suit certain situations better than others, for example: cricket batter's scores (mean), the most common children's shoe sizes in a class (mode), the halfway point in a group of children's heights (median).

Lesson ④

Starter

Write on the board a three-digit number such as 456 and ask: *Will this number divide exactly by 4? How can you tell? What about by 8?* Encourage the children to explain how they worked this out. Revise other tests for divisibility, such as for dividing 348 by 2, 3, 4, 5, 6, 7, 8, 9 and 10.

Main teaching activity

Whole class: On the OHP, show the enlarged conversion graphs. Explain that these types of graphs are called conversion graphs because they are used to change one system of units into another. These particular conversion graphs are very useful when working out the distances involved in foreign travel and the value of money when visiting or taking a holiday in Europe. Emphasise that both graphs must start at zero, as either no distance has been travelled at that point or no money has been exchanged. Stress also that both graphs are straight lines because the distances or amounts of money increase by the same quantity each time. This is known in maths as 'constant proportion'. Tell children that points should be located as accurately as possible and then connected by a line drawn with a ruler.

Paired work: Working in pairs, children construct the two conversion graphs from the data. Provided them with centimetre squared paper and copies of 'Conversion graphs'. Write the following questions on the OHP or whiteboard. *How many kilometres are these distances? 10 miles, 15 miles, 20 miles, 35 miles, 45 miles. How many miles are these distances? 16km, 48km, 100km, 115km. Change these pounds to Euros: £2, £5, £8, £9, £25. Change these Euros to pounds: 3.20€, 8€, 12.80€,16, 60€.*

Differentiation

Less able: Provide help with the construction of the graphs, such as drawing axes, deciding on scale, marking points and so on.

More able: Encourage this group to make other examples of conversion graphs based on topics already worked on in class, such as changing temperatures from °C into °F, converting kilograms into pounds and litres into pints/gallons.

Plenary & assessment

Ask the children: *What do we mean by the term 'conversion graph'? What does the phrase 'constant proportion' mean?* Ask for volunteers to provide answers to the questions set on the conversion graphs.

Lesson ⑤

Starter

Label one end of the counting stick 0 and the other end 1. Count in steps of 0.4 along and back on the stick. Point to any point on the stick and ask the children to say what decimal fits there. Repeat, labelling the stick in steps of 0.6, 0.8 and so on.

Main teaching activity

Whole class: Tell the children they are going to revisit pie charts (see Unit 6, the Autumn Term). Explain that this time they are going to gather information to make their own simple pie charts on the grids provided. Stress that pie charts are increasingly popular as a way of conveying information because of their visual appeal. Remind children that the complete area of the circle represents all the information and is divided into sectors, each of them showing certain categories. Say: *This type of graph is especially good at showing how part of something relates to the whole.* On the OHP, show children examples of the grids they can use for their pie charts. They could have eight sections (45° angles), 10 sections (36° angles), 12 sections (30° angles) or 24 sections (15° angles). Discuss possible topics, including types of trees, surveys of favourite television programmes, or time spent on different activities during the day, with each hour represented by a 15° angle (360° ÷ 24 = 15°). Stress that to make amounts easy to show some rounding off may be necessary.

Paired work: Working in pairs, the children should choose a topic for which to construct a pie chart. Provide them with an appropriate grid from the range provided in General resources. Once the chart has been completed, children should interpret the information shown and write as many statements about it as possible. Statements should include smallest and largest amounts, amounts that are the same, comparison between amounts, and so on.

Differentiation

Less able: Recommend that this group works on pie chart grids with only eight or ten sections. Provide support with rounding off numbers, calculating sectors and drawing lines in the correct places.

More able: Challenge this group to make their own pie charts from blank circles, calculating their own angles and marking them using a 360° protractor.

Plenary & assessment

Look at the examples of the pie charts the children have produced. Mount a class display of them.

Name	Date

In proportion

Copy these grids onto squared paper and colour in the proportions given.

1.

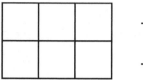

$\frac{1}{3}$ Red

$\frac{2}{3}$ Yellow

2.

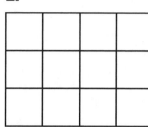

$\frac{1}{6}$ Green $\frac{1}{12}$ Red

$\frac{1}{3}$ Blue $\frac{1}{12}$ Black

$\frac{1}{3}$ White

3.

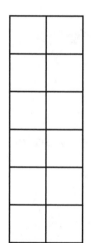

$\frac{1}{2}$ Yellow

$\frac{1}{12}$ Blue

$\frac{1}{4}$ Red

$\frac{1}{6}$ White

4.

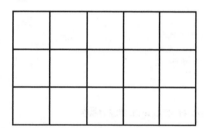

$\frac{3}{15}$ Red $\frac{4}{15}$ White

$\frac{1}{5}$ Blue $\frac{1}{3}$ Yellow

5.

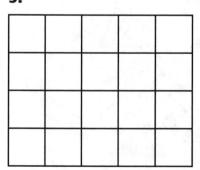

$\frac{1}{2}$ White $\frac{1}{4}$ Black

$\frac{1}{20}$ Red $\frac{1}{5}$ Green

6.

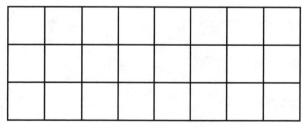

$\frac{5}{24}$ Blue $\frac{1}{24}$ Green $\frac{1}{6}$ Black

$\frac{1}{4}$ Red $\frac{1}{3}$ Yellow

Spring term
Unit 10

Name   Date

Ratio time

Simplify these ratios by putting them in their lowest terms, for example, 3:6 would become 1:2.

1. 2:6   _____

2. 10:15   _____

3. 9:12   _____

4. 20:50   _____

5. 14:21   _____

6. 12:27   _____

7. 75:100   _____

8. 32:20   _____

Put these amounts into the correct ratio.

For example, 20 flowers in the ratio 2:3 would be $\frac{1}{5}$ of 20 = 4, 2 x 4 = 8 and 3 x 4 = 12, so the answer is 8 flowers and 12 flowers.

1. 15 biscuits, ratio 1:4   _____

2. 24 cakes, ratio 3:5   _____

3. 30 sweets, ratio 7:3   _____

4. 36 stickers, ratio 4:5   _____

5. 40 apples, ratio 3:1   _____

6. 50 stamps, ratio 7:3   _____

7. 66 grapes, ratio 5:6   _____

8. 72 currants, ration 2:7   _____

Name		Date	

Number sets

Find the range, mode, median and mean of these sets of numbers.

		range	mode	median	mean
1	9, 7, 2, 2, 10				
2	6, 9, 5, 4, 6				
3	12, 15, 17, 12				
4	9, 21, 20, 18, 9, 9				
5	18, 32, 28, 18, 54				

Make up your own sets of numbers for finding the range, mode, median and mean.

1					
2					
3					
4					
5					

Properties of numbers and reasoning about numbers

Among the number activities investigated are the products of odd and even numbers, simple tests of divisibility and recognising prime numbers. The unit also covers factorising numbers up to 100 into prime factors and using letters as symbols in formulae, for example, finding the area and perimeter of rectangles.

LEARNING OBJECTIVES

		Topics	Starter	Main teaching activity
Lesson	**1**	Properties of numbers and number sequences.	● Consolidate rounding an integer to the nearest 10, 100 or 1000.	● Make general statements about odd and even numbers, including the outcome of products.
Lesson	**2**	As for Lesson 1.	● Round a number with two decimal places to the nearest whole number.	● Know and apply simple tests of divisibility.
Lesson	**3**	As for Lesson 1.	● **Order a mixed set of numbers or measurements with up to three decimal places.**	● Recognise prime numbers to at least 20. ● Find simple common multiples. ● Factorise numbers to 100 into prime factors.
Lesson	**4**	Reasoning or generalising about numbers or shapes	● Order a set of positive and negative integers.	● Develop from explaining a generalised relationship in words to expressing in formula using letters as symbols. Use knowledge of sums, differences, products of odd/even numbers.
Lesson	**5**	As for Lesson 4 and checking results of calculations.	● Count on in steps 0.1, 0.2, 0.25, 0.5 and then back. ● Order fractions such as 2/3, 3/4 and 5/6 by converting them to fractions with a common denominator, and position then on a number line.	● Solve mathematical problems or puzzles, recognise and explain patterns and relationships, generalise and predict.

Lessons   overview

Preparation
Display a chart showing the rules of divisibility (see Lesson 2). Write a set of numbers on the whiteboard for turning into prime factors (Lesson 3).

Learning objectives
Starters
● Consolidate rounding an integer to the nearest 10, 100 or 1000.
● Round a number with two decimal places to the nearest whole number.
● Order a mixed set of numbers or measurements with up to three decimal places
● Order a set of positive and negative integers.
● Count on in steps 0.1, 0.2, 0.25, 0.5 and then back.
● Order fractions such as 2/3, 3/4 and 5/6 by converting them to fractions with a common denominator, and position then on a number line.
Main teaching activities
● Make general statements about odd and even numbers including the outcome of products.
● Know and apply simple tests of divisibility.
● Recognise prime numbers to at least 20.
● Find simple common multiples.
● Factorise numbers to 100 into prime factors.

Vocabulary
number, count, odd, even, product, quotient, multiple of, digit, next, consecutive, sequence, continue, predict, pattern, relationship, rule, sort, classify, property, square number, divisible by, divisibility, factor, factorise, prime, prime factor

You will need:
Photocopiable pages
A copy of 'Quick check' (page 151) for each child.

CD Pages
A set of 1–9 digit cards (which can be made from 'Digit (+ and –) and decimal point cards') for each pair, a copy of 'Factors 1–100' and 'Prime numbers 1–200) for reference; differentiated copies of 'Quick check' for each less able and more able child (see General resources).

Equipment
Table squares for less able children; calculators.

Lesson

Starter

Write some four-digit numbers on the board, such as 1234, 5029, 5209. Ask the children to round each one firstly to the nearest 10, then the nearest 100 and finally top the nearest 1000. Repeat for another set of four-digit numbers.

Main teaching activity

Whole class: Tell the children they are going to establish which rules apply when odd and even numbers are multiplied. Remind them that the word 'product' means the answer to a multiplication calculation, for example, the product of 6 and 3 is 18. Work through several examples of each on the whiteboard or OHP, for example: even x even, 8 x 6 = 48 and 4 x 10 = 40; odd x odd, 7 x 5 = 35 and 9 x 11 = 99; even x odd, 6 x 9 = 54 and 10 x 7 = 70; odd x even, 5 x 14 = 70 and 13 x 6 = 78.

Paired work: Working in pairs, children should divide a set of 1–9 digit cards into odd and even numbers and shuffle them. Choosing cards at random from both or either piles of cards, they should test out the rules that apply to the products of odd and even numbers by trying out as many examples as they can (even x even, odd x odd, even x odd and odd x even). Towards the end of the session they should be able to suggest some general rules.

Differentiation

Less able: Work with the children in this group to check that multiplication calculations are correct, otherwise they may gather confusing results at the investigation stage. Table squares may be needed by some.

More able: Encourage this group to check rules using two-digit numbers. They could go on to check the rules that apply when odd and even numbers are divided, but this should only be carried out with numbers that will divide equally without leaving remainders.

Plenary & assessment

Compare the rules about the products of odd and even numbers with those to do with adding and subtracting odd and even numbers.

Lesson

Starter

Write some numbers with two places of decimals on the board, such as 3.76, 9.03, 8.07. Ask the children to round these firstly to the nearest tenth, and then to the nearest whole number. Repeat for the decimal numbers.

Main teaching activity

Whole class: Tell children that the purpose of this session is to learn about simple tests of divisibility that can be applied to most of the times-tables up to 10. First, go quickly over the rules for dividing by 2 (it must be an even number, eg 158 or 3294), 5 (the last digit will be a 5 or 0, eg 95 and 2730) and 10 (the last digit will be 0, eg 790 and 32570). Then look at divisibility by 3 and 6. Explain these in more detail. Say: A number is divisible by 3 if the sum of its digits is divisible by 3. For example, 87 will divide by 3 since 8 + 7 = 15, and 15 is divisible by 3. Try 345 ÷ 3. 3 + 4 + 5 = 12 and since 12 is in the three time-table, 345 is divisible by 3. A number is divisible by 6 if it is even and also divisible by 3. For example, try 462 ÷ 6. 462 is an even number and 4 + 6 + 2 = 12. Since 12 is divisible by 3, then 462 is divisible by 6. Also try 3744. It is even, and as 3 + 7 + 4 + 4 = 18, which is a multiple of 3, then 3744 is divisible by 6.

Move on to consider divisibility by 4 and 8. A number is divisible by 4 if 4 will divide exactly into the last two digits. Look at 196. 96 is divisible by 4, so the whole number will work. Try 2512. As 12 is a multiple of 4, the whole number will be divisible by 4. A number is divisible by 8 if half the number if divisible by 4 or the last three digits are divisible by 8. For example, 448 halved would be 224, and $224 \div 4 = 56$. 35576 would also work since $576 \div 8 = 72$. Lastly, a number is divisible by 9 if the sum of its digits is divisible by 9. So, since 153 makes $1 + 5 + 3 = 9$ and 4734 makes $4 + 7 + 3 + 4 = 18$, both these numbers are divisible by 9.

Individual/paired work: Set children to work individually or in pairs on the 'Quick check' activity sheet. Calculators should not be used during the main part of the lesson but could be used for quickly checking answers in the plenary session.

Differentiation

Less able: The differentiated version of 'Quick check' focuses on tasks which revise the rules of divisibility by 2, 5 and 10 and then looks at 3. Some children may need the rules to refer to.
More able: This group should be provided with the version of 'Quick check' where they concentrate on tests of divisibility for 6, 8 and 9.

Plenary & assessment

Display each of the rules of divisibility prominently in the classroom so children can refer to them when carrying out calculations in the future. Check through activity sheets to sort out any problems that have occurred.

Lesson ③

Starter

Write on the board a list of numbers such as 3.75, 9.4, 6, 7.123. Invite the children to order the numbers from smallest to largest. Repeat with a set such as 9.27, 5.437, 9.227. Repeat, extending the number range to include some numbers with three places of decimals.

Main teaching activity

Whole class: Revise briefly the work done on factor trees in Spring Term, Unit 3. Remind children that factors are whole numbers that divide exactly into another number without a remainder. For example, the factors of 20 are 1, 2, 4, 5, 10 and 20 as all these numbers divide into 20 without a remainder. Point out that 20 is a multiple of 1, 2, 4, 5, 10 and 20. Practise finding the factors of other numbers if necessary (see 'Factors 1–100'). Also tell children that prime numbers are whole numbers that only have two factors, the number itself and 1. For example, 13 is a prime number as 1 and 13 are the only two numbers that divide into 13 without a remainder. Quickly check that children know all the prime numbers up to at least 20, and further if possible (see 'Prime numbers 1–200'). Then, writing an example on the flipchart or whiteboard, demonstrate how to express a number in

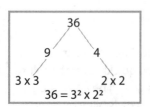

prime factors. Explain that index numbers or indices can be used as a shorthand method to avoid having to repeat the same digits. 12 would become $2^2 \times 3$, 36 would become $3^2 \times 2^2$, and 64 would become 2^6 or 2 to the power of 6.

Group work: Write up on the whiteboard or flipchart the following numbers that children should break down into prime factors. Stress that all stages of the process should be shown and that indices should be used to show the answer in its most concise form: 8, 10, 16, 20, 24; 28, 32, 36, 40, 48.

Differentiation

Less able: This group should focus on the first five numbers in the list. Support may need to be given when listing factors.
More able: Work with this group who should be expected to complete all 15 numbers in the list. They could go on to demonstrate that the final roots of any factor tree will be the same whichever factors are used. For example, $18 = 2 \times 9 = 2 \times 3 \times 3 = 2 \times 3^2$, while $18 = 3 \times 6 = 3 \times 2 \times 3$ which also produces 2×3^2.

Plenary & assessment

Check through some of the numbers given to the class to make sure that prime factors have been correctly found. Ask the following questions: *What does the word 'factor' mean? What are the factors of 24? What are the factors of 35? What does the phrase prime number mean? Give a prime number between 10 and 20. Give a prime number between 40 and 50. What does multiple mean? Why do we use index numbers? How would you show 5 x 5 x 5 using an index number? How would you show 2 x 2 x 3 x 3 x 3 using indices?*

Lessons   overview

Preparation

Prepare examples of number sequences (see Lesson 4) and examples of formulae to write on the whiteboard (Lesson 5).

Learning objectives

Starters

- Order a set of positive and negative whole numbers.
- Count on in steps of 0.1, 0.2, 0.25, 0.5, and then back.
- Order fractions such as 2/3, 3/4 and 5/6 by converting them to fractions with a common denominator, and position then on a number line.

Main teaching activities

- Solve mathematical problems and puzzles, recognise and explain patterns and relationships, generalise and predict.
- Develop from explaining a generalised relationship in words to expressing in formula using letters as symbols.

Vocabulary

predict, relationship, pattern, puzzle, number sentence, formula, symbol, sign, operation, equation, calculation, method, strategy, jotting, what could we try next?, answer

You will need:

Photocopiable pages

A copy of 'Formula 1' and 'Formula 1' (page 152) 'Number sequences' (page 153) for each pair.

CD Pages

Differentiated copies of 'Number sequences' and 'Formula 1' for each less able and more able child (see General resources).

Equipment

Straws, matchsticks, pegboards and calculators for groups of less able children.

Lesson

Starter

Write on the board the following set of numbers: 24, –18, 9, –13. Ask the children to order the numbers from smallest to largest. Repeat for other sets of positive and negative integers.

Main teaching activity

Whole class: Point out to the children that in mathematics, relationships between numbers can be written using symbols – often letters of the alphabet – and that these are often used in simple formulae to help us with certain rules and calculations. Write up a simple example on the whiteboard or flipchart. Say: *We could denote a packet of sweets by the letter 'p'. The cost of each individual packet could be shown by the letter 'c'. If we wanted to find the total cost (t) of a number of packets of sweets we could use the formula t = p x c, or in full, total cost (t) = numbers of packets (p) x cost of one packet (c).* Use another example. Remind children that the area of a rectangle or square can be calculated by multiplying the length by the width. In formula terms this could be written as a (area) = l (length) x w (width). Ask children what other formulae could be developed from this. They should respond that l = a ÷ w and w = a ÷ l. Then ask the class if they can give a formula for finding the perimeter of a rectangle or square. They should produce several alternatives. They could use l + w + l + w in various forms, or (l + w) x 2 or 2 (w + l). From this last example emphasise that in these types of formulae a letter and a number next to each other with no visible sign always means multiply. So, for example, 2t = 2 x t and 5n = 5 x n.

Group work: Provide children with copies of the 'Formula 1' activity sheet to work through.

Differentiation

Less able: Provide this group with the version of 'Formula 1' that deals with using the formula area = length x width only. Support may be needed when the formula is expressed in other ways, such as $w = a \div l$.

More able: This group should work on the version of 'Formula 1' where they use other formulae, namely, circumference of a circle = pi x diameter, and converting degrees in Fahrenheit into degrees in Celsius ($F = 9C \div 5 + 32$).

Plenary & assessment

Check through calculations children have carried out on the activity sheets and ensure figures have been correctly matched to letters in formulae.

Lesson ⑤

Starter

Write on the board the following fractions 1/4, 1/2, 3/8, 7/8. Ask: How can we order these fractions? Encourage the children to find a common denominator and then to order the fractions. Draw an empty number line labelled 0 at one end and 1 at the other. Invite children to place each fraction where they estimate it belongs. Repeat this for another family of fractions, such as 1/3, 4/5, 5/6, 2/5.

Main teaching activity

Whole class: Explain that during the main part of the lesson groups will be working on different number puzzles involving number sequences and patterns. Stress that in solving these puzzles it is important to work from the known to the unknown. Emphasise the importance of looking for relationships between numbers that will help to make generalisations about which rules are being applied. Once rules have been established, this should be used to predict what form the pattern or sequence is taking.

Group work: Children should work on the 'Number sequence' activity sheet. They have to work out the patterns involved in making balanced triangles using single-digit numbers.

Differentiation

Less able: Provide plenty of equipment like straws, matchsticks, pegboards and so on, so that children can work with patterns and sequences in a concrete way first. This will help them make the link between the spatial and the numerical pattern. Children then work on the easier version of 'Number sequence'.

More able: Encourage this group to extend their own number sequences as far as they can once they have completed their version of the activity sheet, which deals with the number sequence associated with Leonardo Fibonacci.

Plenary & assessment

Ask representatives from each group to report back to the others on the number puzzles they have been working on. Put up a display of their work in the classroom. Revise children's knowledge and understanding of common number patterns covered in recent lessons, like odd and even numbers, square numbers, triangular numbers, Fibonacci numbers and so on.

Name	Date

Quick check

- **Which of these numbers are divisible by 3?**

  51   72   91   173   288

  _____   _____   _____   _____   _____

- **Which of these numbers are divisible by 4?**

  162   212   275   268   383

  _____   _____   _____   _____   _____

- **Which of these numbers are divisible by 6?**

  134   186   252   415   462

  _____   _____   _____   _____   _____

- **Which of these numbers are divisible by 9?**

  175   289   342   657   1341

  _____   _____   _____   _____   _____

Name	Date

Formula 1

- **Match the expressions that mean the same thing.**

one less than t	t x l
double t	3t
t times itself	t – l
t	2 x t
treble t	t^2

- **Using the formulae area (a) = length (l) × width (w), l = a ÷ w and w = a ÷ l, solve these rectangle problems.**

1.
l = 12cm

w = 5.5cm

Find the area.

_____

2.
a = 52cm^2

l = 8cm

Find the width.

_____

3.
a = 57.6cm^2

w = 7.2cm

Find the length.

_____

- **Using the formula area of a triangle (a) = base (b) x height (h) ÷ 2, solve these triangle problems.**

1.
h = 10cm

b = 8cm

Find the area.

_____

2.
a = 35cm^2

h = 7cm

Find the base.

_____

3.
a = 48cm^2

b = 6cm

Find the height.

_____

SCHOLASTIC
photocopiable

Name   Date

Number sequence

- **Use the digits 1 to 6 to make each side of the triangle total 9.**

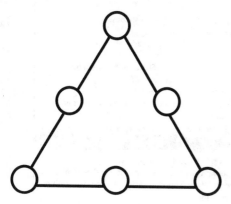

- Rearrange the digits to make balanced triangles with other totals for the three sides

- **Make more balanced triangles here using the digits 1 to 9.**

  Start with making the total for each of the three sides 17.

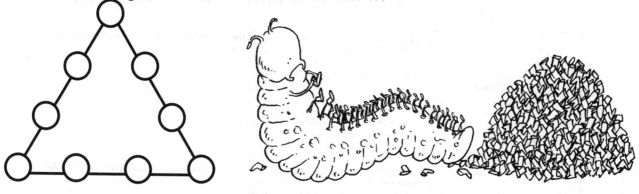

- **This shape is made up of two triangles. Use the digits 1 to 7.**

  Each straight line should total 12.

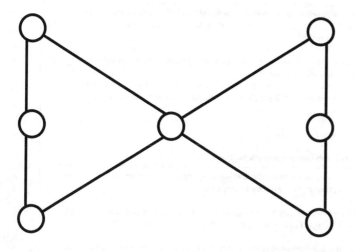

EVERY DAY: Practise and develop oral and mental skills (eg counting, mental strategies, rapid recall of +, –, x and ÷ facts)	
• **Multiply and divide decimals mentally by 10 or 100 and explain the effect.** • Consolidate knowing by heart multiplication facts up to 10 x 10. • Order fractions such as 2/3, ¾ and 5/6 by converting them to fractions with a common denominator, and position them on a number line. • Consolidate rounding an integer to the nearest 10, 100 and 1000. • Round a number with two decimal places to the nearest tenth or the nearest whole number. • Consolidate all mental addition and subtraction strategies from previous years. • **Derive quickly: division facts corresponding to tables up to 10 x 10;** doubles of two-digit numbers including decimals (eg 3.8 x 2, 0.7 x 2) and the corresponding halves.	• Use known number facts and place value to consolidate mental addition and subtraction. • Classify quadrilaterals and other shapes. • Add several numbers mentally. • Use known number facts and place value to consolidate mental multiplication. • Visualise 3-D shapes from 2-D drawings and identify different nets for a closed cube. • Order a set of positive and negative integers. • **Order a mixed set of numbers** or measurements **with up to three decimal places.**

Units	Days	Topics	Objectives
1	3	Fractions, decimals, percentages, ratio and proportion	Order a mixed set of numbers or measurements with up to three decimal places. Reduce a fraction to its simplest form by cancelling common factors in the numerator and denominator. Use a fraction as an 'operator' to find fractions, including tenths and hundredths, of numbers or quantities. Understand percentage as the number of parts in every 100. Find simple percentages of small whole-number quantities.
		Problems involving 'real life', money or measures	Identify and use appropriate operations (including combinations of operations) to solve word problems involving numbers and quantities, including converting pounds to foreign currency and calculating percentages such as VAT.
		Using a calculator	Develop calculator skills and use a calculator effectively.and calculating percentages such as VAT.
2-3	10	Pencil and paper procedures (+ and –)	**Extend written methods to: column addition and subtraction of numbers involving decimals.**
		Pencil and paper procedures (x and ÷)	**Extend written methods to: long multiplication of a three-digit by a two-digit integer; short multiplication of numbers involving decimals.**
		Problems involving 'real life', money and measures.	**Explain methods and reasoning.**
		Check results of calculations	Check with the inverse operation when using a calculator. Check with an equivalent calculation. Estimate by approximating, then check result.
		Shape and space	**Calculate the perimeter and area of simple compound shapes that can be split into rectangles.** **Read and plot co-ordinates in all four quadrants.** Recognise where a shape will be after reflection. Recognise where a shape will be after two translations. Calculate angles in a triangle or round a point. **Use a protractor to measure and draw acute and obtuse angles to nearest degree.** Recognise and estimate angles. Check that the sum of angles of a triangle is 180°, for example, by measuring or paper folding. Check that the sum of the angles of a triangle is 180°: for example, by measuring or paper folding.
4-5	10	Problems involving 'real life', money and measures	**Identify and use appropriate operations to solve word problems involving numbers and quantities** based on 'real life', money… including converting pounds to foreign currency and vice versa. **Explain methods and reasoning.**
		Handling data	**Solve problems by** representing, **extracting and interpreting data in tables, graphs, charts** and diagrams including those generated by a computer. Find the mode and range of a set of data. Begin to find the median and mean of a set of data. Use the language associated with probability to discuss events, including those with equally likely outcomes.
		Measures	Know rough equivalents of lb and kg, oz and g, miles and km.
		Fractions, decimals and percentages	**Solve simple problems involving ratio and proportion.**
6	5	Handling data	**Solve problems by representing, extracting and interpreting data in tables, graphs and charts and diagrams including those generated by a computer.**
		Problem solving	**Solve mathematical problems or puzzles, recognise and explain patterns and relationships, generalise and predict. Suggest extensions asking 'What if?'**
		Reasoning and generalising about numbers and shapes	**Develop from explaining a generalised relationship in words to expressing it in a formula, using letters as symbols.**

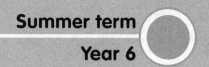
EVERY DAY: Practise and develop oral and mental skills (eg counting, mental strategies, rapid recall of +, –, x and ÷ facts)	
• **Derive quickly: division facts corresponding to tables up to 10 x 10.** • **Order a mixed set if numbers** or measurements **with up to three decimal places.** • Give pairs of factors for whole numbers up to 100. • Recognise prime numbers to at least 20. • **Calculate the perimeter and area of simple compound shapes that can be split into rectangles.** • Use known number facts and place value to consolidate mental multiplication and division. • Recognise squares of numbers to least 12 x 12. • **Multiply and divide decimals mentally by 10 or 100 and explain the effect.** • Count on in steps of 0.1, 0.2, 0.25, 0.5, and then back. • Consolidate knowing by heart multiplication facts up to 10 x 10. • Factorise numbers to 100 into prime factors. • Use, read and write standard metric units (km, m, cm, mm, kg, g, l, ml, cl), including their abbreviations, and the relationship between them.	• Know what each digit means in a number with up to three decimal places. • Recognise the equivalence between the decimal and fraction forms of common fractions. • Order fractions such as 2/3, ¾ and 5/6 by converting them to fractions with a common denominator, and position them on a number line. • **Derive quickly:** doubles of multiples of 100 to 10,000, and the corresponding halves. • Convert smaller units to larger units and vice versa. • **Understand percentage as the number of parts in every 100.** • **Find simple percentages of small whole-number quantities.** • Classify quadrilaterals and other shapes. • Describe and visualise properties of solid shapes. • Recognise where a shape will be after reflection. • Recognise where a shape will be after rotation through 90° about one of its vertices.

Units	Days	Topics	Objectives
7	5	Shape and space	**Calculate the perimeter and area of simple compound shapes that can be split into rectangles.**
		Pencil and paper procedures (+ and –)	**Extend written methods to: column addition and subtraction of numbers involving decimals.**
		Problems involving 'real life', money and measures	**Identify and use appropriate operations (including combinations of operations) to solve word problems involving numbers and quantities** based on 'real life'. **Explain methods and reasoning.**
8-9	10	Fractions, decimals, percentages, ratio and proportion	**Solve simple problems involving ratio and proportion.** **Understand percentage as the number of parts in every 100.** **Find simple percentages of small whole numbers.**
		Problem solving involving 'real life', money and measures	**Identify and use appropriate operations (including combinations of operations) to solve word problems involving numbers and quantities** based on 'real life'. **Explain methods and reasoning.**
		Using a calculator	Develop calculator skills and use a calculator effectively.
		Checking results of calculations	Check with an equivalent calculation. Check with the inverse operation when using a calculator.
		Pencil and paper procedures (x and ÷)	**Extend written methods to: long multiplication of a three-digit by a two-digit integer; short multiplication and division of numbers involving decimals.**
		Making decisions	Choose and use appropriate number operations and appropriate ways of calculating: mental, mental with jottings, written methods, calculator.
10	5	Fractions, decimals, percentages, ratio and proportion	Recognise the equivalence between the decimal and fraction forms of common fractions. **Reduce a fraction to its simplest form by cancelling common factors.** Begin to convert a fraction to a decimal using division. **Use a fraction as an 'operator' to find fractions**, including tenths and hundredths, of numbers or quantities. **Solve simple problems involving ratio and proportion.** Factorise numbers to 100 into prime factors.
11-12	10	Shape and space	**Use a protractor to measure and draw acute and obtuse angles to nearest degree.** **Read and plot co-ordinates in all four quadrants.** Recognise where a shape will be after reflection. Recognise where a shape will be after rotation through 90° about one of its vertices. **Calculate the perimeter and area of simple compound shapes that can be split into rectangles.** Describe and visualise properties of solid shapes. Make shapes with increasing accuracy. Visualise 3-D shapes from 2-D drawings. **Use a protractor to measure and draw acute and obtuse angles to nearest degree.**
		Problems involving 'real life', money and measures	**Identify and use appropriate operations (including combinations of operations) to solve word problems involving numbers and quantities** based on 'real life'.

Decimals, fractions, percentages

This unit revisits and reinforces objectives introduced previously, providing a sound basis for revision for SATs. Care should be taken to ensure that children fully understand the processes involved with decimals, fractions and percentages and that they are able to apply these to 'real-life' situations.

LEARNING OBJECTIVES

	Topics	Starter	Main teaching activity
Lesson 1	Fractions, decimals, percentages, ratio and proportion	● **Multiply and divide decimals mentally by 10 or 100, and integers by 1000, and explain the effect.**	● **Order a mixed set of numbers with up to three decimal places.**
Lesson 2	Fractions, decimals, percentages, ratio and proportion Using a calculator	● Consolidate knowing by heart multiplication facts up to 10 x 10.	● **Reduce a fraction to its simplest form by cancelling common factors** in the numerator and denominator. ● Develop calculator skills and use a calculator effectively.
Lesson 3	As for Lesson 1.	● Order fractions, such as 2/3, 3/4 and 5/6 by converting them into fractions with a common denominator, and position them on a number line.	● **Use a fraction as an 'operator' to find fractions,** including tenths and hundredths, **of numbers or quantities.**
Lesson 4	As for Lesson 1.	● Consolidate rounding an integer to the nearest 10, 100 or 1000.	● **Understand percentage as the number of parts in every 100.** ● **Find simple percentages of small whole-number quantities.**
Lesson 5	Problems involving 'real life', money or measures	● Round a number with two decimal places to the nearest tenth or the nearest whole number.	● **Identify and use appropriate operations (including combinations of operations) to solve word problems involving numbers and quantities** based on money, using one or more steps, and calculating percentages such as VAT.

Lessons   overview

Preparation
Copy 'Multiplying and dividing' onto acetate to display on an OHP. Prepare sets of 'Decimal cards' and '0 and 1 cards' and a blank card for each more able child to write their own decimal on. Copy and cut out the 'Number cards' and 'Fraction cards' (differentiate according to ability) see General resources.

Learning objectives
Starters
● **Order a mixed set of numbers with up to three decimal places.**
● Consolidate knowing by heart multiplication facts up to 10 x 10.
● Order fractions, such as 2/3, 3/4 and 5/6 by converting them into fractions with a common denominator, and position them on a number line.
Main teaching activities
● **Multiply and divide decimals mentally by 10 or 100, and integers by 1000, and explain the effect.**
● **Reduce a fraction to its simplest form by cancelling common factors** in the numerator and denominator.
● Develop calculator skills and use a calculator effectively.
● **Use a fraction as an 'operator' to find fractions,** including tenths and hundredths, **of numbers or quantities.**

Vocabulary
decimal, sixth, tenth, twelfth, hundredth, thousandth, ascending order, descending order, fraction, equivalent, numerator, denominator, cancel, reduced to

You will need:
Photocopiable pages
A copy of 'What fraction?' (page 161) for each child.

CD pages
An OHT of 'Multiplying and dividing', a set of 'Decimal cards' and '0 and 1 cards' for each group, a copy of '1–100 number cards' (1–50 cards for each pair, and 1–100 cards for each more able pair), 'Fraction recording sheet' for each pair and two sets of 'Fraction cards'; differentiated copies of 'What fraction?' for each less able and more able child (see General resources).

Equipment
An OHP; whiteboards and marker pens; magnetic board with digits (optional); blank cards for more able children; pegs and washing line.

Lesson

Starter

Display the OHT of 'Multiplying and dividing'. Tell the children that you are going to give them a number and then point to one of the operators. They must do the operation in their heads and write the answer on their whiteboards to show you. Start with integers, such as 24, 35 and 16, 315, using any of the operators. Then move on to decimal numbers, such as 1.25, 21.3, 10.75, 106.35. Select different children to explain the effect of the operators. If necessary, use the OHT chart to demonstrate.

Discourage children from saying 'move the decimal point' – instead, remind them that each operation results in the digits moving to the left or the right, but the decimal point stays in the same position. Demonstrate this on the board, or use a magnetic board with digits which can be physically moved.

Main teaching activity

Whole class: Write these decimal numbers on the board: 140.125, 0.45, 14.05, 15.045, 1.504, 400.05. Point to a digit (such as 5 in 14.05) and ask the value of the digit. Highlight that this is 0.05 or five hundredths. Compare the 4 digit in each number. Where is it? Point out that in each number there is a digit 4, but in each case the value of that digit is different (forty, four tenths, four, four hundredths, four thousandths, four hundred).

Ask the children to write the numbers in ascending order on their whiteboards. Discuss how they decided upon the order. Point out that they must consider the value of the most significant digit – when comparing numbers, they should consider the place value furthest to the *left* .

Paired/group work: Children should work in pairs or small groups to play 'All in a line'. Provide each group with a set of decimal cards, plus a 0 and a 1 card. The 0 and 1 are placed on the table with space for ten cards between them. The cards are shuffled and children take it in turns to select a card and place it between 0 and 1 in a line. Children may slide cards to the left or right to make a space, but cannot move the 0 or 1. When all the spaces are filled, they may continue with the game by swapping their selected card with one already in the line.

Differentiation

Less able: Select more simple decimal cards, such as those with only one decimal place, and the more common ones (eg 0.25, 0.75). Alternatively, ask children to leave space for only six cards between 0 and 1.

More able: Give these children a blank card, and when their line is completed they can write their own card to three decimal places to swap into the line.

Plenary & assessment

Ask each child to select a decimal card from their pack. Choose two groups of four children to come out to the front, show their cards and arrange themselves in ascending order. Groups should then stand next to each other. Ask the rest of the class to give instructions to combine the two groups to put the numbers in ascending order. They may only ask two children to swap places; they cannot ask them to slide to the left or right.

Lesson

Starter

Tell the children that you are going to give them a mental maths quiz. They should work out the answers, and when you say 'now' they show the answer using their number cards.

Ask questions such as: *What is 6 multiplied by 8?* (48) *What do I need to divide 45 by to get 5?* (9) *Give me a factor of 54.* (1, 2, 3, 6, 9, 18, 27 and 54) *What number is a factor of 63 and 24?* (3).

Main teaching activity

Whole class: Write 1/2 on the board and ask the children to give you an equivalent fraction. If necessary, give an example such as 3/6. Write these on the board. Explain that each fraction can be reduced to the simplest form (1/2) by cancelling common factors in the numerator and denominator. Demonstrate using the examples you have written on the board.

Write a fraction such as 15/20 on the board and ask children what the common factor is (see working in the margin). Explain that the fraction can be 'cancelled down' by dividing both the numerator and the denominator by 5. Point out that the fraction will not always reduce to a unitary fraction, in the example given it is 3/4. Go through similar examples.

Explain that a fraction can be changed to an equivalent fraction by multiplying both the numerator and the denominator by the same number, for example 3/10 can become 30/100 by multiplying numerator and denominator by 10.

Point out that in order to compare fractions it is useful to convert them to fractions with a common denominator, for example 3/8 and 2/5 gives 15/40 and 16/40 (the common denominator is found by multiplying 8 by 5).

Paired/group work: Working in pairs or small groups, children select two cards from a set of 1–50 number cards and use them to make a fraction (eg 25/35), then reduce the fraction if possible. They can record their work on the 'Fraction recording sheet'.

Differentiation

Less able: Give these children a set of number cards 2, 3, 4, 5, 6, 8, 9, 10, 12, 15, 18, 20, 24, 25, 30, 32, 35, 36, 40, 45, 48, 50, 54, 55, 60. They can record their work on the 'Fraction recording sheet'.
More able: This group should use a set of 1–100 number cards. Suggest that they may make improper fractions such as 35/25.

Plenary & assessment

Select two number cards and ask the children whether the fraction they make can be reduced. Discuss strategies. Ask: *What do you try first?* Point out that the fraction can be reduced in a number of steps, for example, 16/20 may be reduced to 8/10, then 4/5. Explain that this can be related to ratio, thus: 4 in every 5, 8 in every 10, 16 in every 20, and so on.

Ask for examples of fractions the children found that could not be reduced. Discuss why.

Lesson ③

Starter

Give each child a fraction card. Select a card from a similar set and hold it up, asking the children to show you a card higher, lower or equal to yours. Children have to show their fraction card if it is appropriate. Repeat. Then select two cards and ask for fractions between these two. Finally, ask children to come up in turns and peg their fraction on a number washing line, in order.

Main teaching activity

Whole class: Write on the board: 3/5 of £625. Point out that the calculation is 3/5 x 625. Ask the children to approximate the answer. Point out that if we are multiplying by a fraction, the answer will be *smaller*. This can often confuse children because they see multiplying as 'making bigger'. Tell them that when we multiply by a fraction we first divide by the denominator, so we divide 625 by 5 to get 125. Then we multiply by the numerator '3' to get 375. Hence, 3/5 of £625 is £375.

Work through a similar example, such as 3/4 of 2m. Remind children that they need to think what units they are going to work in. It is easier to convert 2 metres to 200cm and give the answer in centimetres, but both quantities should be expressed using the same units: 3/4 x 2m = 1.5m or 3/4 x 200cm = 150cm.

Individual work: Introduce the activity sheet 'What fraction?' The children should complete this independently.

Differentiation

Less able: Provide this group with the version of the activity sheet that is limited to halves, quarters and tenths.

More able: Provide this group with the version of the activity sheet using a wider range of fractions, including fifths, eighths, hundredths and thousandths.

Plenary & assessment

Discuss any difficulties that the children have encountered.

Write on the board: *Gemma saved £75. She spent 3/5 on a computer game. How much did she have left?* Ask the children what calculations they need to do to find the answer. Can they solve the problem in their head? Can they do it using jottings? Ask a child to come out and work through the problem, showing their workings.

Make sure that the children understand that they must first divide by the denominator and then multiply by the numerator. Then re-read the question to decide what the answer should be. Point out that they are being asked 'How much did she have left?'

Lessons   overview

Preparation

Copy and cut out sets of cards for each group of children (differentiate according to ability).

Learning objectives

Starters

- Consolidate rounding an integer to the nearest 10, 100 or 1000.
- Round a number with two decimal places to the nearest tenth or the nearest whole number.

Main teaching activities

- **Understand percentage as the number of parts in every 100.**
- **Find simple percentages of small whole-number quantities.**
- **Identify and use appropriate operations (including combinations of operations) to solve word problems involving numbers and quantities** based on money, using one or more steps, and calculating percentages such as VAT.

Vocabulary

decimal, tenth, hundredth, thousandth, percentage, per cent, %, discount

You will need:

Photocopiable pages
A copy of 'Discount store' (page 162) for each child.

CD pages
A set of 'Percentage cards' for each pair; 'Number cards' for each group (1–50, 1–100 according to ability); differentiated copies of 'Discount store' for each less able and more able child (see General resources).

Equipment
An OHP and OHP calculator; whiteboards and pens.

Lesson

Starter

Children will need whiteboards and pens. Tell them that you want them to round numbers, first to the nearest ten, then the nearest hundred and finally the nearest thousand. For example, if the number is 458 children should write 460, 500, 0. Tell them that they should round up from 5. Call out numbers such as 901 (900, 900, 1000) 3045 (3050, 3000, 3000) 2637 (2640, 2600, 3000).

Main teaching activity

Whole class: Ask: *What is 50% of £80? What is 25%?* Remind the children that per cent means per hundred, so 50% is 50 parts out of a hundred. Ask the children to work out 60% of £150, working in pairs and recording their method on whiteboards.

Let children explain how they calculated their answers and discuss which methods were most effective. Possible methods may be to: find 10% (£15) and multiply this by 6; find 10% and 50% and add the two together; find 10%, double it to find 20%, total the two to give 30% then double; find 1% and multiply by 60.

Discuss the simplest strategies to use; encourage children to use jottings and mental methods. Ask: *How would you find 59%?* (suggest taking 1% from 60%) ... *15%?* (10% plus half of 10%) Demonstrate finding 48% of 625 using the OHP calculator: input 625, divide by 100 to find 1% (6.25), then multiply by 48 to find 48% (300).

Individual/paired work: Write some amounts on the board, such as £400, £200, £60, £500. Children work in pairs, each pair with a set of 'Percentage cards'. They should select a percentage card and use it as an operator on each of the amounts on the board. They should do the calculation independently and then compare with their partners. Repeat with another percentage card. Allow the children to check using the calculator calculations they find difficult.

Differentiation

This activity can be differentiated by giving different percentage cards to different ability groups, and by allocating different amounts for the groups to find the percentages of.
Less able: Limit the percentage cards to multiples of 10 (10%, 20 %, 30%, 40%...).
More able: Give more complex amounts to find percentages of, such as £125, £380, £55.

Plenary & assessment

Discuss any difficulties the children had in the lesson. Demonstrate how to find percentages using the calculator percentage key, using the example 25% of £625. Enter the amount (625) press x followed by 25 then the % key.

Lesson ⑤

Repeat the **Starter** for lesson 4, but this time rounding a number with two decimal places to the nearest tenth or whole number. Give numbers such as 4.26 (rounded to 4.3, 4), 15.75 (15.8, 16), 21.36 (21.4, 21), 5.06 (5.1, 5).

In the **Main teaching activity**, explain that VAT is a tax of 17½% which is added onto the price of some items. Remind children of how they found percentages in the previous lesson. Introduce the 'Discount store' activity sheet. There are differentiated versions for more able and less able children. Remind children to approximate first and then to check their answers.

For the **Plenary**, write on the board: £325 less 15%, £340 less 20%. Say: *A bike is in the sale in two shops at these prices. Which is the best deal?* (£325 less 15% = £276.25; £340 less 20% = £272) Check that the children are able to calculate accurately and that they understand the comparisons. Go through any difficulties they had with the activity sheet.

Name   Date

What fraction?

You may use a calculator to help you answer the following questions.

1. How far is $\frac{3}{5}$ of 2km?   _____

2. How many minutes are there in $\frac{1}{3}$ of 4 hours? _____

3. What is $\frac{3}{8}$ of 12kg?   _____

4. Rashid had £650 birthday money. He spent $\frac{7}{10}$ on a new bike.
How much did the bike cost?   _____

5. Rashid then spent $\frac{1}{5}$ of his remaining birthday money on a game.
How much did he have left?   _____

6. Sara entered the long-distance walking race of 24km.
She completed the first $\frac{3}{8}$ in 2 hours. How far did she have left to walk?_____

7. What fraction of £8 is 25p?   _____

8. What fraction of 2 weeks is 5 days?   _____

**Choose a fraction from the first box and use it as an operator on a quantity or measurement
from the second box. Repeat.**

$\frac{1}{3}$ £240

$\frac{1}{8}$ 10km

$\frac{3}{10}$ 2kg

$\frac{7}{100}$

Name	Date

Discount store

'Planet' is having a sale, and all items have been reduced.

Work out the sale price of the following items.

Item	Usual price	Reduced by	Sale price
14-inch colour TV	£125.00	20%	
Portable CD player	£99.00	10%	
Mobile phone	£130.00	15%	

'Discount warehouse' boasts that it has the lowest prices anywhere, but their prices do not include VAT, so you must add $17\frac{1}{2}$% to all the prices.

Work out the full price of the following items.

Item	Usual price	+ VAT	Full price
14-inch colour TV	£72.00	+ $17\frac{1}{2}$ %	
Portable CD player	£80.00	+ $17\frac{1}{2}$ %	
Mobile phone	£96.00	+ $17\frac{1}{2}$ %	

If you bought the three items, what is the least you could pay? _____

The items cost less at one store than the other. If you bought all three items from this store, how much less would you pay than if you bought them at the other store? _____

In this unit methods of calculation are revised, ensuring that children are secure in their understanding of the 'four rules', in preparation for the Key Stage 2 SATs. There is a strong emphasis on applying the rules to calculations involving decimals and 'real-life' situations.

LEARNING OBJECTIVES

		Topics	Starter	Main teaching activity
Lesson	1	Pencil and paper procedures (+ and −) Problems involving 'real life, money or measures Checking results of calculations	● Consolidate all mental addition and subtraction strategies from previous years.	● **Extend written methods to column addition and subtraction of numbers involving decimals.** ● **Explain methods and reasoning.** ● Check with the inverse operation when using a calculator. ● Estimate by approximating, then check result.
Lesson	2	Pencil and paper procedures (+ and −) Checking results of calculations	● **Derive quickly division facts responding to tables up to 10 x 10.**	● **Extend written methods to column addition and subtraction of numbers involving decimals.** ● Check with an equivalent calculation.
Lesson	3	Pencil and paper procedures (x and ÷) Checking results of calculations	Use known number facts and place value to consolidate mental multiplication.	● **Extend written methods to: short multiplication of numbers involving decimals; long multiplication of a three-digit by a two-digit integer.** ● Estimate by approximating, then check result.
Lesson	4	Pencil and paper procedures (× and ÷) Problems involving 'real life, money or measures Problems involving 'real life, money or measures Check results of calculations	● **Derive quickly** doubles of two-digit numbers, eg 3.8 × 2, 0.76 × 2) and the corresponding halves.	● **Extend written methods to: short multiplication of numbers involving decimals; long multiplication of a three-digit by a two-digit integer.** ● **Explain methods and reasoning.** ● Estimate by approximating, then check result.
Lesson	5	As for Lesson 4	As for Lesson 4.	● As for Lesson 4.

Lessons ① ② ③ ④ ⑤ overview

Preparation
Prepare OHTs of 'Column addition','Column subtraction','Multiplication methods' and 'Division methods'.

Learning objectives
Starters
● Consolidate all mental addition and subtraction strategies from previous years.
● **Derive quickly division facts corresponding to tables up to 10 x 10**.
● Derive quickly doubles of two-digit numbers (including decimals) eg 3.8 × 2, 0.76× 2) and the corresponding halves.

Main teaching activities
● **Extend written methods to column addition and subtraction of numbers involving decimals**.
● **Extend written methods to:**
 short multiplication of numbers involving decimals;
 long multiplication of a three-digit by a two-digit integer;
 short division of numbers involving decimals.
● **Explain methods and reasoning**.
● Check with the inverse operation when using a calculator.
● Estimate by approximating, then check result.
● Check with equivalent calculation.

Vocabulary
decimal, decimal position, decimal place, placeholder, approximate, jottings

You will need:
Photocopiable pages
A copy of 'Choosing decimals' (page 168),'Bean growth' (page 169).

CD pages
OHTs of 'Column addition', 'Column subtraction', 'Multiplication methods' and 'Division methods', (see General resources); a set of 'Digit (+ and −) and decimal point cards' (see General resources Spring term); differentiated copies of 'Choosing decimals','Bean growth' and 'Sponsored Walk'.

Equipment
An OHP; whiteboard, pen and number fan for each child; a ten-sided dice (0–9) for each group.

Lesson ①

Starter

Children will need whiteboards and markers to record their answers. Give a selection of addition sums to be done mentally, such as 24 + 56, 79 + 87, 6 +7 +9 + 7, 230 + 90, 123 + 99. Allow no more than five seconds for them to answer.

Main teaching activity

Whole class: Explain that you are going to revisit column addition, looking especially at decimal numbers. Point out that with any calculation the children should first see if they can calculate mentally, then mentally with jottings, before resorting to a standard method.

Write on the board 927.4 + 0.73 + 83.78 and ask a child to come and set this out as a vertical sum and calculate the answer. Demonstrate the different methods, as shown on 'Column addition', which you can display on the OHP.

Stress that care must be taken to ensure that the decimal points are in line and that each digit is written in the correct column. Remind children to check their work by using an inverse operation or alternative method when using a calculator.

Paired work: Introduce the 'Choosing decimals' activity sheet. Children select decimal numbers from boxes, then add them using column addition. Suggest to the children that they could use an approximation and that they should always ask: *Can I do this in my head or with jottings?*

Differentiation

Less able: Give this group the version of the activity sheet that limits calculations to adding two numbers at a time.

More able: Give this group the version of the activity sheet where four or more numbers are added at a time.

Plenary & assessment

Write these examples on the board and ask children to tell you which method they would use.
a) 3899 + 499.5   b) 54.12 + 267.8 + 3.25
c) 12.99 + 312.4   d) 346.2 + 19.93

Remind children that they should look for the method they find quickest and simplest, for example, for a) mental addition with jottings (3900 +500 – 1.5 = 4398.5), b) column addition (325.17), (mental addition (13 + 312.4 – 0.01 = 325.39) and d) mental addition with jottings (346.2 + 20 – 0.7 = 366.13). Also remind them that they can check the addition of several numbers by changing the order.

Lesson ②

Starter

Children will need number fans to show their answers. Give quick-fire division questions such as: *Divide 8.1 by 9. (0.9) Divide 320 by 40. (8) What do I have to divide 72 by to get 8? (9) A box of 24 eggs is divided into 4 cartons. How many are in each? (6) What is one twentieth of 640? (32) Divide 7 into 47. (6R5)*

Main teaching activity

Whole class: Explain that today you are going to re-visit the subtraction methods that children have learned, and look at how these can be applied to decimal numbers. Write 7207 – 3859 on the board and ask the children to calculate the answer in any way they choose, and then discuss their methods. Remind them that they should approximate first, for example by rounding to 7200 – 3900 = 3300. Go through the column methods as shown on 'Column subtraction', which you can display on the OHP.

Stress that it is important, when doing calculations in columns, that the digits are in the correct columns, so units in line with units and so on. Work through an example using decimal numbers. Write on the board 234.4 – 26.75 and ask for an approximation (eg 235 –30 = 205). Ask a child to set the calculation out as a column subtraction and to come and explain how the calculation is done. Again, stress the importance of positioning the digits correctly in the column subtraction.

$$
\begin{array}{r}
234.4 \\
-\ \ 26.75 \\
\hline
207.65
\end{array}
\qquad
\begin{array}{r}
234.40* \\
-\ \ 26.75 \\
\hline
207.65
\end{array}
$$

Point out that they can add a zero to make the decimal places the same and this will not affect the value of the number as it is after the decimal point. Explain that the subtraction can be done in the same way as for integers, and the decimal point is 'in line' in the answer.

Individual work: Children should complete the 'Bean growth' activity sheet. Remind them to take care when setting out the calculations vertically to ensure the digits are in the correct 'columns'.

Differentiation

Less able: Give this group the version of 'Bean growth' with simpler calculations.
More able: This group should work through the 'Bean growth' activity sheet with more difficult calculations.

Plenary & assessment

Ask the children to give examples of subtractions that they did mentally, mentally with jottings, using informal methods, and using formal written methods. Discuss when the different methods are appropriate.

Lesson 3

Starter

Write on the board: 9 x 6 = 54. Ask the children to give examples of related multiplication facts, for example: 9 x 60, 9 x 0.6, 0.9 x 0.6. Discuss the effect of multiplying decimal numbers: 9 x 0.6 = 5.4, 0.9 x 0.6 = 0.54

Main teaching activity

Whole class: Write 4837 x 8 on the board and ask a child to demonstrate a calculation method for this. Remind them that first they should approximate, for example 4800 x 10 = 48, 000. Revisit the grid method and both expanded and contracted short multiplication, as shown on 'Multiplication methods', which you can display on the OHP (cover the bottom half).

Then write on the board: 5.39 x 6. Explain that we can easily use similar methods to multiply decimals. Again, ask the children to approximate first (5 x 6 =30) and demonstrate how it is done on the OHP, uncovering the bottom half of 'Multiplication methods'. Stress that it is important that decimal points line up under each other and that the answer is close to the approximation. You may want to point out that if they count the total number of digits to the right of the decimal point in the numbers to be multiplied, there will be the same number of digits after the decimal point in the answer.

Paired work: Working in pairs, children will need a set of digit cards and a card with a decimal point. A child selects four digit cards and arranges them to make a multiplication sentence, which should also include the decimal point. Both children should work out the answer independently, then agree answers. The second child must then use the same cards to make a different multiplication sentence and predict whether this will give a larger or smaller answer than the previous sentence. Both children work out the answers and compare. If the child predicted correctly, s/he wins that point. They then shuffle the digit cards and repeat the process, taking it in turns to predict whether the second sum will be higher or lower than the first.

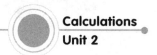
Differentiation

Less able: This group should use digit cards without the decimal point to make their sentences.
More able: Challenge this group to make a multiplication sentence with the highest or lowest total. They should check all possibilities using the digits chosen.

Plenary & assessment

Discuss whether predictions were correct. Ask: *How did you decide the order of digits?* Challenge children to find the highest multiplication total using the digits 1, 2, 3 and 4, multiplying a three-digit number by a one-digit number, first without a decimal point and then with a decimal point, for example: 4 x 321 = 1284, 4 x 32.1 =128.4.

Lesson ④

Starter

Children will need whiteboards and markers. Give quick-fire questions involving doubling and halving decimal fractions. For example, say: *Halve 1.26* (0.63) …*3.90* (1.95) …*8.06* (4.03) …*0.15* (0.075) *Double 0.85* (1.7) …*1.23* (2.46) …*1.8* (3.6) *and double again* (7.2). Discuss any difficulties. Remind children that this can be an effective strategy for mentally multiplying and dividing, for example by 2, 4, 8 and so on.

Main teaching activity

Whole class: Write 543 x 38 on the board. Work through the long multiplication as shown in the margin. Remind the children to approximate, then check the result after completing the long muliplication.

		5	4	3	
	x		3	8	
543 x 30	1	6	2	9	0
543 x 8		4	3	4	4
	2	0	6	3	4

Ask the children what the result of multiplying 54.3 x 38 would be. Point out that as 54.3 is ten times smaller than 543, the answer to the calculation 54.3 x 38 will be ten times smaller than 543 x 30 (2063.4) Ask: *What about 5.43?* Point out that in this example the answer will be 100 times smaller than 20,634 (206.34).

Individual work: Children should work independently through the 'Sponsored walk' activity sheet.

Differentiation

Less able: Give this group the version of 'Sponsored walk' with simpler calculations.
More able: This group should work through the 'Sponsored walk' activity sheet with more difficult calculations.

Plenary & assessment

Discuss methods children used for multiplication. Which calculations did they do mentally? What method did they use to check their answers? One strategy would be to total the amounts per mile and then multiply the total by the number of miles and check that this agrees with the totals.

Lesson ⑤

Starter

Explain that you will write a two-digit number on the board. Ask the children to double it as quickly as they can. Begin with, for example, 36 × 2, 47 × 2 and extend to decimals such as, 7.3 ×2, 0.94 ×2, 0.78 ×2. Ask for the methods chosen for each example and compare for efficiency and effectiveness.

Main teaching activity

Whole class: Remind children how to set out a short division sentence. Write on the board: 274 divide by 6. Ask children to approximate first (270 ÷ 5 = 54), then work through the example on the board and display the OHT of 'Division methods'.

Group work: Working in groups of four, children take turns to roll a ten-sided dice. They record all four digits then have 30 seconds to make up a division sentence, each of which must include a decimal point. First they approximate the answer to their own division sentence, then they calculate the answer. Next, they compare their answers – the winner is the child with the calculation that gives the highest (or lowest) answer (for example, 7, 3, 5 and 6 may give 35.6 ÷ 7 or 6 ÷ 7.35). They repeat this process.

Differentiation

Less able: Tell this group not to include a decimal point in their calculations, for example, 7, 3, 5 and 6 may give 356 ÷ 7 or 63 ÷ 75.

More able: Allow this group to use five digits and try with two decimal numbers, for example, 2, 7, 3, 5 and 6 may give 32.5 ÷ 7.6 or 6.25 ÷ 7.3.

Plenary & assessment

Look at some of the calculations the children have made. Discuss which division methods they used. Ask: *Which were quickest? How did it help you to approximate first?*

Name	Date

Choosing decimals

- Choose three numbers from different boxes and add them together. Remember to set the sum out as a column addition.
- Now choose three more numbers to make a sum.
- Make as many different sums as you can, using three numbers from different boxes every time.

Box A

3.2	5.1	9.3	7.8	4.8	4.7	2.9	8.6	6.4	7.7

Box B

12.5	20.5	32.7	40.3	65.2	98.4	12.3	74.8	82.1	56.3

Box C

215.6	330.4	306.8	999.4	868.4	704.3	550.1	199.9	412.2	603.7

Box D

19.25	39.19	98.12	80.03	64.01	39.22	10.04	98.78	86.31	78.77

| Name | | Date | |

Bean growth

Children in Class 8 have been growing beans.

Each child has measured his or her plant in centimetres. Their results are shown below.

	Ben	Rashid	Ali	Chris
Tuesday	0.35	0.9	0.4	0.25
Wednesday	1.4	1.35	1.02	0.98
Thursday	2.03	2.09	1.99	3.25
Friday	4.68	4.31	3.98	5.06
Monday	8.76	10.06	4.20	11.28

Complete the following table to show how much each plant grew each day.

	Ben	Rashid	Ali	Chris
Tues – Wed				
Wed – Thurs				
Thurs – Fri				
Fri – Mon				
Total growth Tues – Monday				

How much was the total growth for each day?

Tues – Wed _____

Wed – Thurs _____

Thurs – Fri _____

Fri – Mon _____

Shape and space

In this unit a number of shape and space objectives are revisited. Children are reminded how to calculate perimeters and areas, and of the importance of accuracy in measurement is stressed, especially when using protractors.

LEARNING OBJECTIVES

		Topics	Starter	Main teaching activity
Lesson	1	Shape and space Problems involving 'real life', money or measures	● Use known number facts and place value to consolidate mental addition/subtraction.	● **Calculate the perimeter and area of simple compound shapes that can be split into rectangles.** ● **Explain methods and reasoning.**
Lesson	2	Shape and space	● Classify quadrilaterals and other shapes.	● **Read and plot co-ordinates in all four quadrants.** ● Recognise where a shape will be after reflection. ● Recognise where a shape will be after two translations.
Lesson	3	Shape and space	● Visualise 3-D shapes from 2-D drawings and identify different nets for a closed cube.	● As for Lesson 2
Lesson	4	Shape and space	Use known number facts and place value to consolidate mental addition/subtraction.	● **Use a protractor to measure** and draw **acute and obtuse angles to nearest degree.** ● Recognise and estimate angles. ● Calculate angles in a triangle or around a point. ● Check that the sum of the angles of a triangle is 180°: for example, by measuring or paper folding.
Lesson	5			

Lessons overview

Preparation
Copy 'Finding perimeters and areas', 'Shape plots', 'Demonstrating angles' and 'Calculating angles' onto acetate.

Learning objectives
Starters
● Use known number facts and place value to consolidate mental addition/subtraction.
● Classify quadrilaterals and other shapes.
● Visualise 3-D shapes from 2-D drawings and identify different nets for a closed cube.
Main teaching activities
● **Calculate the perimeter and area of simple compound shapes that can be split into rectangles.**
● **Explain methods and reasoning.**
● **Read and plot co-ordinates in all four quadrants.**
● Recognise where a shape will be after reflection.
● Recognise where a shape will be after two translations.
● **Use a protractor to measure** and draw **acute and obtuse angles to nearest degree.**
● Recognise and estimate angles.
● Calculate angles in a triangle or around a point.
● Check that the sum of the angles of a triangle is 180°: for example, by measuring or paper folding.

Vocabulary
reflective symmetry, reflection, mirror line, angle, x-axis, y-axis, protractor, right angle, acute obtuse, reflex, sketch, draw, flat, line, base, rectangular, oblong, isosceles triangle

You will need:
Photocopiable pages
A copy of 'Shape plots' (pages 175–6) for each child.

CD Pages
OHTs of 'Finding perimeters and areas', 'Demonstrating angles' and 'Calculating angles'; an OHT of 'Shape plots', differentiated copies of 'What's the shape?' and 'What's the angle?' for each less able and more able child (see General resources).

Equipment
An OHP; protractors; squared paper; tracing paper; mirrors; if possible, a computer simulation program to demonstrate angle measuring, 1cm-squared grid paper.

Lesson ①

Starter

Play 'Flow chart'. Write on the board a series of instructions: (? + 5) x 100 +16 – 3 = ?. Call out a number to signify the first question mark, such as 13, and children have to follow the instructions and write their answer on their whiteboard ((13 + 5) x 100 +16 – 3 = 1813). Repeat with other starter numbers.

Main teaching activity

Whole class: Display part A of the 'Finding perimeters and areas' OHT. Point out the rectangle and remind the children that the perimeter of the rectangle is the sum of the lengths of each side, which can be written as 2L + 2B (where L = length, B = Breadth). Also, the area can be calculated by multiplying the length by the breadth of the rectangle (L x B). Ask the children to calculate the perimeter of the rectangle shown: (8 + 8 + 6 + 6) = 28cm. Point out that the units represent centimetres. Next, ask them to calculate the area 8 x 6, which is 48cm² – this time the units are square centimetres.

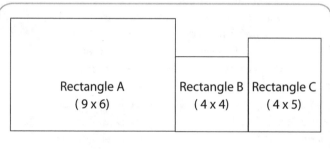

Rectangle A
(9 x 6)

Rectangle B
(4 x 4)

Rectangle C
(4 x 5)

Area = 54 + 16 + 20 = 90 sq. cm²

Explain that the area of a compound shape can be found by splitting it into rectangles, then finding the sum of the areas of the rectangles. Work through example on 'Finding perimeters and areas'. Point out that the length of the base line is 17. Discuss with the children how the shape could be divided into rectangles. Let them calculate the lengths of the unmarked sides, then ask them to tell you the area of each rectangle. Ask the children to calculate the perimeter; make sure that they realise that the perimeter is the perimeter of the whole shape and not the total of the perimeters of the three shapes (6 + 9 + 2 + 4 +1 + 4 + 5 +17 = 48cm). Ask how much more the total of the perimeters of the three shapes will be (point out that there are two sides of rectangle B which are common to each of the other two rectangles).

Paired work: Pair children of similar ability. Give them squared paper to start with and then progress to plain paper. Each child designs a shape that can be divided into rectangles, labelling the lengths of the sides of the main shape. They work out the area and perimeter (writing their calculations on a separate sheet of paper), then swap shapes with their partner and calculate the area and perimeter of this shape. When they have agreed their calculations they swap shapes with another pair and find the solutions.

Differentiation

Less able: This group should use squared paper and initially draw a shape that can be split into just two rectangles.

More able: Provide this group with plain paper and encourage them to draw more complex shapes. They should label as few sides as possible in order for their partner to calculate side lengths as well as area and perimeter.

Plenary & assessment

Compare the ways children have split the shapes into rectangles. Discuss how they calculated the lengths of sides which were not given. Show part C of the 'Finding perimeters and areas' OHT. Ask: *Can you find the perimeter?* (40 cm) *Can you find the area?* (5 x 8 + 3 x 6 + 4 x 3 = 40 + 18 + 12 = 70 cm²)

Ask children to explain how they calculated side lengths and why they divided the shapes as they did. They may choose to calculate the area of the rectangle (12 x 8) and then subtract the two smaller rectangles (3 x 2 and 4 x 5).

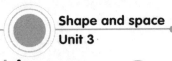
Lesson ②

Starter

Play 'What's the shape?' Emphasise identifying quadrilaterals – include square, rectangle, parallelogram, kite, trapezium, rhombus. Give clues. Children have to work out which quadrilateral the clues apply to, for example: *This shape has four sides. All four sides are of equal length. Opposite angles are equal. The diagonals bisect each other. One diagonal is longer than the other.* (rhombus)

Select a child and give them the name of a shape; they must then give clues to the rest of the class. Make sure that the children know the names and properties of all quadrilaterals.

Main teaching activity

Whole class: Explain to the children that they will be reading and plotting co-ordinates in all four quadrants. Using the OHT of the first sheet of 'Shape plots', remind children about the four quadrants and about the x and y co-ordinates. Point out that where the axes cross is the point 0, 0, which means that the value of the x co-ordinate is 0 and the value of the y co-ordinate is 0. Point to the point D in the top right quadrant and ask the children to give the co-ordinates (8, 3). Remind them that the x co-ordinate comes first. Point out that the value of all co-ordinates in this quadrant will always be positive. Ask: *What is the value of the point marked X in the top left quadrant?* (−2, 1) Ask what generalisation they can make about values of co-ordinates in this quadrant (x values are negative and y values are positive). Ask about values in the remaining two quadrants (bottom right: x positive, y negative; bottom left: both x and y negative).

Hand out copies of the first sheet of the 'Shape plots' activity. Ask the children to look at it carefully and label the co-ordinates for the points A (0,3), B (2,1), C (6,1) and D (8, 3), and then join the points ABC and D to make a quadrilateral. Ask them to name the quadrilateral (trapezium). Demonstrate on the OHP. Next, ask the children to mark the points (5, 7), (5, 4), and (3,3) and join them. Say: *Now join the point (5, 4) to the point (5,3).* (This will give the outline of a sailing boat.) Demonstrate on the OHP.

Individual work: Tell the children that you now want them to continue with the activity sheet and to plot the reflection of the shape in the y-axis. The first point X, which is already marked on the sheet, is the reflection of point B.

Hand out the second sheet of the activity. Children should use this to draw their own shape and plot its reflection. They should also extend the activity to include two translations.

Differentiation

Less able: This group should just reflect in one axis using 'Shape plots'.

More able: Encourage the more able group to draw more complex shapes and to calculate the co-ordinates of the reflection before drawing the translation.

Plenary & assessment

Show the OHT of the second sheet of the activity and ask a child to draw a simple shape in the bottom left quadrant. Then ask other children to come out and give the co-ordinates of the shape, and the co-ordinates of the shape reflected in the other three quadrants.

Lesson 3

Starter

Play 'What's the shape?' again, this time putting the emphasis on 3-D shapes. Show the children some 2-D drawings of these shapes and ask them to name them. Include shapes like cube, cuboid, cylinder, sphere, tetrahedron, Egyptian pyramid and various kinds of prism. Ask the children to draw possible nets for a closed cube on their whiteboards.

Main teaching activity

Whole class: Remind the children of the activities from the previous lesson and tell them that for this lesson you want them to plot their own shapes.

Paired work: Children work in pairs to plot their own shapes. They then give the co-ordinates of their shape to their partner to draw. The partner must then draw a reflection of the shape and tell the first child the co-ordinates of this shape for them to draw.

Differentiation

Less able: Suggest that the children keep to simple shapes. They should draw them first on plain paper and ensure that there are no more than four or five lines making up the outline. Make sure that they start with either a horizontal or a vertical line.

More able: Set the challenge for them to design shapes which do not have any vertical or horizontal lines.

Plenary & assessment

Show the second sheet of 'Shape plots' again. Draw a simple triangle with co-ordinates A (2, 3), B (4, 6) and C (4, 2). Say: *Give me the co-ordinates for A reflected in the y-axis. (–2, 3) …reflected in the x-axis. (2, –3)* Ask: *What would be the co-ordinates of A when reflected in the line x = 1? (0, 3).* If necessary, children can use tracing paper or a mirror to check this. Discuss the effect of reflecting in other mirror lines.

Lesson 4

Starter

Tell children you are looking for pairs of numbers that total 100. Give a number and ask the children to write their answer on their whiteboards. Give numbers such as 40, 70, 35 67. Remind them how to quickly calculate the number, for example, 35: add 5 to units to make 40, add 60 to reach 100, hence add 65.

Main teaching activity

Whole class: If possible, use a computer simulation program to demonstrate angle measuring. Show the OHT of 'Demonstrating angles'. Say: *Look at the angle A. Is it more or less than 90º?* (less) *So what sort of angle is it?* (acute) *Look carefully at the angle. You know how big 90º is, so can you estimate the size of this angle?* (30º) Point out that it is less than half of 90º.

Demonstrate how to use a protractor to measure an angle. Point out that the protractor must be positioned correctly, with the + placed accurately on the intersection of lines making the angle. Ensure that the measurement is done using the correct scale on the protractor. Say: *Look at angle B. Is this an acute angle?* (No, it is greater than 90º.) *Is it greater than 180º?* (No, so it is an obtuse angle.) Do the same with angle C (a reflex angle measuring 240º). Children should be able to recognise these angles, but if they do not, remind them of the terms acute, obtuse and reflex angles. Show the other examples if necessary: D is an acute angle measuring 65º, E is an obtuse angle measuring 98º, and F is an obtuse angle measuring 125º.

Say: *Draw a line 5cm long and label it AB. Now draw the next line starting at B, at an angle of 35° to the line AB. This line should be 8cm long. Now complete the triangle ABC. How long is BC? Measure the angle at B and the angle at C.*

Paired work: Explain to the children that they will be working in pairs on the 'What's the shape?' activity sheet. Supply each child with 1cm-squared paper to draw their shapes on. Each child draws a simple shape without showing their partner and labels the shape alphabetically in clockwise order. They follow the instructions on the sheet and then give the measurements to their partner to draw the shape. When the shapes are completed, children should compare them with the original design. If they are not the same, the children should measure each other's shapes and compare.

Differentiation

Less able: Provide this group with the less demanding version of the activity sheet.
More able: Provide this group with the more demanding version of the activity sheet.

Plenary & assessment

Ask children to show some of their shapes. Ask: *What did you find most difficult? How did you know if their measurements were correct?* Stress how important it is to measure accurately. Demonstrate how a variation of 1 or 2 degrees can make a big difference.

Lesson

Starter

Play 'Quick pairs', to revise two-digit pairs of numbers that total 100. You say a two-digit number up to 50 and children have to tell you the number that will make the total 100. Talk to the children about how they can use this knowledge to help them find pairs of numbers that total 90.

Main teaching activity

Whole class: Remind children that in the Spring Term they checked that the sum of the angles of a triangle is 180°, and explain that they are going to use this information to calculate the angles of a triangle. Show the OHT of 'Calculating angles' and point to A. Say: *If we know that the sum of the angles of a triangle is 180°, then 40 + 80 + C = 180, so angle C is 180° – (40 + 80)°, or 180° – 120°, which is 60°.*

Look at example B. Ask the children to work out what they think angle C is (55°), then ask a child to come and show his/her calculations. Work through some other examples if necessary. Now point to example C. Say: *Look at the point marked X. How big do you think the angle on the line is at that point?* (180°) If necessary, demonstrate by placing two right angles together.

Finally, look at example D and ask: *How big do you think this angle is?* Point out that it is the same as three right angles, so is 270°. Ask: *What would the size of the angle be if it continued all the way around the point?* Point out that it would be four right angles (360°). Explain that the sum of angles at a point is 360°.

Individual work: Children should complete the 'What's the angle?' activity sheet.

Differentiation

Less able: Provide this group with the less demanding version of the activity sheet.
More able: Provide this group with the more demanding version of the activity sheet.

Plenary & assessment

Discuss any difficulties. Go through the second part of the activity sheet and ask children to demonstrate how they calculated the angles.

Name   Date

Shape plots

1. Some points are marked on this grid, write down their co-ordinates,

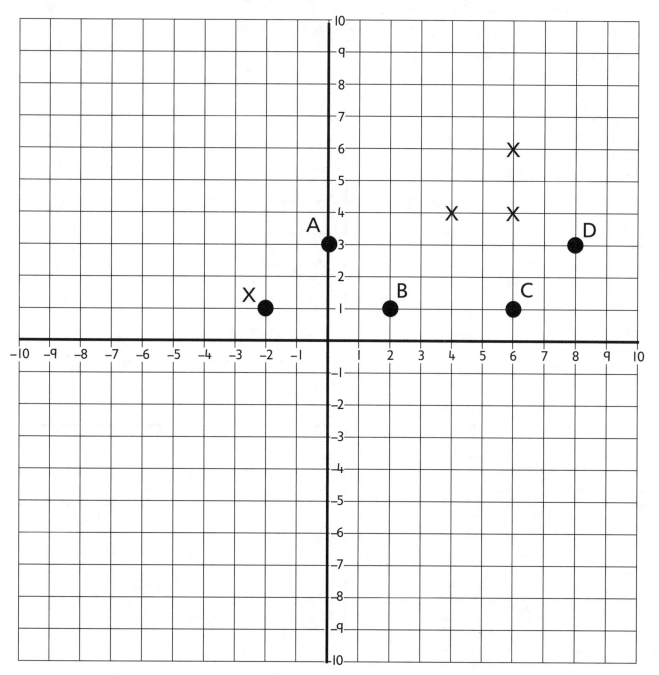

A _____ B _____ C _____ D _____ X _____

- Now mark the points (5, 7), (3, 4) and (5, 4).
- Finally, join the point (5, 7) to the point 5, 3.
- Plot the reflection of the shape through the y-axis (one point has been done for you).

Name	Date

Shape plots continued

2. On the grid below:

- draw a shape in the top left quadrant
- label the co-ordinates of the shape and then plot its translation 3 units to the right and 2 units down.
- label the co-ordinates of the translations.

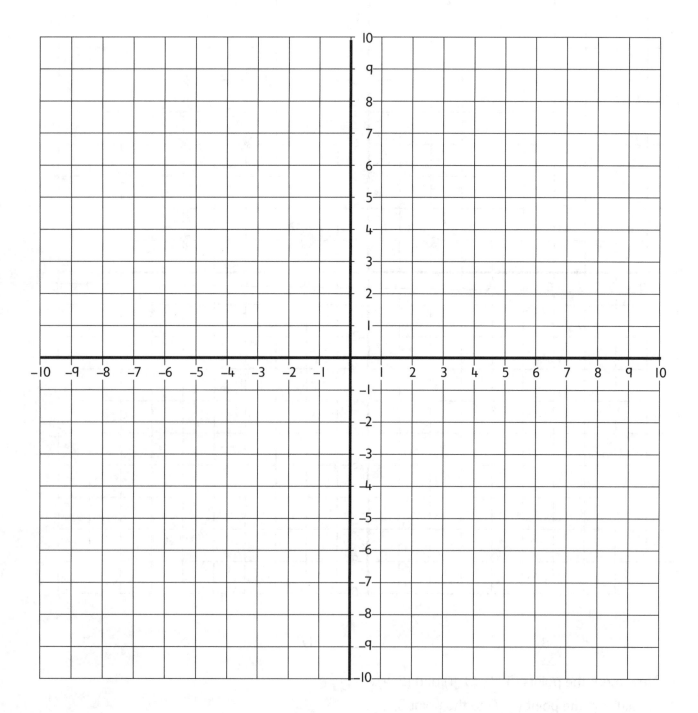

Problem solving 1

This is the first of two units based on a 'holiday' theme. After SATs this will give children the opportunity to apply their mathematics with a thematic approach. Many children will have experience of continental holidays, and they are asked to consider aspects of planning for a holiday abroad, including currency conversions.

LEARNING OBJECTIVES

	Topics	Starter	Main teaching activity
Lesson 1	Handling data	● Add several numbers mentally.	● **Solve a problem by** representing, **extracting and interpreting data in tables, graphs and charts** and diagrams including those generated by a computer. ● Find the mode and range of a set of data. Begin to find the median and mean of a set of data.
Lesson 2 Lesson 3	Handling data Problems involving 'real life', money or measures	● Read and write whole numbers in figures and words, and know what each digit represents. (Year 5)	● **Solve a problem by** representing, **extracting and interpreting data in tables, graphs and charts and diagrams including those generated by a computer**. ● Find the mode and range of a set of data. Begin to find the median and mean of a set of data. ● Use the language associated with probability to discuss events, including those with equally likely outcomes ● **Explain methods and reasoning.**
Lesson 4 Lesson 5	Measures Problems involving 'real life', money or measures	● Order a set of positive and negative integers.	● Know rough equivalents of lb and kg, oz and g, miles and km, litres and pints or gallons. ● **Identify and use appropriate operations (including combinations of operations) to solve word problems involving numbers** and quantities based on 'real life', money or measures (including time) using one or more steps, including converting pounds to foreign currency. ● **Explain methods and reasoning.**

Lesson overview

Preparation
Children will need data on weather from newspapers and other sources, including the Internet.

Learning objectives
Starters
● Add several numbers mentally.
Main teaching activities
● **Solve a problem by** representing, **extracting and interpreting data in tables, graphs and charts and diagrams including those generated by a computer**.
● Find the mode and range of a set of data. Begin to find the median and mean of a set of data.

Vocabulary
mode, mean, range, table, chart, diagram, data, database, statistics

You will need:
Photocopiable pages
A copy of 'What's the weather?' (page 182) for each child.

Equipment
Individual whiteboards and marker pens; access to the Internet for weather data; calculators; audio tape recorder.

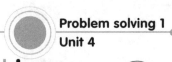
Lesson ①

Starter

Children will need a whiteboard each. Give them four numbers to add together. Ask them to write the answer on their whiteboard and show it. They then have to divide the total by four to find the mean, for example, 25, 14, 26 and 31: total = 96, mean = 24. Repeat this with different sets of numbers

Main teaching activity

Whole class: Explain to the children that over the next two weeks they will be looking at planning for a holiday in the sun. Today you will be checking weather information. Discuss where this kind of information may be obtained, for example, five-day weather forecasts for some cities in Europe can be obtained from CEEFAX (BBC1) and from the Internet.

	Daytime maximum	Night-time minimum
Monday	27	18
Tuesday	28	17
Wednesday	28	17
Thursday	30	19
Friday	26	14

Show the data in the table below and explain that this is the five-day weather forecast for Malaga for the first week in June. Ask children if they can remember how to find the mean maximum daytime temperature (add the five entries and then divide the total by five: total = 139, mean = 27.8). This will give the average or mean daytime temperature. Ask about the range of temperatures. Remind children that this is the difference between the greatest and least of the data (30 – 26 = 4). Remind them that the median is the middle value (28).

Go through the same process looking at the night-time temperatures

Paired work: Hand out copies of 'What's the weather?' and ask children to find the range, the mode and the mean for each data set. Working with a partner they should discuss what the weather would be like for the week.

Differentiation

Less able: This group should just work with one destination. Allow them to use a calculator. They may make a tape recording of their weather forecast rather than write it.
More able: Children in this group should ensure that they use all the information for their destination in their weather script.

Plenary & assessment

Ask the children to think about what the data tells them. Let some children read or play their weather forecaster's script. Compare scripts. Ask: *Have you interpreted the information in the same way? If there are differences, why? How might the script change if it was for a holiday programme promoting the resort?*

Lessons ② ③ overview

Preparation

Copy 'Malaga weather information' onto acetate to show on the OHP. Decide how children are going to gather data for the activity in Lesson 3.

Learning objectives

Starters

● Read and write whole numbers in figures and words, and know what each digit represents. (Year 5)

Main teaching activities

Solve a problem by representing, **extracting and interpreting data in tables, graphs and charts and diagrams including those generated by a computer.**

● Find the mode and range of a set of data. Begin to find the median and mean of a set of data.
● Use the language associated with probability to discuss events, including those with equally likely outcomes.
● **Explain methods and reasoning.**

Vocabulary

mode, mean, range, average, probability, risk, doubt, equally likely

You will need:

CD Pages
An OHT of 'Malaga weather information' and a copy for each child (see General resources).

Equipment
An OHP; materials for making posters.

Lesson ②

Starter

Ask the children to work with a partner. Explain that they will take turns to write the number that you say in numerals and in words. Say, for example: *One of you write the number 3947 in figures, the other one write it in words. Now check each others' answers. Do you agree?* For the next number the children swap roles. Use numbers such as 700,089; 9,456,013 and so on.

Main teaching activity

Whole class: Show the OHT of 'Malaga weather information'. Discuss what other weather information a holidaymaker would like to know about a holiday destination. Point out that weather forecasts are not infallible – they give an indication of the weather and enable us to decide on the probability of good weather. Ask probability questions related to the information, such as: *What is the probability of snow?* (unlikely) Go through the different probability terms, such as 'certain', 'likely', 'possible', 'unlikely', 'no chance', 'risk', 'doubt'. Some children may say that it is impossible to have snow, so point out that although it would be extremely unlikely, there is a possibility that there could be freak weather conditions, so it is not impossible. Ask children to give examples of conditions for the various terms, for example: *It is likely that it will be sunny every day in the first week in July. There is an even chance that Wednesday will be warmer than Tuesday. It is unlikely that London will be hotter than Malaga in September.* Remind children of terms such as 'equally likely' and 'even chance'. Ask for examples, such as: *There is an even chance that it might rain (or be sunny) today.*

Group work: Hand out the individual copies of 'Malaga weather information', plus copies of 'Holiday hotspots'. Children should pose questions for each other from the activity sheet. Encourage them to consider all the information they have been given.

Differentiation

Children should work in mixed-ability groups and should be encouraged to discuss the activity and explain their thinking. The teacher should join each group and pose questions such as: *How did you decide upon that question? What do you think the probability of a week with no rain will be?* Ensure that all children contribute by establishing ground rules for the mixed ability group: each child should pose a question and each must have the opportunity to answer and explain their reasoning.

Plenary & assessment

Discuss some of the questions that children have posed. Ask: *Is there any information which will enable you to predict a certain outcome? What more information would you need to be reasonably certain about the weather that you could expect on holiday?* (information over several months, years) *What is the likelihood that it will be hot and sunny in this week in July?* (likely, information from five-day forecast) *How will this kind of information help you when you plan a holiday? What other weather information would you like to have? Does everyone want the same kind of weather when they go on holiday?* Point out that some people don't like too much sun or heat.

Lesson ③

Repeat the **Starter** for Lesson 2. This time ask what specific digits in the numbers represent. For example, for 6,013,295, say: *What does 0 represent?*

In the **Main teaching activity**, explain that for this lesson you want the children to research a holiday destination of their own choice. Children will need access to weather data. This may be information they have collected for homework, or they could access data on a computer during the lesson.

Working in ability pairs or small groups, they should identify a holiday destination and look at the weather data that is available. Write the following instructions on the board.

● Choose a holiday destination and look at the weather information that you have available.
● Produce a poster giving as much weather information about your destination as you can.
● Include the range of temperatures that holidaymakers should expect for both daytime and night-time, as well as the expected mean temperatures.

Encourage children to present their information in the best way they can – this may involve graphs or charts.

Lower ability groups will need support in this activity. Encourage more able groups to use more complex graphs and charts to present their data.

For the **Plenary**, ask the children to present their group's information to the rest of the class.

Lessons   overview

Preparation
Copy and cut out the 'Digit (+ and –) and decimal point cards'.

Learning objectives
Starters
● Order a set of positive and negative integers.
Main teaching activities
● Know rough equivalents of lb and kg, oz and g, miles and km, litres and pints or gallons.
● **Identify and use appropriate operations (including combinations of operations) to solve word problems involving numbers and quantities** based on 'real life', money or measures (including time) using one or more steps, including converting pounds to foreign currency.
● **Explain methods and reasoning.**

Vocabulary
grid, axes, horizontal, vertical, money, pence, penny, pound (£), coin, note, label, title

You will need:
Photocopiable pages
A copy of 'Money matters' (page 183) for each child.

CD Pages
A set of 'Digit (+ and –) and decimal point cards' for each pair (see General resources Spring term); differentiated versions of 'Money matters' for each less able and more able child.

Equipment
1cm-squared paper.

Lesson

Starter
Explain that you will write a list of integers onto the board, including negative numbers. Write up, for example, –25, 8, 15, –31, –14. Ask the children to order these, lowest number first. Repeat for other examples, such as 21, –21, 13, 27, –4, –19.

Main teaching activity
Whole class: Tell the children that if we are travelling abroad we need to be able to convert currency as well as metric and imperial units. Remind them that we tend to measure in miles, but in Europe they use kilometres. We use pounds sterling, but much of Europe uses Euros.

Explain that they are going to draw a conversion graph to help them to convert kilometres into miles and vice versa. If we know that 100km = 62 miles, we can easily draw a conversion graph. Draw the axes of the graph on the board (see diagram below). Say: *We are going to label the vertical axis miles, and put in the values from 0 to 100, in steps of 10. The horizontal axis will be kilometres from 0 to 100. We know that 0km = 0 miles, so we can mark the point 0.0. We also know that 100km = 62miles.*

Ask a child to show you where 100km is on the horizontal axis, and where 62 miles is on the vertical axis. Say: *This gives us the point on the graph where we know the values are equal. We can now draw a line from 0, 0 to 100, 62. At any point on that line we can find the relative values for kilometres and miles.*

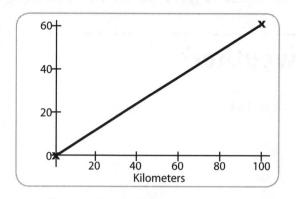

Demonstrate finding values for conversions from kilometres to miles and vice versa. Ask children to come out and find conversion values. Check that they are able to convert from kilometres to miles and vice versa.

Individual/paired work: Children should work individually or in pairs to draw their own conversion graphs, then answer the questions on 'Money matters' related to the graph. Remind children that there are 100 cents in one Euro, and that this makes conversion simpler. They then make up conversion questions to ask their partner.

Differentiation

Less able: Give this group the version of 'Money matters' where the conversion rate chosen is simpler (1.4 Euros to the pound) and the questions are amounts that will convert easily using the graph.

More able: Give this group the version of 'Money matters' where the questions are more complex and involve amounts outside the range of the graph. Children will have to break these amounts down in order to convert them. There is also a further challenge asking how to convert smaller amounts of currency, which may involve a second graphs with a smaller scale.

Plenary & assessment

Discuss any difficulties that the children have had. Ask children how they could convert a larger amount of currency, such as £350 (it could be broken down into smaller amounts). Ask: *How would you convert values less than £1. Would the graph you have drawn be accurate enough?* Suggest to children that they draw another graph for values up to £1. Ask them to suggest the values to use and invite a child to draw the graph on the board. Use this to convert small amounts of money, such as 35p or 28 cents.

Lesson ⑤

Repeat the **Starter** for Lesson 4. This time draw an empty number line on the board, and mark the mid-point zero. Invite children to plot the positive and negative integers that you write on the line.

For the **Main teaching activity**, discuss with children what other conversation graphs we may need for the holiday (pounds to kilograms, degrees Celsius to degrees Fahrenheit). Ask the children what the approximate conversation for kg to lbs would be (approximately 2.2lbs = 1kg). Ask them to suggest how they could use this information to draw a conversion graph.

Children should work with their groups from Lesson 4 to prepare other conversion graphs for the holiday destination they have chosen. This may include other currency graphs. You might like to let the children look at other currencies. For the **Plenary**, children should show their graphs and calculate conversions suggested by the rest of the group.

Name	Date

What's the weather?

Here are some five-day weather forecasts for some cities in Europe.

Lisbon

Maximum	27	28	29	30	26
Minimum	13	15	19	17	16

Amsterdam

Maximum	21	22	23	25	23
Minimum	4	10	11	12	13

Rome

Maximum	25	26	26	21	25
Minimum	14	16	17	18	17

Athens

Maximum	27	27	28	28	24
Minimum	18	15	18	19	17

● Calculate the mean, mode and range for each city, for both the maximum and minimum temperatures.

	mean	mode	range
Lisbon Maximum			
Lisbon Minimum			
Amsterdam Minimum			
Amsterdam Maximum			
Rome Maximum			
Rome Minimum			
Athens Maximum			
Athens Maximum			

● Choose one destination and write a script for the television weather forecaster to describe the expected weather for the week.

Name   Date

Money matters

The exchange rate for pounds to Euros fluctuates.
Using a rate of 1.44 Euros to the pound, draw a conversion graph for values up to £100.00

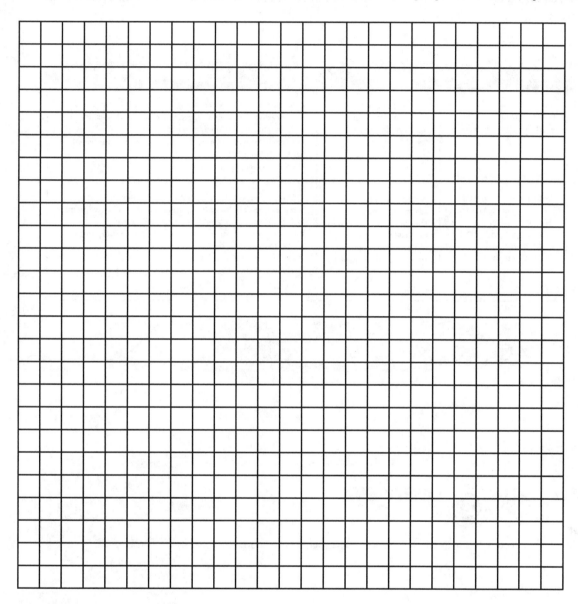

Use your graph to solve these problems.

1. John has £55 sterling. How many Euros will he get in exchange? _____

2. The hotel bill comes to 146 Euros. How much is this in sterling, to the nearest pound? _____

3. The restaurant bill is 37 Euros. What would this cost in pounds sterling? _____

4. Make up some conversion questions for your partner to solve.

_____

_____

Problem solving 2

This unit is based on a holiday theme and is continued from Unit 4. Children develop their own holiday project file, costing a holiday from one or more brochures and comparing alternative brochures and independent travel. Children should be encouraged to research their own information and to access the Internet for travel and hotel costs in order to make comparisons.

LEARNING OBJECTIVES

	Topics	Starter	Main teaching activity
Lesson 1 / Lesson 2	Handling data Problems involving 'real life', money and measures	● Use known number facts and place value to consolidate mental calculations.	● **Solve a problem** by representing **extracting and interpreting data in tables, graphs, charts** and diagrams, including those generated by a computer. ● **Identify and use appropriate operations to solve word problems based on 'real life'.** ● **Explain methods and reasoning.**
Lesson 3 / Lesson 4 / Lesson 5	Problems involving 'real life', money or measures Handling data Solving problems Fractions, decimals, percentages, ration and proportion	● **Order a mixed set of numbers** or measurements **with up to three decimal places.** ● Consolidate rounding an integer to the nearest 10, 100 or 1000.	● **Solve a problem** by representing **extracting and interpreting data in tables, graphs and charts** and diagrams, including those generated by a computer. ● **Identify and use appropriate operations to solve word problems** based on 'real life'. ● **Explain methods and reasoning.** ● **Solve simple problems involving ratio and proportion.**

Lessons   overview

Preparation
Copy 'Beauty villas' onto acetate to use as an OHT. Collect travel brochures and copy extracts if needed.

Learning objectives
Starters
● Use known number facts and place value to consolidate mental calculations.
Main teaching activities
● **Solve a problem** by representing **extracting and interpreting data in tables, graphs and charts** and diagrams, including those generated by a computer.
● **Identify and use appropriate operations to solve word problems** based on 'real life'.
● **Explain methods and reasoning.**

Vocabulary
discount, price, cost, buy, bought, sell, sold, spend, spent, pay, change, dear, costs more, more/most expensive, cheap, costs less, cheaper, less/least expensive, how much…?, how many …?, total, amount, value

You will need:
CD Pages
An OHT of 'Beauty villas'; a copy of 'Best buy holidays' for each child and differentiated copies for each less able and more able child (see General resources)

Equipment
An OHP; a holiday brochure (or copies of details from brochures) for each child.

Lesson

Starter

Give the children a target number such as 353. The aim is to find a product of two numbers that is as close as possible to the target number. You may allow some children to use a calculator. Let children compare their suggestions to see which is the closest and explain the mental calculations they used. Repeat.

Main teaching activity

Whole class: Explain to the children that they are going to be looking at holiday brochures and working out how to cost a holiday. Display the OHT of 'Beauty villas', showing the first page of the two extracts from the holiday brochure. Ask the children to look carefully at the first extract, showing prices for 'Beauty villas'. Point out that in this brochure the dates are written across the top of the table, and information for one bedroom (four adults sharing, then for the first child and the second child) is given on the left-hand side, with prices for seven nights and 14 nights. Point out that it is important to read the 'small print' to find conditions for child discounts and any supplements that may be payable.

Ask: *Who can give me the price for two adults staying seven nights with a departure between 13 December and 14 December?* The answer £259 per person will probably be given, but point out that this is in an apartment for four people, so if only two people stay there they will have to pay an under-occupancy supplement. There are three rates for supplements, depending upon whether it is high, medium or low season; this holiday is low season, so the supplement is £2 per person per night. Ask: *How much extra is that for each person for a week?* (£14) So, this increases the cost per person to £273.

Explain that there are often reductions for children, with the first child usually being the cheapest. Ask: *Who can give me the price that this family would have to pay to take their two children with them for that week?* (first child £99, second child £99 = £198)

Individual work: Give each child a copy of 'Best buy holidays'. Remind them to read the information carefully and to make sure they calculate and include any supplements that are payable. Answers will vary depending on the choices of dates, locations, types of board required and sleeping arrangements. Children will need to show you their workings out as there will be many permutations!

Differentiation

Less able: Give this group the version of 'Best buy holidays' where they are directed towards a particular holiday and have fewer decisions to make and simpler calculations.
More able: Give this group the more demanding version of 'Best buys holidays' where they have to calculate different alternatives in order to find the most economical, and which also includes an extension activity.

Plenary & assessment

Go through the answers for each version of the activity sheet and discuss any difficulties. Display the whole of the 'Beauty villas' OHT and ask the children what differences they notice with the way the information is presented in the second table from the first. (Dates are down the side and there are different accommodation options and different holiday length options.)

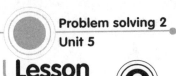

Lesson ②

Starter
Repeat the Starter from Lesson 1, but stipulate that the answer must be the product of two two-digit numbers.

Main teaching activity
Whole class: Hand out details from holiday brochures to each child. Tell them that today they will choose a holiday and cost it from the brochures they have. The holiday must be for a family of two adults and two children and they must be sure to include all the necessary extras such as insurance and any flight supplements. Remind them to read the information carefully, especially the 'small print'. Point out that they may have to look in different places in the brochure for information such as the cost of insurance and the flights.

Individual work: Explain to the children that when they have identified 'their holiday' they should make a leaflet giving as much information as possible about their chosen holiday destination. It should include the cost for their family holiday and show how this is made up.

Differentiation
Less able: Limit the choice of destination for this group and provide them with data for that particular area.

More able: The task for this group should be more open ended. Encourage them to consider a range of possibilities and to justify their choices.

Plenary & assessment
Look at the different holiday brochures that children have used and compare the way in which information is presented. Discuss different holiday destinations that have been chosen and other ways of travelling to these destinations.

Lessons ③ ④ ⑤ overview

Preparation
Copy 'Ferry crossings and mileage information' onto acetate to use as an OHT. Collect travel brochures and copy extracts if needed. Prepare a list of Internet sites for children to visit to find prices of flights, hotels, car hire and so on.

Learning objectives
Starters
● **Order a mixed set of numbers** or measurements **with up to three decimal places.**
● Consolidate rounding an integer to the nearest 10, 100 or 1000.
Main teaching activities
As for Lessons 1 and 2 plus:
● **Solve simple problems involving ratio and proportion.**

Vocabulary
as for lessons 1 and 2.

You will need:
CD Pages
An OHT of 'Ferry crossings and mileage information', plus a copy for each child (see General resources); a copy of 'Which ferry' and 'How far is it?' for each child and differentiated copies for each less able and more able child.

Equipment
An OHP; whiteboards and pens; atlases; computers to access the Internet.

Lesson 3

Starter

Write a set of mixed numbers onto the board, such as: 4.37, 14.2, 6.97, 6.9. Ask the children to order these largest to smallest. Repeat for another set, including up to three decimal places, such as 6.665, 6.656, 6.566, 6.576. This time ask the children to order these smallest to largest. Repeat for other sets of numbers.

Main teaching activity

Whole class: Explain to the children that they have looked at costing package holidays, but many people prefer to travel independently. In this lesson they will be looking at costing ferry crossings. Ask the children about any channel crossings they know about (eg Dover – Calais, Portsmouth – Le Havre). Discuss which are the shortest and the longest, and reasons why people may choose a longer route rather than the quickest. Consider where the starting points are in the UK.

Show the first part of the 'Ferry crossings and mileage information' OHT with costs for Dover – Calais and Poole – Cherbourg. Talk about the way the information is presented, reminding children that they need to read everything, as the overall price is usually made up of several different parts, for example the cost for a vehicle, adult and child passengers. Discuss the reasons why the prices vary at different times of the year. You may work through some examples of costs if you feel the children need support.

Individual/paired work: Give children the 'Which ferry?' activity sheet and a copy of 'Ferry crossings and mileage information'. Tell them they will need to refer to the latter for the prices for the activity. Point out that they must read the 'small print'. Children may work independently or in pairs to complete the activity.

Differentiation

Less able: Give this group the version of 'Which ferry?' that guides them through the task.
More able: This group should work from the more demanding version of 'Which ferry?', which asks them for two different routes and to cost alternative routes.

Plenary & assessment

Go through the answers to the activity sheet and ask children to explain their calculations. Make sure that they have included all parts of the costing and used the correct prices. Ask them to explain how they built up the cost of the ferry. Work through one example, asking children to contribute at each stage. Ask questions such as: *How many passengers are there? How many are children under 15? Is the driver included in the cost for the car? Is the cost of the return leg the same as the outward leg? Would there be any savings if the family travelled back in September?*

Lesson 4

Starter

Ask the children to round the following integers to the nearest 10: 396, 9945, 101,345. Repeat this for rounding to the nearest 100.

Main teaching activity

Whole class: Continuing from Lesson 3, show the OHT of 'Ferry crossings and mileage information', focussing on the mileage charts at the end of the sheet. Discuss the different ferry routes and identify them on a map. Point out that when deciding which ferry route to take, people usually consider the mileage involved on either side of the ferry journey. Some people may like to drive longer distances and have a shorter ferry journey, and the mileage costs will vary depending upon the vehicle.

Consider a trip for a family from Bristol to Faro in Portugal. Tell the children you are going to calculate how many miles driving there would be if the family used the Dover – Calais route. Ask: *How many miles is it from Bristol to Dover?* (206) *…and then from Calais to Faro?* (1293) So the total mileage is 1499 miles. Ask the children how much the overland cost would be if the average costs per mile is 20p for their car. Invite a child to explain how to work this out (1499 x 20p = £299.80). Remind children to think about the method for calculation and to choose the most suitable – in this example it is easiest to say 1500 x20p = £300 and then take away 20p.

Individual/paired work: Give children the 'How far is it?' activity sheet and a copy of 'Ferry crossings and mileage information'. Children may work independently or in pairs to complete the activity.

Differentiation

Less able: Give this group the version of 'How far is it?' where the cost per mile is given as 20p, making an easier calculation. Children may need help identifying the distances when using the mileage chart.
More able: This group should work from the more demanding version of 'How far is it?', where calculations are more difficult and they are asked to calculate additional alternative routes.

Plenary & assessment

Discuss the costs of the various routes and make sure that children understand that the mileage costs given are based on average fuel consumption for the vehicle. Discuss what other costs would have to be taken into account, for example overnight accommodation on the longer routes.

Lesson ⑤

Starter

Repeat the Starter for Lesson 4, this time including rounding to the nearest 1000. Write a list of numbers on the board and ask the children to round each to the nearest 10, 100 and 1000.

Main teaching activity

Whole class: Explain to the children that they will continue working on their holiday brochures.
Paired/group work: Working in pairs or small groups they should use the information that they have been looking at in the previous lessons to plan their overland route to the holiday destination of their choice. They will need to refer to maps to find driving distances. They should choose their ferry route and cost the journey accordingly. They should add the information to the holiday booklet they are producing on the destination of their choice. It may be necessary for them to research other ferry routes, for example from Barcelona to Majorca, which will be available on the Internet or from holiday brochures.

Differentiation

Less able: Work with this group to help them decide which route to choose. Direct them towards the appropriate costings and the rate per mile that they should use.
More able: Encourage this group to extend the activity by researching other routes and comparing costs. They may research the cost of rail or air travel to their chosen destination.

Plenary & assessment

Discuss any difficulties that children have had. Give some questions based on the information sheet, such as, *How far is it from Manchester to Bordeaux, via Portsmouth?* and work through, ensuring that all the children understand. Give examples of the various routes. Discuss, pointing out that although one may be shorter in miles the ferry crossing is much longer.

Division, decimals and problem-solving

This unit is designed to make children think and apply logical thinking. It does not initially look like the 'conventional' maths that they are used to, and also allows children to extend investigations to their own level of ability. There are a number of activities that involve children interpreting information and making deductions.

LEARNING OBJECTIVES

	Topics	Starter	Main teaching activity
Lesson 1	Handling data Problem solving	● **Derive quickly division facts corresponding to multiplication tables up to 10 x 10.**	● **Solve a problem by extracting and interpreting information presented in tables, graphs and charts.**
Lesson 2			● Solve mathematical problems or puzzles, recognise and explain patterns and relationships, generalise and predict. Suggest extensions asking 'What if?'
Lesson 3	Reasoning and generalising about numbers and shapes	● Give pairs of factors for whole numbers to 100.	● Develop from explaining a generalised relationship in words to expressing it in a formula, using letters as symbols.
Lesson 4	Problem solving	● **Order a mixed set of numbers with up to three decimal places.**	● Solve mathematical problems or puzzles, recognise and explain patterns and relationships, generalise and predict. Suggest extensions asking 'What if?'
Lesson 5	Problem solving	● Recognise prime numbers to at least 20.	As for Lesson 4.

Lessons   overview

Preparation
Copy the 'Favourite snacks' sheet onto acetate to show on the OHP.

Learning objectives
Starters
● **Derive quickly division facts corresponding to multiplication tables up to 10 x 10.**
● Give pairs of factors for whole numbers to 100.
Main teaching activities
● **Solve a problem by extracting and interpreting information presented in tables, graphs and charts.**
● Develop from explaining a generalised relationship in words to expressing it in a formula, using letters as symbols.

Vocabulary
square number, one squared, two squared

You will need:
Photocopiable pages
A copy of 'High street kids' (page 194) for each child.

CD Pages
An OHT of 'Favourite snack'; differentiated versions of 'High Street kids' for each less able and more able child, and a copy of 'High Street kids' template for each less able child (see General resources).

Equipment
An OHP; whiteboards and marker pens.

Lesson ①

Starter

Ask the children to write the answers to the following questions on their whiteboards: *Divide 4.8 by 6.* (0.8)
How many sevens in 35? (7) *What is one twentieth of 380?* (19) *What is 9 multiplied by 0.7 divided by 3?* (2.1)
Check the answers and then ask each child to devise a question involving division which can be solved
mentally. They should then give it to their partner to solve.

Main teaching activity

Whole class: Explain to the children that they are going to be solving problems, but they will be
given some information to help them. Show the 'Favourite snacks' problem on the OHP and ask a
child to read out the information. Explain that from the clues it is possible to deduce information in
order to solve the problem.

Say: *It is useful to draw a grid and mark on the grid the information that you are given and what you
can deduce from that information.* Go through the problems with the children, ticking and crossing
the relevant boxes as you go. Say: *From the first piece of information, we know that one of the boys is
called Jon Smith, so we can tick the box for Jon Smith. This means that we can put crosses in some of the
other boxes, because if Jon's name is Smith it cannot be Brown or Moore and similarly, neither Ben nor
Sam can be Smith. Jon Smith doesn't like crisps, so his snack cannot be crisps, nor does he like football, so
his sport cannot be football, so we can put crosses in two more boxes.*

We are next told that Ben's favourite snack is chocolate. Ask: *Which box can we tick?* Remind
children that this means that neither Sam's nor Jon's snack is chocolate. Ask: *Which other two boxes
can we cross?* (Ben – biscuits and crisps) We now know that Jon Smith's snack can't be chocolate or
crisps, so it must be biscuits (so we can tick this box), which means that Sam's snack must be crisps
(so we can tick this box). We are also told that Brown is the rugby ace, which means he does not play
cricket or football, and Moore and Smith do not play rugby.

The final clue is that the first name of Moore is not Sam, which means it must be Ben, hence
we have Jon Smith and Ben Moore, so Sam's name must be Brown. We know that Sam (Brown) has
crisps for his snack and Jon Smith has biscuits, so Ben Moore must have chocolate. We know that
Sam Brown is the rugby ace and Jon (Smith) doesn't play football, so he must play cricket, which
means that Ben Moore must play football. So we have found out that Ben Moore eats chocolate and
plays football, Jon Smith eats biscuits and plays cricket and Sam Brown eats crisps and plays rugby.

Paired work: Tell the children that you want them to work together on the 'High Street kids' activity
sheet. Point out that sometimes they will be given information that they may not need in order to
solve the problem – they have to select the relevant information.

Differentiation

Less able: The activity sheet for this group has fewer criteria, limiting the amount of information
needed.

More able: Give this group the more complex version of the activity sheet, with five different sets
of data and some extra information. They have to decide which facts are relevant to the task.

Plenary & assessment

Ask children from the lower-ability group to demonstrate how they solved their problem. Share the
solutions of the other two groups, discussing any difficulties.

Lesson

Starter

Write a selection of at least ten number properties on the board, such as: a square number, a triangular number, a prime number between 10 and 50, an even number that is a multiple of 7, an odd number that is not a multiple of three, a factor of 64, a prime number greater than 50, a multiple of both 9 and 4, a number divisible by both 3 and 5.

Tell the children to draw a 3 x 2 grid. They write a number corresponding with one of the properties in each section of the grid. Children then swap grids with their partner. Call out the different properties and children have to mark off on their grid any numbers that match the properties.

Main teaching activity

Whole class: Remind children that in the previous lesson they solved problems from given facts. Today you want them to design their own problem, following the pattern of the one they had been doing. Remind them that the problem should involve having to deduce information. Suggest that they start with the solution and then think of how they can present some of the information. They will complete this activity in the next lesson, so they only need to make a start on it in this lesson.
Group/paired work: Children can work in pairs or small groups to design their problem. When they are happy with their problem they should give it to another pair to solve.

Differentiation

Less able: Give this group the blank template version of 'High Street kids' to complete first. If they are able to do this they should then start to design their own problem.
More able: Encourage this group to include superfluous information in order to make their problem more complex. For example, use extra adjectives: 'the tall girl', 'the boy with black hair'.

Plenary & assessment

Ask one pair or group to show their problem so far. Let the class discuss how to solve it. Make sure that the children understand how each piece of information 'feeds into' the whole picture. Ask them to suggest other ways the information could be presented.

Lesson

Starter

Write 72 on the board. Ask the children to write down as many pairs of factors of 72 as they can in one minute. At the end of the time, ask for suggestions of factors and write these on the board. Encourage the children to check that nothing has been missed out. Repeat for 84.

Main teaching activity

Whole class: Revise the work covered in Unit 11, lesson 5, showing that in mathematics, relationships between numbers can be written using symbols and often letters of the alphabet, and that these are often used in simple formula to help us with certain rules and calculations, for example, area of a rectangle = length x width ($a = l \times w$).
Group work: Children work in pairs and play the missing number (h) game to check they remember the rules about using letters and symbols. Ask them to make up statements and give them a formula, for example: *Add 5 to the missing letter.* ($h + 5$) *Take the missing number away from 8.* ($8 - h$) Square the missing number. (h^2 or $h \times h$) Halve the missing number. ($h \div 2$)

Differentiation

Less able: Work with this group to assist with correct recording.
More able: Challenge the children to replace 'n' with a number and work out solutions, as per the example shown n the night.

if n = 4
n + 5 = 9
8 - n = 4
n² = 16
n ÷ 2 = 2

Plenary & assessment

Check how the children have converted a statement into a formula. Collect examples. Ask the more able group to share some of their answers with the class as well.

Lessons   overview

Preparation
Copy 'Happy and sad numbers' and 'The farmer and his cows' activity sheets onto acetate to show on the OHP.

Learning objectives
Starters
- **Order a mixed set of numbers with up to three decimal places.**
- Recognise prime numbers to at least 20.

Main teaching activities
- Solve mathematical problems or puzzles, recognise and explain patterns and relationships, generalise and predict. Suggest extensions asking 'What if?'

Vocabulary
predict, pattern, strategy, prime

You will need:
CD Pages
OHTs of 'Happy and sad numbers' and 'The farmer and his cows', a copy of 'Happy and sad numbers' and 'The farmer and his cows' for each child and differentiated copies for each less able and more able child (see General resources).

Equipment
An OHP; whiteboards and marker pens; counters or other 'counting' objects for pairs of less able children; a one hundred square for each child.

Lesson

Starter
Ask the children to write down ten decimal numbers, each with three digits. They should then pass their list to their partner who must write them in ascending order.

Choose two children to give you one of their numbers. Then ask the other children to give you one of their numbers which is between these two numbers and very close to one of them. Let the children decide which is the closest and order any other numbers that have been suggested.

Main teaching activity
Whole class: Give each child a copy of 'Happy and sad numbers'. Explain that in order to do the activity they will be investigating different numbers to find out whether they are happy or sad. Display the activity sheet on the OHP and go through the example with the class: *Starting with 32, we need to square each of the digits: 3 (to get 9) and 2 (to get 4). We then add together 9 and 4 to get 13. Then, continuing from 13, the squares of 1 and 3 are 1 and 9, added together give 10. Continuing from 10, the sum of the squares of 1 and 0 is 1. As we have reached 1 this is the end of the chain, so 32 is a happy number. Some numbers seem to go round in circles. These are called sad numbers.*
Work through the process for 14, asking the children to work out each step: 14 gives 1 + 16 = 17, then 1 + 49 = 50, 25 + 0 = 25, 4 + 25 gives 29, 4 + 81 = 85, 64 + 25 = 89, 64 + 81 = 145, 1 + 16 + 25 = 42, 16 + 4 = 20, 4 + 0 = 4, 16, 1 + 36 = 37, 9 + 49 = 58, 25 + 64 = 89, which 'loops back' into the chain. Hence, 14 is a sad number.

Ask: *From these two chains, can you tell me any other numbers that you know will be either happy or sad?* Children may suggest that all numbers in the chain will be happy if the starting number is happy, and all the numbers will be sad if the starting number is sad. If they do not notice this, draw it to their attention, hence: 32, 13 and 10 are all happy; 14, 17, 50, 25, 29, 85, 89, 145, 42, 20, 4, 16, 37 and 58 are all sad.

Individual work: Children should continue with the investigation using their own copies of 'Happy and sad numbers'. Some children may wish to extend the investigation further.

Differentiation

Less able: Children should work in pairs, and start by investigating only the numbers up to 10.

More able: These children should be encouraged to look for patterns and to try and predict which numbers will be happy.

Plenary & assessment

Discuss the strategies that the children used. Did they notice that there were pairs of numbers, for example if 32 is happy then 23 must also be happy, and if 14 is sad then 41 must also be sad? Did they notice any patterns in the investigation? Talk to children about investigative techniques. Remind them that an investigation can be ongoing.

Lesson

Starter

Write the integers 1 to 20 on the board. For each of these invite the children to say whether the number is a multiple or is prime. Where the number is a multiple ask the children to say the multiplication fact.

Main teaching activity

Whole class: Point out to the children that when they are carrying out an investigation there is often more than one 'answer' and there may be different ways to take the investigation forward. They should be asking the question 'What if?' Remind them that in the 'Happy and sad numbers' investigation they could stop at the stage where they feel they have found out something, or they may like to investigate other possibilities.

Show the 'Farmer and his cows' activity sheet on the OHP and explain to the children that they may use models or symbols to help them investigate the problem. Encourage children to pose questions and look for alternatives, such as 'What if there were more fields?'

Individual work: Some children may like to continue investigating 'Happy and sad numbers'. Alternatively, they can work through the 'Farmer and his cows' activity sheet.

Differentiation

Less able: It is helpful to provide some apparatus, such as counters, for the children to work with so that they can physically move the 'cows' from field to field.

More able: The more demanding version of the activity sheet includes suggestions for children to extend this investigation. There are a number of 'open' questions which enable them to investigate a wide range of possibilities.

Plenary & assessment

Discuss the children's solutions. Can they think of any variations to the problem, for example, more cows in each field? Ask the children to suggest a variation and work through it as a class. Ask questions such as: *For the farmer to see the largest number of sheep from each window, which fields need to have the most sheep?* (the corner fields) *What about if he wants to see the fewest sheep?* (corner fields should have fewest sheep) *Why do you think the number of sheep in the corner fields is the most important?* (the corner fields are seen from two windows)

Name	Date

High Street kids

Only three bikes were hired from the Bike Hire shop on High Street on a sunny Sunday in June.

From the clues given below, can you work out the name of the boys who hired the bike at each of the three times and how long they kept each bike? Use the table below to help you sort out the information. Remember to complete as many boxes as you can.

- The city bike went out for 45 minutes.
- Peter went out for a shorter time than the boy who hired the bike at 10.30am.
- The racing bike which was hired at 1.15pm was out longer than Ali's bike, which was not the mountain bike.

	Ali	Peter	Rick	Racing bike	Mountain bike	City bike	30 mins	45 mins	60 mins
10.30a.m									
1.15p.m.									
2.00p.m.									
30 mins									
45 mins									
60 mins									
Racing bike									
Mountain bike									
City bike									

Write your solution in the boxes below.

Name	Departure time	Bike	Duration

Summer term
Unit 6b
Perimeter, area, calculation and problem-solving

This unit brings together work that children have done in previous units. It is based on real-life situations involving scale drawing and simple plans. Children have to make decisions about layouts and cost different options.

LEARNING OBJECTIVES

	Topics	Starter	Main teaching activity
Lesson 1	Shape and space Pencil and paper procedures (+ and −)	● Calculate the perimeter and area of simple compound shapes that can be split into rectangles.	● Calculate the perimeter and area of simple compound shapes that can be split into rectangles. ● Extend written methods to column addition and subtraction of numbers involving decimals.
Lesson 2	Problems involving 'real life', money and measures	● Use known number facts and place value to consolidate mental multiplication and division.	● Identify and use the appropriate operations (including combinations of operations) to solve word problems involving numbers and quantities. ● Explain methods and reasoning.
Lesson 3 Lesson 4 Lesson 5	Shape and space Problems involving 'real life', money and measures	● Recognise squares of numbers to at least 12 x 12.	● Calculate the perimeter and area of simple compound shapes that can be split into rectangles. ● Identify and use the appropriate operations (including combinations of operations) to solve word problems involving numbers and quantities and ● Explain methods and reasoning.

Lessons   overview

Preparation
Prepare an OHT of 'Super playground design'. Collect pricelists for garden/playground materials. Measure playground or site to be redesigned. Prepare a list of Internet sites for children to visit to find prices of materials, plants etc.

Learning objectives
Starters
● **Calculate the perimeter and area of simple compound shapes that can be split into rectangles.**
● Use known number facts and place value to consolidate mental multiplication and division.
● Recognise squares of numbers to at least 12 x 12.
Main teaching activities
● **Calculate the perimeter and area of simple compound shapes that can be split into rectangles.**
● **Extend written methods to column addition and subtraction of numbers involving decimals.**
● **Identify and use the appropriate operations (including combinations of operations) to solve word problems involving numbers and quantities.**
● **Explain methods and reasoning.**
● **Identify and use the appropriate operations (including combinations of operations) to solve word problems involving numbers and quantities.**
● **Explain methods and reasoning.**

Vocabulary
area, perimeter, how did you work it out?

You will need:
Photocopiable pages
A copy of 'Super playground' (page 199) and 'How much will it cost?' (page 200).

CD pages
An OHT of 'Super playground design'; differentiated copies of 'Super playground' and 'How much will it cost?' for each less able and more able child (see General resources).

Equipment
An OHP; whiteboards and pens; squared paper.

Lesson ①

Starter

Give the children a series of questions related to perimeters and ask them to write their answers on whiteboards. Ask questions like: *What is the perimeter of a rectangle 7m x 6m? (26m) In a rectangle with a perimeter of 24cm, and one side length 3cm, what is the length of the other side? (9cm).*

Main teaching activity

```
  30.7m
  30.7m
  16.5m
+ 16.5m
  94.4m
   1 2
```

Whole class: Explain to the children that in this unit they will be using skills and strategies that they have already learned to design and plan a redevelopment of the playground (or a particular area relevant to your school). Say: *In this lesson we are going to look at finding area and perimeter.* Draw a simple rectangle on the board with length 7 and breadth 5. Ask the children to tell you the area and the perimeter and explain how they calculated each. (Area = 7 x 5, which is length times width = 35 square units. Perimeter = 2 x (7 + 5) = 24 units.) Make sure that the children remember the difference between perimeter and area and stress that the units of area are two-dimensional, so are square units, whereas the units for perimeter are units of length. Also mention that perimeter can be calculated solely by addition. Use an example involving decimal numbers and add in a column, for example, the perimeter of a rectangular field 30.7m by 16.5m would be (see left).

Remind the children how to find the area and perimeter of a simple irregular shape by splitting the shape into rectangles (see Summer Term, Unit 3, Lesson 1). Tell the children that the activity they will be doing in their group work is in preparation for the next lesson, when they will need the measurements for the area and perimeter in order to cost improvements.

Group/paired work: Introduce the 'Super playground' activity sheet. Children could work in pairs or small groups to discuss their plans. Point out that we often use the term 'area' to describe a part of the playground such as seating area, but in this case they should calculate the area as a measurement. Remind children to think carefully about boundaries and to discuss with their partner whether the boundaries should be marked in any way.

Differentiation

Less able: Give this group the version of the activity sheet with simpler measurements.
More able: Give this group the more demanding version of 'Super playground', where they have to fit areas of their own design into the space using given dimensions.

Plenary & assessment

Show the OHT of 'Super playground design' and ask children to show how they calculated areas and perimeters. Point out that the less able group did not have the paved area. Make sure that they understand that the length of the planted area is 50 + 50 + (80 – 4) + 30 = 206, giving an area of 412m². When they have shown how they calculated the different areas, draw in the paved area and discuss any difficulties that arose with this. Discuss how the design would relate to your school's playground. Ask: *Do you think that the areas chosen by Park School would have been your choice? What would you like to see done to our school grounds? What would be your ideal school playground?*

Lesson ②

Starter

Give the children some money multiplication sums to be done mentally, such as: 12 x 25p (£3), 4 x £12.50 (£50). Ask children to explain the strategies they used to calculate the answers.

Main teaching activity

Whole class: Remind the children of the activity from the previous day and explain that they will need to use their calculations of area and perimeter in order to complete this lesson's activities. Show the OHT of 'Super playground design' and explain that in this lesson the class will be calculating costs related to the design. Ask the children to tell you the things that would need to be costed (hard area surface, grass or turf, paving slabs, surface for seated area, seating, plants, trees, fencing, small walls and so on).

Explain to the children that together you are going to work through the costing for the football pitch area. The football area is 40m x 20m, which is 800m². There is a choice of turf: superfine garden turf is £2.50/ m², general purpose turf is £2.00/m² and extra tough turf is £2.25/m². Discuss which is the best choice: *For football we would probably choose extra tough. We may also choose this for the other grass area but we may decide that the general purpose turf would be suitable. If we choose extra tough turf, it is £2.25/m², so how do we calculate the cost of turf?* (800 x £2.25 = £1800.00)

When you calculate the cost of paving slabs you need to calculate how many slabs are needed and then price them accordingly. Ask: *If we have an area 5m x 6m and the slabs are 400cm x 400cm, how can we work out how many slabs we need?* Children may need to draw this on squared paper, but encourage them to calculate the length of the area divided by the length of the slab (6m ÷ 0.4 = 15), then the width of the area divided by the width of the slab (5m ÷ 0.4 = 12.5). Point out that this should be rounded up to 13, so the total number of slabs is 15 x 13 = 195. Children may suggest that the slabs could be cut in half, which would then give 15 x 12.5 = 187.5 slabs, rounded up to 188 slabs. Agree that either amount is an acceptable answer as long as they point out that they will be cutting the slabs in half in the second example.

Group work: Working in the same groups or pairs, the children develop the work done in the previous lesson using the 'How much will it cost?' activity sheet. They should select the items they need for the playground, check the prices and work out the relevant costs. Remind them to look carefully at the way the price is quoted, and to look for bulk buying discounts. They need to think carefully about the quantities they need, and to read the small print on the price list.

Differentiation

Less able: Give this group the version of the activity sheet with simpler amounts and fewer choices of materials. Allow them to use calculators.

More able: Give this group the more demanding version of 'How much will it cost?'

Plenary & assessment

Ask the children, using the information they have, to calculate the cost of a paved area 3m by 4m using the cheapest slabs available. Discuss any difficulties they have encountered in the lesson. Ensure that they have checked the price guides carefully, checked dimensions and checked the reasonableness of answers.

Lessons ③ ④ ⑤

Starter

Play 'Guess my square number'. Ask a child to write a square number and show it to you; the others have to try and work out what the number is by asking questions to which the answer can only be yes or no. Suggest possible questions, such as: Is the number even? *Is the number less than 100?* Discuss which are the most useful questions to ask. Repeat this starter for Lessons 4 and 5.

Main teaching activity

Whole class: Explain to the children that the **next three lessons** will be spent on redesigning your own school playground or an area of the school grounds (or, alternatively, working on their dream playground). Using 'The ideal playground' activity sheet, children will work in mixed ability groups to agree a design and draw an accurate scale plan showing all the relevant dimensions, taking into account existing features. Discuss the kinds of issues that need to be considered in relation to your own setting. Is there an area for outdoor apparatus? Is this something to be considered for your school? Is there a shaded area? Talk about the kinds of materials that would be appropriate for your school and encourage children to share information they have on prices.

You may prefer to work on the whole design as a class and then give each group a different part of the plan to work on. If it is not appropriate to use your own grounds for this exercise, let the children work on their 'dream playground'. Tell them that by the end of the first lesson they should have agreed and drawn their scale plan. The next two lessons should be spent identifying materials and costing the project.

Group work: Agree with the children some ground rules for group working, to ensure that all members of the group participate. They should use 'The ideal playground' activity sheet to plan and cost their designs; however, they may prefer to work on squared paper for their plan.

Differentiation

Children should agree to undertake different tasks within the group, thus enabling tasks to be allocated to children of all abilities. Check that task allocation has been organised in a way that will benefit the less able and more able children.

Plenary & assessment

At the end of each lesson, ask one group to give an update on their progress and share their ideas with the class. Discuss any general difficulties. Each group should have the opportunity to show their ideas. For the final lesson, each group should make a presentation to the rest of the class showing their designs and the costs.

Name	Date

Super playground

Park School is planning to improve the school grounds. They need:

- a hard play area for playground games
- a quiet seating area
- a grass area big enough for a five-a-side football pitch
- and they also want some planted areas with flowers and trees.

The overall size of plot is 50m x 80m.

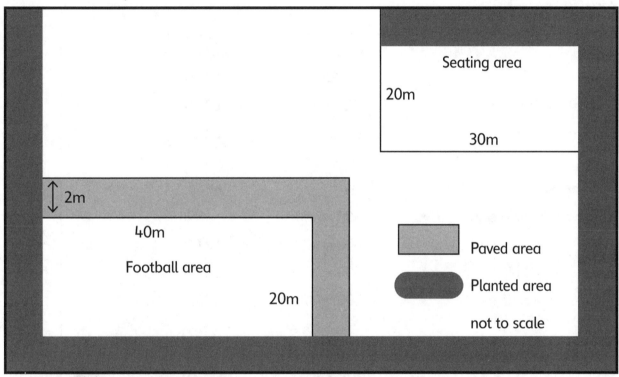

Football area is 20m x 40m; seating area is 20m x 30m; planted area is 2m wide; there is a paved area 2m wide separating the football area from the grass and hard surface; the remaining area is half grass and half hard surface.

1. Look carefully at each area and calculate the area and perimeter of each part of the playground:

planted area _____

paved area _____

seating area _____

hard surface _____

grass area (including football area) _____

2. With a partner, discuss what else you may need in the playground and think about how you would improve your own playground.

Name	Date

How much will it cost?

Now you have worked out the dimensions for the playground you have to calculate how much the improvements are going to cost. This is 'Super DIY Stores' pricelist.

SUPER DIY STORES

Price List

Turf

	Price per m² for up to 50m	Price per m² purchases over 50m
Superfine turf	£ 2.95	£2.50
General purpose turf	£.2.35	£2.00
Extra tough turf	£ 2.65	£2.25

Paving slabs

	Size	Price each
Plain white budget slab	400 x 400cm	99p
Coloured standard quality concrete	600 x 600cm	£2.00
Stone effect – buff	600 x 400cm	£3.99
Stone effect – buff	400 x 400cm	£3.20

Tarmac playground surface – complete service – supplied and laid.

Surface area	Cost per m²
Up to 25 m²	£10.00
25–50 m²	£ 9.25
Over 50 m²	£ 8.00

Delivery costs: £25.00 for total order.

- Calculate the cost for the paved area, the grassed areas and the hard play area if you buy materials from 'Super DIY Stores'. You will have to choose which materials to use and explain why.
- What is the total cost for these areas? (State which materials you have chosen.)
- What other items will still have to be costed?

Calculation, percentage, ratio and problem-solving

This unit is based on the theme of planning an end-of-term party. Children are required to make decisions about what would be appropriate for the function and to find costs for items. They will compare prices for different options and calculate the costs of various items.

LEARNING OBJECTIVES

	Topics	Starter	Main teaching activity
Lesson 1 / Lesson 2	Fractions, decimals, percentages, ratio and proportion Problems involving 'real life', money and measures Using a calculator Checking results of calculations	● Multiply and divide decimals mentally by 10 or 100 and integers by 1000, and explain the effect.	● Solve simple problems involving ratio and proportion. ● Identify and use the appropriate operations (including combinations of operations) to solve word problems involving numbers and quantities. ● Explain methods and reasoning. ● Develop calculator skills and use a calculator effectively. ● Check with an equivalent calculation.
Lesson 3 / Lesson 4 / Lesson 5	As for Lessons 1 and 2	● Count on in steps of 0.1, 0.2, 0.25, 0.5 and then back.	● Understand percentages as the number of parts in every 100. ● Find simple percentages of whole-number quantities. ● Identify and use the appropriate operations (including combinations of operations) to solve word problems involving numbers and quantities. ● Develop calculator skills and use a calculator effectively. ● Check with an equivalent calculation.

Lessons overview

Preparation
Identify website addresses for supermarkets and online shopping. Prepare OHTs of 'Fruit punch recipe', 'Photo prices' and 'Trendy T-shirts'. Children need to research costs, so will either need to access this information on line or be supplied with catalogues or price lists.

Learning objectives
Starters
● **Multiply and divide decimals mentally by 10 or 100 and integers by 1000, and explain the effect.**
● Count on in steps of 0.1, 0.2, 0.25, 0.5 and then back.
Main teaching activities
● **Solve simple problems involving ratio and proportion.**
● **Understand percentages as the number of parts in every 100.**
● **Find simple percentages of whole-number quantities.**
● **Identify and use the appropriate operations (including combinations of operations) to solve word problems involving numbers and quantities.**
● **Explain methods and reasoning.**
● Develop calculator skills and use a calculator effectively.
● Check with an equivalent calculation.

Vocabulary
for every, in every, profit, loss

You will need:
Photocopiable pages
A copy of 'Party hotdogs' (page 205).

CD pages
OHTs of 'Fruit punch recipe' and 'Photo prices'; an OHT of the core version and the less able version of 'Trendy T-shirts', and a copy of 'Trendy T-shirts' and 'Disco discount' for each child, differentiated copies of these and 'Party hotdogs' for each less able and more able child (see General resources).

Equipment
Whiteboards and marker pens; access to the Internet or catalogues and price lists for food and other party supplies; calculators; counting stick.

Lesson ①

Starter

Children will need whiteboards and pens. Ask them to divide the board into five columns, labelled as follows: divide by 100, divide by 10, starting number, multiply by 10, multiply by 100. Explain that you are going to give them a list of starting numbers and they have to complete the table. For example, starting number 62.5 gives: 0.625, 6.25, 62.5, 625, 6250. Give a range of starting numbers, such as 47.3, 901, 1.25, and so on. After a given amount of time children should swap boards and check each other's answers.

Main teaching activity

Whole class: Explain to the class that over the next few lessons they will be planning and costing an end-of-term party. Discuss what tasks will need to be undertaken, such as working out how much food is required, the costs of the food, a disco or group, hire of a hall and leaving presents. Say: *In this lesson we will be working out quantities of food and drink and the costs of these.* Ask: *If we know that one bottle of coke will serve six people, how many bottles will we need to buy for 40 people?* (seven) If there are any children who do not give the correct answer, ask another child to explain the reasoning. Point out that we divide 40 by 6 to give 6.66, but this must be rounded up to 7, so we will buy seven bottles.

Individual/paired work: Children work individually or in pairs on 'Party hotdogs'. Explain that they should first work out the quantities needed for the disco and then calculate the costs. Children may use a calculator. They should be encouraged to estimate their answers first and to check their calculations with an equivalent calculation.

Differentiation

Less able: This group should work from the version of the activity sheet where simpler quantities are used.

More able: On the more advanced version of 'Party hotdogs' an extension activity is included which involves discounts and percentages.

Plenary & assessment

Discuss any difficulties that have been encountered during the lesson.

Show the OHT of 'Fruit punch recipe'. Ask: *How much orange juice would be needed for 20 people?* (2 1/2 litres) Discuss how this is calculated, asking children to explain their method. Ask: *How many oranges would be needed for 20 people?* (10) If further assessment is needed, ask them to calculate other quantities, such as how much blackcurrant cordial is needed (5/6 of a litre).

Lesson ②

Repeat the **Starter** from Lesson 1. For the **Main activity**, children should work in small groups to decide what food they would like for their party – they might prefer a barbecue. They need to consider how many people will be at their party. Is it just their year group, or are others invited? They should decide how much food they will need, make a shopping list and cost it for the amounts required. They will need price lists, or they could use the Internet to visit online supermarkets to find out prices and delivery costs. You may decide to set a budget for them or a cost per head. For the **Plenary**, children should compare their shopping lists and discuss what would be a reasonable cost per head.

Lesson ③

Starter

Give a starter number and then, as a class, repeatedly halve the number, for example: 36, 18, 9, 4.5, 2.25, 1.125. Then give a decimal number as a starter, for example: 5.3, 2.65, 1.325. Ask the children to write their answers on their whiteboards. They can stop at three decimal places. Alternatively, do this exercise orally by asking individual children to do the next step. Repeat several times with different numbers.

Main teaching activity

Whole class: Discuss possible ideas for gifts for the leavers, such as T-shirts, autograph books, photos and so on. Point out that when they are calculating the costs for these, there are a number of things they should consider, such as: Are there bulk discounts or special offers? Do prices include VAT and any other extras? How will they decide between different options? Show the OHT of 'Photo prices'. Ask the children: *Which would be the best option if there are likely to be 20 people who want the photos?* (Option 1= £290, option 2 =£300, so option 1 would be better.) *What if 50 people are likely to want photos?* (Option 1= £650, option 2 = £500, so option 2 would be better.) Point out that they have to estimate how many people they think will want photos.

Group work: Show the OHT of the core version of 'Trendy T-shirts' and discuss the content. Remind children that they will need to consider different options before they make their decisions. They should work in pairs or groups and discuss their ideas and responses to the questions. Children should be allowed to use calculators and encouraged to check their results.

Differentiation

Less able: Work with this group, discussing the options on the less demanding version of the activity sheet.

More able: Give these children the more demanding version of the activity sheet.

Plenary & assessment

Show the OHT of the less demanding activity sheet and ask a child to talk through the steps that they followed. Make sure that they used *all* the relevant information. Discuss the different options with the whole group. Do they agree where assumptions have been made? How many people missed out parts of the information, such as the 'set-up' fee? Were they surprised by any of their results?

Lesson ④

Starter

Label one end of the counting stick 0 and the other end 1. Count in steps of 0.1 along and back on the stick. Point to any point on the stick and ask the children to say what decimal fits there. Repeat, labelling the stick in jumps of 0.2, 0.25, 0.5, 0.6… and so on.

Main teaching activity

Whole class Discuss with the children what sort of entertainment might be needed for the party, such as a disco, a group, an entertainer or a DJ. Ask: *What is the best way to decide? Will a committee be organised?* Explain that there are a number of things to consider when booking entertainment; ask for suggestions. Answers might include: how many hours they will be needed for, start and finish times, any discounts that may be available, extra costs such as VAT.

Show the 'Disco discount' activity sheet and explain that these two examples are typical of what may be on offer. Ask them to identify the most important pieces of information to help them choose between the two. They should suggest working out the price for different group sizes and calculating the cost per individual. The cheapest may not be the best, so if they choose a more expensive option they should be able to justify their decision.

Paired work: Tell the children that you want them to use the information on 'Disco discount' to decide which entertainment they would choose for their party. Point out that they should make sure they include all the costs, and they should be able to justify their choice.

Differentiation

Less able: Give this group the more straightforward version of the activity sheet.
More able: Give this group the version of 'Disco discount' where they have a choice of three discos and have to include VAT.

Plenary & assessment

Discuss any difficulties encountered during the lesson. Ask someone from each level to explain the steps they followed to decide which option to go for.

Lesson ⑤

Repeat the **Starter** from Lesson 4, choosing different jump intervals.

For the **Main teaching activity** children should work in groups to plan their own end-of-term party. They may decide to use the food that they budgeted for in Lesson 2. They should also plan for the other aspects of the party, such as the disco or the entertainment. They will need to consult price lists to find different prices. When they have costed the whole event they should decide what they will charge per head, or alternatively how they will raise the money to pay for the event.

For the **Plenary**, ask the children to share their ideas with each other and agree on the plans and costs for their end-of-term party.

Name	Date

Party hotdogs

For each hotdog we need one roll, one sausage, spread, onions and sauce. We will also need a serviette to serve it in.

We have calculated that:

- one tub of spread is enough for 30 rolls
- one kilogram of onions is enough for 25 hotdogs
- one large bottle of tomato sauce is enough for 50 hotdogs.

There will be 75 people at the barbecue who would like two hotdogs each.

1. Calculate the quantities of each ingredient that we have to buy and then work out the total cost based on the prices below.

	Price	Quantity	Cost
Sausages (pack of 24)	£2.50		
Rolls (pack of 36)	98p		
Spread per tub	46p		
Onions per kilo	75p		
Tomato sauce	£1.25		
Serviettes (pack of 200)	£1.45		
Total cost			

2. At least 50% of the selling price of the hotdogs must be profit. What would be a good price for the hotdogs?

The theme of this unit is redecorating and carpeting a room. It introduces a number of practical mathematical aspects that apply when home decorating. Children have to calculate the number of rolls of wallpaper needed by reading a chart. They are required to decide upon the most economical way to choose the size of carpet, as well as calculating costs within a budget

LEARNING OBJECTIVES

	Topics	Starter	Main teaching activity
Lesson 1 **Lesson 2**	Pencil and paper procedures (× and ÷) Problems involving 'real life', money and measures Using a calculator Checking results of calculations	● Consolidate knowing by heart multiplication facts up to 10 x 10.	● **Extend written methods to: short multiplication and division of numbers involving decimals; long multiplication of a three-digit by a two-digit integer.** ● **Identify and use the appropriate operations (including combinations of operations) to solve word problems involving numbers and quantities.** ● **Explain methods and reasoning.** ● Develop calculator skills and use a calculator effectively. ● Check using equivalent calculation. ● Check with the inverse operation when using a calculator .
Lesson 3 **Lesson 4** **Lesson 5**	Problems involving 'real life' money or measures Making decisions Using a calculator Checking results of calculations	● Factorise numbers to 100 into prime factors. ● Use read and write standard metric units (km, m, cm, mm, kg, g,l,ml ,cl), including abbreviations, and relationships between them.	● **Identify and use the appropriate operations (including combinations of operations) to solve word problems involving numbers and quantities.** ● **Explain methods and reasoning.** ● Choose and use appropriate number operations to solve problems and appropriate ways of calculating: mental, mental with jottings, written methods, calculator. ● Develop calculator skills and use a calculator effectively. ● Check using equivalent calculation. ● Check with the inverse operation when using a calculator

Lessons   overview

Preparation
Prepare an OHT of 'Wallpaper dimensions'. Collect brochures, catalogues and newspaper advertisements with prices for wallpaper, soft furnishings and timber.

Learning objectives
Starters
● Consolidate knowing by heart multiplication facts up to 10 x 10.
● Factorise numbers to 100 into prime factors.
● Use read and write standard metric units (km, m, cm, mm, kg, g,l,ml ,cl), including abbreviations, and relationships between them.

Main teaching activities
● **Extend written methods to:**
  short multiplication and division of numbers involving decimals;
  long multiplication of a three-digit by a two-digit integer.
● **Identify and use the appropriate operations (including combinations of operations) to solve word problems involving numbers and quantities.**
● **Explain methods and reasoning.**
● Choose and use appropriate number operations to solve problems and appropriate ways of calculating: mental, mental with jottings, written methods, calculator.
● Develop calculator skills and use a calculator effectively.
● Check using equivalent calculation.
● Check using inverse operation.

Vocabulary
area, perimeter, square metre (m²), edge, distance

You will need:
Photocopiable pages
A copy of 'How many rolls?' (page 210) and 'Shelf fit' (page 211).

CD Pages
An OHT of 'Wallpaper dimensions' (see General resources); a copy of 'Fully carpeted' for each child; differentiated copies of 'How many rolls?', 'Shelf fit' and 'Fully carpeted' for each less able and more able child.

Equipment
Whiteboards and pens; calculators, 1–9 digit cards.

Lesson ①

Starter

Play times-tables bingo. Children write down six two-digit numbers on their whiteboard, making it a 'bingo card'. Call out different multiplication questions, such as 4 x 9 and 7 x 7. If the answer is one of the numbers on a child's 'bingo card' they can cross it out. The winner is the first to cross out all six numbers.

Main teaching activity

Whole class: Explain that this week's lessons are about redecorating a room. Discuss what might need to be done, such as wallpapering, changing the carpet, installing fitted cupboards, hanging new curtains, and so on. Talk to the children about what measurements they would need to take and how they would calculate quantities. Ask the children what would they need to consider if they were to use wallpaper. Show the OHT of 'Wallpaper dimensions'. Explain that the chart will help them to calculate how many rolls of wallpaper would be needed. Ask them to calculate the perimeter of a rectangular room which measures 2.5m x 3m (11m). Ask: *If the height of the walls is 2.5m, how many rolls of paper will be needed?* (six) Ask a child to explain how they have used the chart. Point out that they need to go to the next value up on the chart.

Individual work: The children should work individually on 'How many rolls?' to calculate the amount of wallpaper needed. They also have to calculate the cost of the wallpaper. Encourage them to use calculators and to check their answers.

Differentiation

Less able: This group should work in pairs on the less demanding version of the sheet.
More able: Give this group the version of 'How many rolls?' with more complex calculations.

Plenary & assessment

Discuss any difficulties the children had in the lesson. Ask them to think about anything else they would need to consider when wallpapering a room. Explain that the chart is only a rough guide. Ask: *Why may you need more rolls of some paper than another?* Discuss the facts that pattern matching may result in wasted paper, and that paper will be saved if there are big windows and doorways.

Lesson ②

Starter

Using a set of digit cards, select pairs of cards for children to multiply together. Allow five seconds and then select the next pair. Children should write their answers on whiteboards and check with their partners after ten pairs of numbers have been shown.

Main teaching activity

Group work: Discuss with the children what fitted furniture they may want in the bedroom, such as fitted wardrobes or built-in cupboards and shelves. Tell them that for this lesson they will be thinking about putting some shelves into the room. Explain that timber comes in various lengths and qualities. Sometimes it is easier to buy several shorter lengths and cut off any surplus, or it may be possible to buy fewer longer lengths and cut them to size.

Individual work: Explain that you want the children to calculate the cost of shelves using the 'Shelf fit' activity sheet. When they have completed the activity sheet, they should design their own shelf unit for a bedroom and list the timber they need.

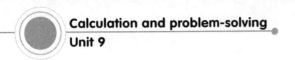

Differentiation

Less able: Give this group the less demanding version of the activity sheet. Ensure that they understand that the timber is priced per metre, but comes in 2m lengths.

More able: Give this group the more demanding version of the activity sheet. Point out that often VAT is not included in the price of materials when they are bought from a wholesale outlet, so the cost has to be added.

Plenary & assessment

Ask the children to show their designs for shelves. Discuss what other timber may be needed if the shelves are not going to be fitted in an alcove – they may need side panels or a back panel, for example.

Lesson

Starter

Children will need whiteboards and pens. Give them a number (such as 72) and ask them to write down as many factors of it as they can in 30 seconds. Then ask individuals what factors they have found and make a list on the board. Repeat for another number, such as 100.

Main teaching activity

Whole class: Tell the children that in this lesson you will be looking at how to calculate the amount of carpet needed and the cost of different carpets. Draw a diagram on the board of a rectangular room roughly 2.8m x 3.9m, showing a door and window on opposite walls. Ask children how they would calculate the area of carpet that is needed for this room. Explain that this is not just about calculating the area – the carpet will come in particular widths, so the task is to choose the most economical width of carpet to avoid too much wastage. Point out that sometimes the carpet fitter will join a carpet, but for the purpose of this activity you want a carpet without any joins.

Tell the children that the carpet chosen for this room comes in widths of 3m or 4m. Ask them to discuss with their partner which width they should choose and then to decide what length of carpet is required (3m width, × 3.9m or 4m length x 2.8m). Explain that there may be some wasted carpet, but it is sold in lengths so still has to be paid for. Point out to the children that the cost of carpets is usually calculated by the square metre, so ask them to calculate which of these two options will be the cheaper (3m width is 11.7m², 4m width is 11.2 m², so 4m width is more economical). Finally, ask a child to explain how they would calculate the cost if the carpet is £10.50 a square metre.

Paired work: Give the children the 'Fully carpeted' activity sheet and explain that you want them to complete this activity thinking about the most economical way to choose the carpet. Point out that often there are additional charges, such as for fitting and carpet gripper. Children may work in pairs and can use a calculator to check their results.

Differentiation

Less able: Provide this group with the version of 'Fully carpeted' with simpler calculations.

More able: This group should work on the more demanding version of 'Fully carpeted', where they are also asked to include the cost of VAT.

Plenary & assessment

Tell the children to think about a room that is 4.2m x 6m. The carpet available only comes in widths of 3m or 4m. Ask them for suggestions about where they would join a carpet. Children may suggest using two 3m widths with a join in the middle, or a 4m width with 0.2 'fill in'. Point out that the decision may be different depending upon whether the carpet is plain or patterned, and how well the type of carpet will join.

Lesson

Explain to the children that in this and the following lesson they will have the opportunity to plan and design their own bedroom.

Repeat the **Starter** from Lesson 3. For the **Main teaching activity**, discuss with children what features they would like in their ideal bedroom. They should work individually to plan their own room using the 'Ideal bedroom' activity sheet. They should calculate the amount of wallpaper and carpet that would be needed.

For the **Plenary**, children should compare their plans with their partner's, discuss improvements and consider each other's suggestions.

Lesson

The children will need catalogues and price lists for soft furnishings, wallpaper and so on.

For the **Starter**, invite the children to put up their hands to say metric units of length. Invite the child who responds to write the unit as a word, and to write its abbreviated form. Ask: *How many … in a …?* Repeat this for mass and capacity metric units.

For the **Main teaching activity**, children should use the catalogues and price lists to gather information on prices of carpets, curtains, wallpaper and so on to cost their ideal room. They may also include fitted bedroom furniture. By the end of the lesson, they should have made a complete costing for their room. For the **Plenary**, allow children to show their designs and costings to the class and discuss.

Name   Date

How many rolls?

You are going to wallpaper your bedroom.

Your room measures 2.4m x 3.6m.

The height of the walls is 2.35m.

The wallpaper costs £8.25 per roll.

You will also need wallpaper paste, which costs £1.35 for a packet that is sufficient for up to 8 rolls of paper.

● Use the table below to calculate how many rolls of wallpaper you will need. _____

● Calculate the cost for wallpapering this room

Height of walls in metres	Length in metres, of walls including doors and windows						
	8.53	9.75	10.97	12.19	13.41	14.63	15.85
2.13–2.29	4	4	5	5	6	6	7
2.30–2.44	4	4	5	5	6	6	7
2.45–2.55	4	5	5	6	6	7	7
2.56–2.74	4	5	5	6	6	7	7
2.75–2.90	4	5	6	6	7	7	8

SCHOLASTIC

photocopiable

Name	Date

Shelf fit

1. You want to fit some shelves into the alcove in your bedroom.

Each shelf will be 0.85m and you would like four shelves.

The timber comes in three different lengths:
- 1m lengths are £5.75 per metre
- 2m lengths are £5.45 per metre
- 3m lengths are £4.95 per metre.

Work out how much the timber will cost using the most economical sizes.

---

2. It would be useful to make a moveable bookcase. You could make the same four shelves into a bookcase by adding side pieces. The side panels can be made from the same timber.

Each of the side panels should be 1.5m long.

Work out the cost of the additional timber using the most economical sizes of timber.

Fractions, proportion, ratio and problem solving

In this unit the children revisit fractions, decimals and proportion, securing their learning in preparation for moving towards the Year 7 programme. Children are reminded of the common decimal fraction equivalences and begin to convert fractions to decimals and vice versa. Common denominators of fractions are introduced, laying the foundation for addition of fractions. Children are given practice in applying their understanding.

LEARNING OBJECTIVES

	Topics	Starter	Main teaching activity
Lesson 1 Lesson 2	Fractions, decimals, percentages, ratio and proportion	● Know what each digit represents in a number with up to three decimal places. ● Use known facts and place value to consolidate mental multiplication and division.	● Recognise the equivalence between the decimal and fraction forms of common fractions. ● **Reduce a fraction to its simplest form by cancelling common factors.** ● Begin to convert a fraction to a decimal using division.
Lesson 3	Fractions, decimals, percentages, ratio and proportion	● Recognise the equivalence between the decimal and fraction forms of common fractions.	● Factorise numbers to 100 into prime factors.
Lesson 4	Fractions, decimals, percentages, ratio and proportion	As for Lesson 3	● **Use a fraction as an 'operator' to find fractions of numbers or quantities (eg 5/8 of 32, 7/10 of 40).**
Lesson 5	Fractions, decimals, percentages, ratio and proportion	● Order fractions. ● **Order a mixed set of numbers with up to three decimal places.**	● **Solve simple problems involving ratio and proportion.**

Lessons overview

Preparation
Prepare sets of 0–10 digit cards from the resource sheets. Copy 'Fraction boxes' onto acetate.

Learning objectives
Starters
● Know what each digit represents in a number with up to three decimal places.
● Use known facts and place value to consolidate mental multiplication and division.
Main teaching activities
● Recognise the equivalence between the decimal and fraction forms of common fractions.
● **Reduce a fraction to its simplest form by cancelling common factors.**
● Begin to convert a fraction to a decimal using division.

Vocabulary
numerator, denominator, common denominators, thousandths

You will need:
CD pages
A set of 0–10 digit cards from 'Digit (+ and –) and decimal point cards' (see General resources, Spring term) for each child, an OHT of 'Fraction boxes'; a copy of 'What percentage?' for each child and differentiated copies of 'What percentage?' for each less able and more able child (see General resources).

Equipment
Calculators, individual whiteboards and marker pens; an OHP.

Lesson ①

Starter

Play 'Which digit?' Each child will need a set of digit cards. Write a decimal number on the board with at least four digits, such as 1.246, then ask which digit is in the hundredths position (4) or the units position (1). Children should use their digit cards to show the relevant digit.

Main teaching activity

Whole class: Explain to the children that you will be looking at the relationship between fractions and decimals. Remind them that they know decimal equivalents for many common fractions. Ask them for the decimal equivalent of some common fractions, such as 1/2 (0.5), 1/4 (0.25), 3/4 (0.75). Similarly, they will know that 3/10 is equivalent to 0.3, so ask: *What is the decimal equivalent of 4/10? … 7/10?* and so on. Point out that 7/10 is also equivalent to 70/100 or 700/1000.

Write 0.265 on the board. Explain that this is the sum of 0.2 + 0.06 + 0.005. Ask: *What is 0.2 as a fraction?* (2/10, which is equivalent to 20/100 or 200/1000) *What is 0.06 as a fraction?* (6/100, which is equivalent to 60/1000) *What is 0.005 as a fraction?* (5/1000) If we look at the decimals' equivalents that are in thousandths, we can then add them together. Hence: 0.2 + 0.06 + 0.005 = 200/1000 + 60/1000 + 5/1000 = 265/1000.

Remind children that to find the percentage equivalent for a decimal it is necessary to multiply by 100, as 'per cent' means parts per hundred. Hence, the percentage equivalent of 0.265 would be 26.5%.

Individual work: Children should work independently on the 'What percentage?' activity sheet. Show the sheet and explain that children should complete the three columns to show the fraction, the decimal and the percentage. Point out that when they have completed the given examples they should add some of their own.

Differentiation

Less able: Give this group the version of the activity sheet where the fractions used are common simple fractions. Go through the worked example with the children and encourage them to use this as a structure to follow.

More able: This group should work from the more demanding version of the activity sheet, where more complex fractions are used. Children have to think about recurring decimals such as 0.3333. Ask them to think about why there are recurring numbers in decimals.

Plenary & assessment

Write the fraction 1/3 on the board. Ask children to use their calculators to work out the decimal. Ask what is show in the calculator display (0.3333333). Explain that with some fractions, such as 1/3, there will not be an exact decimal equivalent because there would be an infinite number of 3s following the decimal point. We usually write decimals rounded to an agreed number of places so, for example, to two decimal places 1/3 would be 0.33.

Ask the children to use the calculator to work out 2/3 rounded to three decimal places (0.667). Point out that in this instance it was necessary to 'round up'. Give some other examples of fractions for the children to convert, such as 3/5, 1/6.

Lesson ②

Starter

Play 'Target 100'. Give the children a number such as 19 and ask them to multiply it by another whole number to get as close as possible to 100 (5). Let them show that number on their whiteboards, then ask them to use a decimal number to get even closer (5.263). Repeat with other numbers, such as 37 and 41.

Main teaching activity

Whole class: Remind the children that in the previous lesson they looked at converting 0.265 to a fraction by splitting the decimal into 0.2, 0.06 and 0.005, then converting each digit of the decimal to a fraction (2/10, 6/100 and 5/1000) and then converting all the fractions to thousandths so that they could be added.

Ask: *What is the sum of 1/4 and 1/2 ?* Most children will readily answer 3/4. Point out that when adding 1/4 and 1/2 they have actually converted the 1/2 to 2/4 and then added. Explain that we can convert any fraction to an equivalent fraction by multiplying the numerator and the denominator by the same value: Hence: $\dfrac{1 \times 2 = 2}{2 \times 2 = 4}$

This can be applied to any fractions so that you can convert them to fractions with common denominators. Hence the common denominator when adding 1/2 and 1/4 is 4 (we convert the 1/2 to quarters).

Ask the children to try adding together 1/3 and 1/6. Invite a child to demonstrate on the board how to convert 1/3 to 2/6 and then add this to 1/6 to get 3/6. Point out that the answer 3/6 is also the equivalent of 1/2

Individual/paired work: Show the OHT of 'Fraction boxes'. Tell the children that you want them to select pairs of fractions from boxes A, B or C and, by finding a common denominator, add them together. Children may work with partners and suggest pairs of fractions for their partner to add, and then check each other's work. Children may then try adding three fractions together.

Differentiation

Less able: Initially limit the children to working with fractions from box A; when they are confident with these they may then use the fractions in box B.

More able: Children should be free to combine fractions from any of the boxes; they should then be encouraged to find the sum of several fractions.

Plenary & assessment

Ask children how they would add together 1/2 and 1/3. Explain that in this example both fractions have to be changed to equivalent fractions, which have a common denominator. How did they decide which denominator to use? Encourage a child to demonstrate how they converted both fractions to sixths, and hence had 3/6 + 2/6, giving the answer 5/6. Ask: *How could you calculate 1/2 – 1/3?* Discuss any difficulties that the children encountered.

Lessons overview

Preparation
Prepare a set of fraction cards for each group from the resource sheet.

Learning objectives

Starters
- Recognise the equivalence between the decimal and fraction forms of common fractions.
- Order fractions.
- **Order a mixed set of numbers with up to three decimal places.**

Main teaching activities
- Factorise numbers to 100 into prime factors.
- **Use a fraction as an 'operator' to find fractions of numbers or quantities (eg 5/8 of 32, 7/10 of 40).**
- **Solve simple problems involving ratio and proportion.**

Vocabulary
as for lessons 1 and 2

You will need:
CD pages
A set of fraction cards for each group ; differentiated copies of 'How many parts?' for each child and differentiated copies for each less able and more able child (see General resources).

Equipment
Counting stick (metre stick marked in tenths); calculators, individual whiteboards and marker pens.

Lesson ③

Starter

Using the counting stick, count in tenths, saying that the starting point is 0 and the end is 1. Then ask children to identify different points on the stick, for example, 7/10, 1/2, 3/4. Then ask where different decimal values are, such as 0.3, 0.8, 0.75.

Main teaching activity

Whole class: Revise the work done in Spring Term Unit 11, Lesson 3. Check the children remember that a factor is a number that goes into another number exactly without leaving any remainder. Also, highlight the fact that numbers can be reduced to prime factors and that the use of indices will help to shorten these, for example: $24 = 8 \times 3 = 2 \times 2 \times 2 \times 3 = 2^3 \times 3$. Show the children other examples, such as:

$30 = 6 \times 5 = 2 \times 3 \times 5$ and $45 = 9 \times 5 = 3 \times 3 \times 5 = 3^2 \times 5$

Hence:

$$\frac{1 \times 4}{2 \times 4} = \frac{4}{8}$$

Group work: Children should work in pairs. Write the following numbers on the board for the children to break down into prime factors. Ensure children record all the stages they go through. 54, 60, 64, 70, 75, 80, 84, 92, 96, 100.

So:

$$\frac{3 \times 3}{8 \times 2} = \frac{6}{16}$$

Differentiation

Less able: Consolidate work on numbers under 50. The 'Table squares' general resources may be needed to help with the factorising process.

More able: Encourage this group to try factorising numbers over 100 to see if they can be broken down into prime factors.

Plenary & assessment

Check through the responses produced by the children. Emphasise that the final roots of any factor tree will be the same whichever factors are used.

Lesson ④

Starter

Repeat the starter from Lesson 3, but change the range, for example from 0 to 0.5, or 1 to 2.

Main teaching activity

Whole class: Children will need a calculator and individual whiteboards and pens. Tell them that in this lesson they will be looking at using fractions as an operator. They will be familiar with finding simple fractions of amounts, such as ½, 1/3 and ¼. Ask: *What is ¾ of 60?* (45) Children should show their answers on their whiteboards. Invite a child to explain how s/he did the calculation. Encourage them to check the calculation using a calculator, pointing out that we enter the amount 60, divide by 4 and then multiply by 3.

Ask children to work out 3/8 of 40. They may use their calculators and should show their answers on their whiteboards. Again invite a child to work though this example for the class, ensuring that they understand how to us the calculator appropriately.

Individual work: Introduce the 'How many parts?' activity sheet. Explain to the children that they will be using fractions as operators; they should try and calculate the answers and then check their calculation using their calculators. Children should work independently on this activity,

Differentiation

Less able: Provide this group with the version of the sheet where the questions are simplified by working with easier values and tasks are structured to show how to solve the problems. Talk to the children about how they should approach each step, ensuring that they understand where they are finding the information they need.

More able: Provide this group with the version of the sheet where the values used in the questions are more complex. Encourage them to devise some questions of their own to test a partner.

Plenary & assessment

Ask the children to find 3/10 of 450. (135) Can they do the calculation mentally? Ask a child to explain how. Give other questions, such as 4/5 of £3 (£2.40). How did they work it out? Is it easier with money? Try 3/8 of 200 (75).

Lesson ⑤

Starter

Play 'Order them'. Children will need whiteboards and pens. Draw a blank number line on the board, mark 0 at the start and 1 at the end. Write some fractions and decimal values between 0 and 10 on the board and ask the children to write them in order on their whiteboards, for example: 1/2, 0.35, 0.76, 1/4, 0.09, 1/10 (0.09, 1/10, 1/4, 0.35, 1/2, 0.76). Children should then show their whiteboards. Write the numbers in order on the blank number line for the children to check their own work. Ask children to suggest other numbers to add to the line, which they also position on their own line.

Main teaching activity

Whole class: Tell the children that in this lesson they will be solving problems involving ratios. Work through the following example: *If, in a packet of 30 orange and lemon drops, we know that orange and lemon are in the ratio 3:2, how many sweets of each colour are there?* Ask the children to discuss with their partners how they could solve this problem, then ask for suggestions and discuss their ideas. Tell them that you want them to use what they have been learning about fractions as operators. The question tells us that for every three orange sweets there are two lemon ones. To find the number of orange sweets, we need to calculate how many there are as a fraction of the total (which is 3/5, or 3 in every 5). We then multiply 30 by 3/5 to find the number of orange sweets (18). Similarly, the number of lemon sweets is 2/5 of 30, which is 12.

Individual/paired work: Children should complete the 'Ratio problems' activity sheet individually and then work together to pose ratio questions for each other.

Differentiation

Less able: Discuss with the children the stages that they need to go through to solve the problems. If necessary, talk through each problem before they tackle it so that they know exactly what is required. For the second part of the activity, suggest that they use the questions they have just answered as a basis for their own questions by changing the amounts.

More able: Encourage these children to think of more complex ratio problems to pose to each other, for example, extending the problem to include costs.

Plenary & assessment

Give the children an example to work through independently to assess their understanding, such as: *In a class of 36 children there are four boys for every two girls. How many girls are there in the class?* (12) You may choose to use examples that the children have devised. Encourage the children to explain their working out. Ask: *How did you check your answers?*

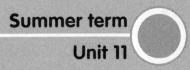

Summer term
Unit 11
Angles, graphs and problem-solving (1)

Children revise using a protractor to measure and draw angles. They also have the chance to extract information from charts and graphs of different kinds.

LEARNING OBJECTIVES

	Topics	Starter	Main teaching activity
Lesson 1 / Lesson 2	Shape and space	● **Derive quickly:** doubles of multiples of 100 to 10, 000 and the corresponding halves.	● **Use a protractor to measure** and draw **acute and obtuse angles to the nearest degree.**
Lesson 3	Shape and space	Convert smaller to larger units and vice versa.	● **Read and plot co-ordinates in all four quadrants.**
Lesson 4 / Lesson 5	Handling data	● Use the units of time (Year 5). ● **Understand percentage as the number of parts in every 100.** ● **Find simple percentages of small whole-number quantities.**	● **Solve a problem by** representing, extracting and interpreting data in tables, graphs and charts.

Lessons  overview

Preparation
Squared paper needed for angle drawing in Lesson 1.

Learning objectives
Starters
● **Derive quickly:** doubles of multiples of 100 to 10 000 and corresponding halves.
Main teaching activities
● **Use a protractor to measure** and draw **acute and obtuse angles to the nearest degree.**

Vocabulary
angle, is a greater/smaller angle than, right angle, obtuse, acute, reflex, degree, angle measurer, protractor, data, statistics, pictogram, bar chart, bar line chart.

You will need:
CD Pages
Differentiated copies of 'Map reading' for each child.

Equipment
Protractors (angle-measurers); OHP protractor or board protractor; whiteboards; squared paper.

Lesson ①

Starter

Explain that you will say a multiple of 100. Ask the children to write the double of this on their whiteboards. Say, for example: *What is double 9600?* Repeat for halves. *What is half 8400?*

Main teaching activity

Whole class: Revise with the children how to measure an angle. Demonstrate using the OHP protractor or use a large board protractor on the whiteboard. Emphasise placing the protractor in the right position and reading the correct scale. Talk about the definitions of an acute angle (less than 90°), an obtuse angle (between 90° and 180°) and a reflex angle (between 180° and 360°). Show the children examples.

Paired work: Children work in mixed-ability pairs. Both the children in the pair should draw a variety of acute and obtuse angles, say eight or ten of them. They should then swap their work with their partner who should name the angles and measure them accurately with a protractor. Encourage children to check each others' work.

Differentiation

Less able: Check that these children are able to use the protractor accurately, especially avoiding confusion between the inner and outer scales. Encourage double checking, for example, if an angle measures 54° it cannot be labelled obtuse.

More able: When these children have completed the task involving acute and obtuse angles, encourage them to move on to examine reflex angles.

Plenary & assessment

Check that children are able to differentiate between the three types of angles considered. *What is an acute angle? What is an obtuse angle?* What is a reflex angle? Ask one of the more able children to demonstrate how to measure a reflex angle. Point out that often it is easier to measure the acute angle formed and then subtract from 360°.

Lesson ②

Starter

Write a list of measurements on the whiteboard and ask children to convert them to larger units. For example, convert 2356m to km, 9124mm to m, 15325g to kg and 69540ml to l. Write another list and ask children to convert these from smaller to the larger units, such as 8.456km to m, 7.403kg to g and 4.103l to ml.

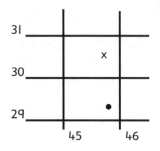

Main teaching activity

Whole class: Explain to the children that in this lesson they are going to revise their knowledge and understanding of coordinates by accurately reading and plotting the position of places on a map. Use the diagram on the left to illustrate important teaching points. Point out that spaces are being used as the coordinates now, rather than the points where lines cross. Explain that position x would be given as (45,30) because it is in square 45 going across and square 30 going up. Remind children about putting references inside brackets to keep them separate and the use of a comma between the two numbers. Go on to show that even more accurate positions can be given using six-figure references.

The black dot would have a reference of (458,292). It is in position 45 and 8/10 going across and position 29 and 2/10 going up. Show other examples if necessary.

Individual/group work: Children can either work individually or in small mixed-ability groups. Provide copies of the 'Map reading' activity sheet. Children should answer all the questions given on the sheet.

Differentiation

Less able: Remind this group that horizontal references should be read first and then vertical references Provide the version of the sheet that includes four-figure references only.

More able: Provide the version of the sheet that includes six- figure references only. If time allows, encourage these children to make up their own maps and to devise games like battleships using six-figure grid references.

Plenary & assessment

Put some large blank grids up on the whiteboard. Ask pairs of children to come and work with them. One should use a cross to make a point within the grid system while the other should give its reference, using four figures at first and then six figures. Repeat this process several times. Ask: *Why is the six-figure reference much more accurate than the four-figure one?*

Lessons   overview

Learning objectives

Starter

- Convert smaller to larger units and vice versa.
- Use the units of time (Year 5).
- **Understand percentage as the number of parts in every 100.**
- **Find simple percentages of small whole-number quantities.**

Main activities

- **Read and plot co-ordinates in all four quadrants.**
- **Solve a problem by** representing, **extracting and interpreting data in tables, graphs and charts.**

Vocabulary

grid, row, column, coordinates, represent, list, chart, table, label, title, axis, axes, pie chart, diagram

You will need:

CD pages

'Pie charts 4 (15°)' (see Spring term General resources) for each child; a copy of 'Test time' and 'Minibeasts' for each child and differentiated copies for each less able and more able child (see General resources).

Equipment

Whiteboards.

Lesson

Starter

Explain that you will say a time, such as 20 minutes to 4 in the afternoon. Ask the children to write this as a 24-hour digital clock time (15:40). Repeat for other times such as half past midnight, four minutes to noon and quarter past 8 in the evening.

Main teaching activity

Whole class: Explain to the children that during the next three lessons they will be solving problems by representing, extracting and interpreting data from different kinds of tables and charts. Remind them that mathematical information, often known as data or statistics, can be shown in many different ways. Revise their understanding of the expressions pictogram, bar chart, bar line graph and pie chart. Tell them in this lesson they will be helping you to appreciate how the children in a class have done in their English, Maths and Science tests. Encourage children to read questions carefully and to read off accurately the information given .

Group work: Children should work in pairs or small groups using the information and questions on the 'Test time' activity sheet.

Differentiation

Less able: Stress that this group should concentrate on the first seven questions on the activity sheet, and the list of pupils' marks could be shortened to five or six.

More able: Encourage this group to move on quickly to the true/false section of the activity sheet and then ask them to make up more true/false statements of their own.

Plenary & assessment

Check through the answers with the children. Which questions did they find easiest? Which questions were the most difficult? Can they explain why? Can they suggest a way of showing the information that would make it easier to read?

Lesson

In the **Starter**, ask children to express the fractions that you write on the board as percentages. Write 1/2, 1/4, 3/5, 9/10 on the board. Repeat, this time writing the percentage and asking children to write the fraction. Use percentages such as 50%, 25%, 75%, 40%.

For the **Main teaching activity**, provide children with resource sheet 'Pie Charts 4 (15°)'. This was introduced during the Spring Term and splits the circle into 24 equal parts. Ask them to record on the pie chart the following information about 24 children and their favourite colours: red (8), blue (2), purple (5), green (6), orange (3). They should also write about the information shown on the completed pie chart, for example, ask: *Which colour was most popular? Which colour was least popular?*

Review the children's results in the **Plenary**. Can the children give the results of the survey in fraction terms (eg red 8/24 or 1/3)? Discuss the advantages and disadvantages of showing information on a pie chart.

Lesson

During the **Starter** ask the following: *What is 10% of £800?* (£80) *So how could we find 20% of £800?* Agree that this can be found by doubling 10%. Ask the children to find 40% and 80% by doubling. Repeat for another quantity like 600 metres.

In the **Main teaching activity,** give out copies of the 'Minibeasts' activity sheet. This shows how mathematics is also an important aspect of other curriculum areas, in this case science. Children should study the information shown on the table and use it to answer the questions given. There is also a bar chart to complete. Check the children's responses in the **Plenary** session. Discuss and investigate how the information in the table could be converted into a computer database and used to find answers to the same questions.

Angles, graphs and problem-solving (2)

In this unit children are looking at patterns and tessellations. This involves them considering reflections and rotations, and developing an understanding of the sum of angles at a point and on a straight line. They will look at properties of regular polygons and begin to calculate the angles in these.

LEARNING OBJECTIVES

	Topics	Starter	Main teaching activity
Lesson 1 / Lesson 2	Shape and space	● Classify quadrilaterals. ● Describe and visualise properties of solid shapes.	● Recognise where a shape will be after reflection. ● Recognise where a shape will be after a rotation through 90º about one of its vertices.
Lesson 3	Shape and space Problems involving 'real life', money and measures	● Recognise where a shape will be after reflection. ● Recognise where a shape will be after a rotation through 90º about one of its vertices.	● **Calculate the perimeter and area of simple compound shapes that can be split into rectangles.** ● **Identify and use the appropriate operations (including combinations of operations) to solve word problems involving numbers and quantities** based on 'real life'.
Lesson 4 / Lesson 5	Shape and space	As for Lesson 3	● Describe and visualise properties of solid shapes. ● Make shapes with increasing accuracy. ● Visualise 3-D shapes from 2-D drawings. ● **Use a protractor to measure** and draw **acute and obtuse angles to the nearest degree.**

Lessons overview

Learning objectives

Starters

● Classify quadrilaterals.
● Describe and visualise properties of solid shapes.
● Recognise where a shape will be after reflection.
● Recognise where a shape will be after a rotation through 90º about one of its vertices.

Main teaching activities

● Recognise where a shape will be after reflection.
● Recognise where a shape will be after a rotation through 90º about one of its vertices.
● **Calculate the perimeter and area of simple compound shapes that can be split into rectangles.**
● Describe and visualise properties of solid shapes.
● Make shapes with increasing accuracy.
● Visualise 3-D shapes from 2-D drawings.
● **Use a protractor to measure** and draw **acute and obtuse angles to the nearest degree.**
● **Identify and use the appropriate operations (including combinations of operations) to solve word problems involving numbers and quantities** based on 'real life'.

Vocabulary

angle, vertical, diagonal, perpendicular, equilateral triangle, compasses, dodecahedron, octahedron, pentagon, pentagonal, hexagon, hexagonal, octagon, octagonal, perimeter, regular, irregular, reflective symmetry, line symmetry

You will need:

CD Pages

A copy of 'Will it fit?', 'How many tiles?' and 'Using equilateral triangles' for each child and differentiated copies of 'How many tiles' and 'Using equilateral triangles' for each less able and more able child.

Equipment

2cm-squared paper, whiteboards and marker pens; a protractor and a pair of compasses for each child; polydron or similar to make 3-D shapes; solid shapes, including a tetrahedron, octahedron, icosahedron and dodecahedron; a piece of A4 card.

Lesson ①

Starter

Play 'What's my shape?' Select a 2-D shape such as a regular pentagon. The children have to identify the shape from a list of clues, such as: *All the sides are the same length. The angles are all the same. Each angle is 108°.* Children should take turns to select a shape and give clues to the rest of the class; agree that if the shape is regular they are not allowed to say how many angles or sides the shape has.

A

B

Main teaching activity

Whole class: Tell the children that in this lesson you will be looking at patterns and shapes. The children will need some 2cm-squared paper. Tell them to draw a square on the squared paper that is 8cm x 8cm. Ask where the lines of symmetry are (two diagonals and vertical and horizontal). Explain that you want them to design patterns, which are symmetrical, by drawing straight lines within the square and using the grid lines as a guide. Show an example like those in the margin, where A shows rotational symmetry and B shows reflective symmetry. Ask the children where the lines of symmetry are. Can they identify whether or not there is 90° rotation in the shape?

Individual work: Children should use the grid paper to design symmetrical patterns. It may be useful to colour different sections, keeping the symmetry of the shape. Remind them of the importance of drawing the lines accurately.

Differentiation

Less able: Encourage the children to start each of their lines at a corner of the square and then repeat the process at each of the other corners; this will give rotational symmetry through 90°. Make sure that they understand the concept of rotational symmetry by physically rotating their squares and checking that the pattern is the same.

More able: Ask the children to identify which angles are the same in their pattern – they should measure them to check. Can they calculate the size of any angles?

Plenary & assessment

Look at the designs and patterns that children have produced. Ask them to look at the angles at the intersections. Can they calculate the sizes of the angles, remembering that a right angle is 90° and that angles at a point add up to 360°? Do they notice that the diagonals of the square bisect the right angle, giving angles of 45°?

Lesson ②

Starter

As in Lesson 1, play 'What's my shape?' This time a child should choose a 3-D shape and give clues until the shape is identified.

stick

Cut along here

Main teaching activity

Whole class: Ask the children what the word 'tessellate' means (shapes that will fit together exactly to cover an area). Ask: *Do you know which regular shapes tessellate?* (square, equilateral triangle, hexagon) *Which other shapes will tessellate?* (parallelogram, rhombus, trapezium, triangle, rectangle) Point out that other shapes will also tessellate. Show a piece of A4 card – starting at one corner of the paper, draw a wavy line to the next corner. Cut along this wavy line, then stick the piece that has been cut off to the other end of the A4 card (see diagram in the margin). Ask children to show you how this new shape will tessellate.

Individual/paired work: Children will need a range of different shapes. Using the 'Will it fit?'

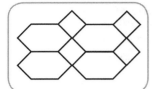

activity sheet, they should investigate which shapes will tessellate. Ask the children to design a tile pattern; this may be simple or can involve more than one shape (see diagram in the margin).

Differentiation

Less able: These children will need 2-D shapes so that they can test whether or not they will tessellate. These should initially be limited to the shapes shown on the activity sheet.
More able: Encourage this group to investigate using several shapes that will combine to make a larger shape that will tessellate.

Plenary & assessment

Ask: *How do you know which shapes will tessellate? Will only regular shapes tessellate?* (no) Show different shapes and ask the children to decide whether or not they will tessellate, such as a regular hexagon (yes), regular octagon (no, but will if combined with a square), right-angled triangle (yes), isosceles triangle (yes), pentagon (no).

Lesson ③

Starter

Children will need 2cm-squared paper. Tell them they have one minute to draw as many different shapes as they can using four squares, with the stipulations that all squares must have at least one side in common with another, and each arrangement must be different and cannot be a reflection or a rotation of another. (There are five possible different shapes.) Ask children to come out and draw their different arrangements on the board.

Main teaching activity

Whole class: Ask the children where they are most likely to see tiles (floors, walls, kitchens). Tell them that you are going to be looking at the way to calculate how many tiles are needed. For the first activity you will be using square tiles. Say: *Imagine you want to tile a floor that is 3m x 2m, and the tiles you want to use are 25cm x 25cm. How could you calculate the number of tiles needed?* Invite children to discuss this with their partner and then ask for their ideas. They may suggest finding the total area of the floor (6m^2) and then dividing by the area of the tile (625cm^2 or 0.0625m^2), which makes 96 tiles. Also, if the children do not suggest it, ask them how many tiles will be needed for 1m^2 (16). They may need to draw this on squared paper. If they know that there are 16 tiles for each square metre, then the total required is 16 x 6 = 96.

Ask them then to think about a border tile to go all around the edge of the floor. These tiles are 25cm long. How many tiles will they need? Again ask the children to discuss this with their partner. Remind them that they will need to calculate the perimeter of the floor and then decide how many tiles are needed. Ask a pair to come out and show how they calculated the perimeter (2 x (3 + 2) = 10m) and then the number of border tiles required (tiles are 25cm long, divide 10m by 0.25m = 40 tiles).
Individual work: Give the children the 'How many tiles?' activity sheet and explain that with this activity they need to calculate the number of tiles needed and the cost of the tiles. Remind them to read the information carefully and to check the sizes of the tiles.

Differentiation

Less able: Give this group the less demanding version of the activity sheet, plus some squared paper so that they can 'draw out' the plan for the wall tiles.
More able: Give this group the version of the activity sheet with the more complex wall plan. Remind them to think carefully about the different methods that they will use to calculate how many tiles are needed for the main part of the wall and how many for the border.

Plenary & assessment

Ask the children to calculate the number of tiles needed for 1m^2 when the tiles are 20cm x 25cm (20). Discuss any difficulties with this.

Ask: What if you wanted a border around the one square metre. How would you calculate the length of border tiles needed? (You would need to know the depth of the border tile.) If the border tiles are 20cm x 5cm, how many would you need? (21, but one would have to be cut in half.)

Lesson

Starter

Repeat the starter from the previous lesson, but this time the children make arrangements with five squares. Children should then compare their arrangements.

Main teaching activity

Whole class: Show a tetrahedron and ask the children to describe it to you (it has four faces, all of which are equilateral triangles). Ask about the angles on the faces – children should remember that the equilateral triangle has three 60° angles and that all the side lengths are the same.

Ask if they know of another three-dimensional shape that has equilateral triangular faces. They will probably name the octahedron. Tell them that there is another regular shape which has just equilateral triangles for its faces. Ask is any one can think how many faces the shape will have. Show the icosahedron and then count the faces (20).

Tell the children that there are five regular 3-D shapes: the tetrahedron (four faces), the cube (six faces), the octahedron (eight faces), the icosahedron (twenty faces) and the dodecahedron, which has 12 pentagonal faces. Show these shapes.

Group work: In this lesson children will be investigating the shapes with equilateral triangular faces. Explain that the 'Using equilateral triangles' activity sheet shows possible nets for the tetrahedron and the octahedron. They should either cut the shape out or copy it onto card to make the shape. They are then asked to explore different nets for these shapes. They should then try and to draw these shapes to enlarge them, taking care to measure the angles accurately.

Differentiation

Less able: Provide this group with polydron or something similar in order to make the shapes practically. They may use triangular paper to draw the enlarged shapes, but should be encouraged to check the measurement of the angles.

More able: This group should be encouraged to attempt to construct their nets using a pair of compasses; they are also asked to investigate how to make the icosahedron.

Plenary & assessment

Ask children to show any shapes they have made. Show the net for the icosahedron (see margin). Ask how many faces meet at each vertex (5).

Show the dodecahedron, which has twelve pentagonal faces. Ask: *How big are the angles in a regular pentagon?* (108 degrees) Children may measure this or they may calculate it.

Lesson

Repeat the **Starter** from Lesson 1. For the **Main teaching activity** show further solid shapes and discuss the shapes of the different faces. Children should then make their own solid shapes. Remind them to allow for tabs to stick the shapes together, and to be careful to draw and cut accurately. For differentiation, suggest that less able pupils make the nets of prisms, such as octagonal or hexagonal prisms. Encourage them to try and make the shapes first using polydron or similar. Where possible, the more able children should try to construct the shapes. For the **Plenary**, show the different solid shapes and see how many the children can name. Discuss the properties of the different shapes, asking questions such as: *How many faces meet at each vertex? How many edges are there?*